S0-AHF-384

WHAT THE REVIEWERS SAY

"Dr. Day writes the story of Hawaii and its people with verve and definite affection. He takes it chronologically from the early Polynesian migrations to the Hawaii of Kamehameha to the Republic of Sanford B. Dole (1894) to the Hawaii of the sugar and pineapple aristocracy and Harry Bridges' ILWU."

William Hogan, San Francisco *Chronicle*

"A. Grove Day's Hawaiian book shows the light and dark sides of life in the islands, and offers good pictures of Hawaii's growth from a laboratory of democracy to a territory and state."

Los Angeles *Times*

"Combined talents for absorbed research, clear organization, and a lively expression make his book the most readable and up to date of recent studies.... While the book is an orthodox spanning of the time periods, its focus is often sharp and dramatic."

Virginia Kirkus *Bulletin*

"Day writes with grace and wit, and in good narrative style. His descriptions are graphic and, because of his knowledge of Pacific literature, he has the ability to select the apt quotation from the tons of source material at hand . . . ."

Honolulu *Star-Bulletin*

"*Hawaii and Its People* is a history aimed squarely at the popular reader. Largely through anecdote and incident it depicts the changing life patterns of the islanders from arrival of the first inhabitants to the time when Hawaii is overdue for statehood. In essence it is social history, but not completely divorced from other branches such as political and diplomatic."

Pacific Historical Review

"This is a book, therefore, which entertains while it informs. It is also a book which is likely to create a sympathetic feeling for the Hawaiian people and their problems."

Mississippi Valley Historical Review

"A highly readable, well organized story of the history of the Hawaiian Islands."

Clare Boothe Luce, *Travel & Leisure*

"Professor Day drew upon the most authentic sources available, utilizing missionaries' memoirs, biographies, accounts of sea captains and travelers, and literary sketches by such authors as Mark Twain, Robert Louis Stevenson, and Jack London. He stresses social history rather than the political side."

Pasadena *Independent*

"This is a book for the layman. Its informal style and approach serve best in descriptions of early trade and business, warfare and political intrigue, the elegant manners and social habits of the resident foreign community, and the personal affairs of the monarchs, ministers, and prominent families."

U.S. Quarterly Book Review

"Being on the campus enables Professor Day to feel into the hopes and some of the frustrations of hundreds of students from all the islands and from all racial groups ....Day gives the story fully and accurately, and catches something of the eagerness and dedication of the missionaries. Nowhere does he make them halo-decked paragons. Nor does he fall into the opposite danger of corroding their motives because their children and children's children have given much of the economic leadership to the islands."

Allen Hackett, *Christian Century*

HAWAI'I
and Its People

A. Grove Day
with illustrations by John V. Morris

MUTUAL PUBLISHING

Copyright © 1955, 1960 by A. Grove Day
Copyright renewed 1983 @ by A Grove Day.
Reprint © 1993 by A. Grove Day

THIS BOOK CONTAINS THE COMPLETE TEXT OF THE ORIGINAL
HARDBOUND EDITION

No part of this book may be reproduced in any form or by any electronic or
mechanical means, including information storage and retrieval devices or systems,
without prior written permission from the publisher, except that brief passages may
be quoted for reviews.

All rights reserved

ISBN 1-56647-705-0

Library of Congress Catalog Card Number: 2004118073

Cover design by Emily Lee

First Printing, February 2005
1 2 3 4 5 6 7 8 9

Mutual Publishing
1215 Center Street, Suite 210
Honolulu, Hawaii 96816
Ph: (808) 732-1709
Fax: (808) 734-4094
email: mutual@mutualpublishing.com
www.mutualpublishing.com

Printed in Australia

To the citizens of

THE STATE OF HAWAII, U.S.A.

this book is affectionately dedicated

Contents

Hawaii and Its People

The Discoverer and the Conqueror

NOBODY IN THE OUTER WORLD SUSPECTED THAT ANY ISLANDS WERE there.

Europeans, through two and a half centuries, ever since the days of Magellan, had voyaged in the Pacific, the world's largest ocean. Through two centuries, the Spanish had each year sent their Manila galleons from the Philippines to Mexico, but they kept to routes north and south of those islands, and the Spanish knew no more about them than had Ferdinand Magellan or Francis Drake or Abel Tasman. No American keels had yet cut those waters; the United States was only a year and a half old.

Now the world's greatest navigator, an English sea captain on his third voyage of discovery in the Pacific, was cruising that ocean from south to north. He had already found scores of islands. What he was now looking for was something that did not exist. He was seeking the mythical Northwest Passage, a navigable strait that would lead from Europe to Asia right through the top of North America. What he found, he stumbled upon by chance. And on the shores he found, he was fated to be worshiped as a god. There he was to leave his bones.

The Floating Islands

HE WAS JAMES COOK. A PLAIN ANGLO-SAXON NAME, FOR A MAN OF plain beginnings, born fifty years before in a farm cottage in Yorkshire. As a boy, he had been drawn by the smell of the sea to an apprenticeship on a North Sea collier. He worked hard and learned navigation. In 1755, when war broke out, he left a post as mate in the merchant service to volunteer as ordinary seaman in the British Navy. Soon promoted to master's mate, he served in American waters in the French and Indian Wars, and for four years surveyed the coast of Newfoundland.

Then, in 1768, an expedition was formed to send a ship to Tahiti so that some astronomers could observe the transit of the planet Venus across the sun. Cook was made captain of that ship, the *Endeavour*, and set forth on his first voyage to the Pacific, during which he explored the shores of Australia and New Zealand and circumnavigated the globe. This was the first of three voyages in the next ten years — a decade in which he became the foremost man of his time in Pacific discovery.

Hence, on his third voyage, even a war was of less importance to the world than Cook's explorations. England was fighting France, Spain, and the United States — but the ships of those countries had orders not to fire on Captain Cook.

Toward the end of 1777, Cook's two ships, the *Resolution* and the *Discovery*, left the Society Islands and headed for the Arctic. In mid-January they sighted tropic birds, man-of-war birds, and boobies. Then Cook jotted down in his journal in unexcited terms:

"All these are looked upon as signs of the vicinity of land. However, we discovered none till daybreak, in the morning of the 18th, when an island made its appearance, bearing northeast by east; and soon after, we saw more land, bearing north, and entirely detached from the former. . . . On the 19th, at sunrise, the island first seen bore east, several leagues distant. This being directly to windward, which prevented our getting near it, I stood for the other, which we could reach; and not long after, discovered a third island, in the direction of west-northwest." These islands were thus for the first time observed by Western eyes. They were Oahu, Kauai, and Niihau, pearls of the Hawaiian Archipelago.

Cook headed for the green hills of Kauai, and many canoes came offshore to greet him, their occupants speaking, surprisingly, in a dialect of the language he had learned at Tahiti. The paddlers came alongside but at first refused to climb aboard. Cook, at the rail of the *Resolution*, tied some brass medals to a rope and dangled it over one of the canoes. The brown-skinned men, wearing loincloths "curiously colored in white, black, and red," took the metal and good-naturedly tied some small fish on the rope in return. Barter had begun.

These Stone Age men of Kauai were especially avid for iron, which they had never owned except in the form of fragments from drift logs. For some small nails they now exchanged a few more fish and one of the yams for which Kauai was to become celebrated. A native even offered for sale the malo* he wore around his waist. The inhabitants of Hawaii had, for the first time, engaged in commerce with the outside world.

The market for iron was brisk. Captain Charles Clerke of the *Discovery* wrote with amazement: "A moderate sized nail will supply my ship's company very plentifully with excellent pork for the day, and as to the potatoes and taro, they are attained upon still easier terms, such is these people's avidity for iron." The natives wanted the nails to make their own very effective brand of fishhook.

* For a glossary of frequently used Hawaiian terms, see Appendix B.

Some of the natives prayed before they came aboard. Others, safe on deck, "sung and made motions with their hands," greeting Captain Cook with a hula dance.

The amazement of the natives made it clear that they had never seen any white-skinned strangers or sailing ships or other foreign possessions. They soon learned that the newcomers owned iron tubes that made a noise and killed from a distance. The leading boat of a party sent to discover a suitable anchorage was met on the beach by a shouting crowd and was lifted from the waves — a friendly gesture. Lieutenant John Williamson saw one of them grab a boat hook; he fired point-blank, the boat dropped back into the water, and the dying native was carried, with great clamor, into the trees. This first act of English hostility, of a sort that had always enraged the common sense of Captain Cook, was a sign of worse to come.

But now everything was friendly. That afternoon the two ships anchored off the village of Waimea, and Cook went ashore. He stood for a moment alone — the first European ever to touch the volcanic soil of the Hawaiian group. The throng of inhabitants promptly fell on their faces, just as they did before their highest chiefs. This man in the salt-stained, three-cornered hat must be a demigod, at least. Thereafter, whenever Cook went ashore he was followed at a distance by a venerating crowd.

Trading continued. Some articles of barter were rich cloaks of red and yellow feathers; others were the crested helmets of ceremonial feathers worn by the chiefs. At first the natives showed a tendency to appropriate anything about the ships that they fancied; but the watchful sailors soon hindered that.

After a few days at Kauai, the two ships went to the islet of Niihau, where Cook obtained a load of yams and salt, and where he gave the people some livestock — a ram goat and two ewes, an English boar and sow pig — and also some seeds to plant — melon, pumpkin, and onion. The white men left another and less welcome gift. A party of twenty men sent ashore to trade was held there by a storm for two days and two nights. Despite Cook's strong orders, the terrible gift that his men left among the native women was one that they had carried in their blood as a reminder of the trollops of Plymouth docks.

Cook named his newly discovered islands in honor of his patron, the First Lord of the Admiralty, the fourth Earl of Sandwich. One wonders why that lazy and corrupt politician, who did more to ruin the British Navy than could the guns of any enemy, should deserve such an honor. His name is also perpetuated in a common article of the luncheon menu, which the earl invented so that he would not lose time eating away from the gaming table. At any rate, Cook's discovery was known for a long time — and in England is known still — as the Sandwich Islands.

Cook sailed north after a fortnight in these islands, and beat up the northwest coast of America to the Bering Sea and beyond, touching the Asiatic mainland. He was the first man in history ever to place foot on every continent. But he found no passage, and as the Arctic winter approached, the memory of the Sandwich Islands beckoned more strongly. He decided to return to those hospitable shores.

The news of Cook's visit, during the ten months since he had left Kauai, had spread to the windward islands that Cook had not seen. After much pondering, the natives had decided who he really was.

Once there was a king of Hawaii named Lono. He had killed his wife in a fit of anger. He had gone mad with grief, and had wandered through all the islands, boxing and wrestling with anyone he met. Then he had set out, "in a singularly shaped canoe," for foreign lands, and his people had made him a god, in whose honor annual games were held in the season of *makahiki*, or harvest. The sails of Cook's ships had looked like the procession banners that hung from the image of Lono. Now, as these ships returned, again in the *makahiki* season, and made a leisurely progress along the shores of the other islands, the people hailed him everywhere as their god Lono, come again.

Blown from their course, Cook's ships found themselves on the morning of November 26, 1778, off the north coast of Maui. "In the country was an elevated saddle hill, whose summit appeared above the clouds." This "hill" was the towering mass of Haleakala, House of the Sun, ten thousand feet high, the largest extinct volcano crater in the world. Later in the day they caught a distant view of the island of Molokai.

Gossip had drifted from Kauai about these ships, or "floating islands," on which lived strangers — haoles — whose loosely fitting skins held slits from which they pulled dazzling gifts. The foreigners had white brows and sharp corners on their heads; they spoke in a strange babble; smoke came out of their mouths. The king of Maui, Kahekili, had heard the stories. Next afternoon he went aboard the *Discovery* and presented Captain Clerke with a red feather cloak.

A few days later, off the east end of Maui, Kalaniopuu, the old king of the Big Island to the south, who was occupied in carrying on a war against Kahekili, came to visit the *Resolution*. His chiefs, looking in their feather capes and gourd helmets like huge birds, followed in his train. Some of the chiefs stayed on the ship overnight. One of them was the king's nephew, a young warrior who watched the strangers with curious eyes. His name was Kamehameha.

Then for six weeks Cook cruised along the coasts of the large island to windward. It was called Hawaii. The sailors saw the lovely emerald Hamakua Coast, ribboned with silver waterfalls leaping down from the slopes of snowcapped Mauna Kea, rising almost fourteen thousand feet in the sky. Unfavorable winds kept them from landing anywhere, but the natives always pushed out in canoes and traded fairly for provisions (which sometimes included, as a great delicacy, live octopus). Cook, always interested in the prevention of scurvy, took aboard some sugar cane and from it brewed a "very palatable beer," but the sailors almost mutinied when asked to drink such unconventional grog.

On around the desert Kau shores, jagged with old lava flows, they ran, through gales and calms, with the titanic slopes of Mauna Loa to starboard. Canoes came off to them still; some of these islanders thought little of venturing out as far as fifteen miles. Off South Point, the Hawaiians brought with them not only hogs but women, about whom Cook made his most monumental understatement: "No women I ever met with were less reserved. Indeed, it appeared to me that they visited us with no other view than to make a surrender of their persons."

David Samwell, surgeon of the *Discovery*, found that some of the native girls were marked with the disease of Venus. He assumed, mistakenly, that it could not have spread this far to windward from Kauai in less than a year. The captain's orders to control infection were quickly forgotten. Cook had discovered the cure for scurvy, but this was another matter.

No safe harbor was found until, on January 17, 1779, the two ships dropped anchor off the western coast, in the district of Kona. Ten thousand Hawaiians, shouting and singing, swimming "like shoals of fish" or riding on canoes and surfboards, welcomed them to Kealakekua Bay. Never before had Cook seen such a large crowd in the Pacific. No wonder that he now wrote that they had made a discovery "in many respects the most important that had hitherto been made by Europeans throughout the extent of the Pacific Ocean." Those were the last words he was ever to enter in his journal.

The Death of a God

KEALAKEKUA MEANS "THE ROAD OF THE GODS," AND AS SOON AS he went ashore, Captain Cook was officially greeted as the god Lono. A skinny, ancient priest named Kuaha, red-eyed from drinking too much awa, led him and his officers to mount the heiau, or temple platform, of Hikiau, greatest shrine of Lono in all the islands. Its flat top was "surrounded by a wooden rail, on which were fixed the skulls of the captives sacrificed on the death of their chiefs." Embarrassed, the British commander was led to the top of a rickety scaffold and there was wrapped in a red cloth and requested, by signs from Kuaha, to kiss one of the wooden images whose horrible features grinned down on the scene. Perhaps Cook did not understand until the last moment of his life what this ceremony meant. It was the most dangerous act of his career. From now on, he must be more than human. He must be a god.

The most powerful force in Hawaiian religion was the idea of tabu, which these people pronounced *kapu*. At Kealakekua, Cook again saw its strength. The nobles and the priests exercised this power of prohibition without challenge from the commoners. When, for instance, a crowd of visiting natives clung to one side of the *Discovery* in such numbers that the ship began to heel, a friendly young chief named Palea was told about the danger; he gave an order, and everybody promptly jumped overboard. When a camp for astronomical observations was set up ashore in a sweet-potato patch, the priests placed the area under a *kapu*, and the district was at once deserted. Since women could not enter the temple precincts, the astronomers were given, according to a later voyager named Manby, a large house about sixty yards from their residence, "where they might entertain their female friends and observe the beauties of Venus whilst the other planets were obscured by clouds."

The Hawaiians had priests and nobles, and a king. Soon he would come; until then, the entire bay was put under a strong *kapu*, and no canoes went out. King Kalaniopuu returned from Maui on January 25 and next day made a ceremonious progress to the ships. Behind the king's canoe came a load of chanting priests with their idols — enormous figures of wickerwork, ornamented with gay feathers; their eyes were large oyster shells with a black nut in the center, and their hideous mouths were edged with the fangs of dogs. The monarch gestured to the officers to come ashore to the village of Kaawaloa. There, following an old Polynesian custom, he exchanged names with Cook, and presented him with several feather cloaks and a supply of hogs, sugar cane, coconuts, and breadfruit. Then Kalaniopuu boarded the *Resolution* and was presented with a linen shirt, Cook's own cutlass, and, later on, a complete tool chest.

Throughout their stay, the haoles were bountifully supplied with fresh provisions. It seemed a harmless idea to pay for them with two-foot iron daggers, made by the ships' blacksmiths on the pattern of the wooden *pahoa* of the Hawaiian warriors, pointed at both ends. The natives crowded about the forges to watch the beating of the hot metal, and then went ashore to try for themselves to practice, pounding with stones at a campfire, the art of the smith.

There were exhibitions of boxing and wrestling by the Hawaiians — a fitting celebration in honor of the return of Lono. Then Cook gave an evening band concert, after which the cliffs surrounding the bay were illuminated by the first, but not the last, display of fireworks on the islands.

An expedition was sent to the hilly uplands, composed of Mr. Nelson, the botanist; a young midshipman, George Vancouver; and Jack Ledyard, corporal of marines, an American lad who had been to Dartmouth College. They climbed into the forests and visited the huts of canoe-builders and bird-catchers. Priests went along to see that the strangers came to no harm.

The priests did not protest even when Cook, wanting firewood for the ships, decided on February 2 to tear down the railing around their sacred heiau. If Lono wanted to chop down Lono's fence, they implied, even to carry away the twelve wooden idols within — well, that was Lono's privilege.

Everything was now shipshape and fresh provisions were stowed aboard. During the fortnight of their stay, the country had been drained of supplies, and the king began audibly wondering when the visitors would be on their way. When Lieutenant James King of the *Resolution* had tried to explain the white man's mission, the

"Indians" of Hawaii already knew the answer. "They supposed we had left our native country on account of the scantiness of provisions and that we had visited them for the sole purpose of filling our bellies." Now those bellies were rounded and sleek. The *makahiki* season was over. The haoles were invited to come again, at the next breadfruit harvest.

Three days before the ships were to set out on their return to the Arctic, an old gunner named William Watman was found dead in his hammock. He was buried in a hole dug in the heiau terrace. A wooden idol served as a headstone. Some of the chiefs watched the burial with interest. At least one of these strangers was mortal. Perhaps even Lono could die.

After an overwhelming farewell feast and more gifts, Cook and his crews sailed north on February 4. Then the muse of tragedy played her hand. A sudden kona storm hit them at midnight four days later. The foremast of the *Resolution* collapsed, and planking began to leak. Here was anticlimax. The ships of the god would have to creep back to the roadstead of Kealakekua to make major repairs.

As the *Discovery* was returning to the bay, Chief Kamehameha, who from the first had shown great interest in the weapons of the strangers, came on board and swapped his red feather cloak for seven of the iron daggers made by the armorers.

On their return, although the king was still friendly, the bay was empty and the air full of foreboding. Why had the haoles come back? But the priests were obliging, as always, and offered the use of the ground about their heiau. There the mast was laid out, with a guard of marines camped nearby to protect the carpenters and sailmakers at their work. Astronomer Bayly again set up his instruments on the temple platform.

Some stealing had taken place during their earlier stay, but Cook had found this not unnatural. Now, on the afternoon of Saturday, February 13, trouble came. A watering party on shore was being helped by some natives when several chiefs came and brusquely ordered them away. Cook was summoned, and managed to smooth things over. But as he and Lieutenant King were starting back to the ships, they heard shots fired from the *Discovery* and saw a canoe heading for the beach. They guessed what had happened — another cursed bit of thieving! They dashed ashore and tried, in vain, to catch the escaping natives, although they wandered three miles inland.

The chase had started when a native daringly grabbed a pair of tongs and a chisel from the ship's forge and jumped overboard, then climbed into a waiting canoe. Tom Edgar, master of the *Discovery*, leaped into a ship's boat and chased the canoe to the beach. Young Palea followed to help, and at once he managed to get back the stolen tools. But Edgar foolishly decided to confiscate what he thought was the guilty canoe. The one he picked out belonged to Palea. There was a scuffle. Palea was hit over the head with an oar, and then two hundred angry Hawaiians began throwing chunks of jagged lava, forcing the boat's crew to wade to a rock offshore. But the blow to Palea had not damaged his dignity or his good sense. He put a stop to the conflict, restored the scattered equipment, and sent off the sailors with apologies for the whole affair.

Cook, when he came back, was worried. These islanders must not imagine that they had gained an advantage. "I am afraid," he told King, "that these people will oblige me to use some violent measures." One must not lose face.

The night passed uneasily. A shot was fired at creeping figures by a marine at the shore camp. Next morning it was found that, in spite of Cook's orders to keep careful watch, the single-masted sailing cutter, anchored a dozen yards off the *Discovery's* bow, had been stolen in the night. Some of Palea's people might have been responsible.

Cook decided to take vigorous action. His men were outnumbered a hundred to one; their party was divided, and the mast was still ashore. A valuable boat had now been lost; other needed equipment might follow. The natives must be taught a lesson. Since Captain Clerke was ill with tuberculosis, Cook himself took charge. He loaded both barrels of his gun, one with harmless birdshot, the other with deadly ball.

The commander decided to use a strategem that he had used with success in other parts of the Pacific. His plan was to get the king on board and hold him as a hostage until the cutter was restored. Placing a cordon of boats to guard the entrance to the bay, he headed early in the morning for the village of Kaawaloa in a six-oared pinnace with Lieutenant Molesworth Phillips and nine marines, accompanied by the launch under the command of Lieutenant Williamson.

Cook and the marines jumped to the rocky shore — there was no beach — and marched to the king's house. The friendly greeting he received made it clear that Kalaniopuu, who had just wakened, was innocent of any plot, and the king and his two sons readily agreed to go aboard. But before the party reached the shore, the queen, Kanekapolei, and several chiefs surrounded their ruler and begged him not to go farther. Lono — if this were truly Lono — had never acted this way before.

The plan came to a halt. A great crowd of natives gathered; brown arms brandished clubs, spears, and the iron daggers made by the foreign smiths. As the king sat and pondered, bad news came. A survivor of a skirmish on the bay rushed up and reported that one of Palea's brothers, running the blockade on the water, had been killed by a shot from one of the boats.

Women and children disappeared, and the men began tying on their armor of matting. Cook decided that his scheme would not work now. His retreat to the ships was almost cut off by the crowd. The marines withdrew and formed a line on the rocks by the waterside. Their muskets might not hold back the throng, for none of these natives had ever seen a bullet kill a man.

A burly native, Palea's eldest brother, made a stab at Cook with an iron *pahoa*. Cook fired the charge of birdshot, which fell harmlessly from the woven armor and only enraged the Hawaiians, who grew bolder. Phillips struck down an attacker with his gun butt. Another aimed at Cook, who fired the second barrel. The man fell dead. The sailors fired from the launch, but the noise was drowned out by the shouts of the natives. The marines also fired a volley; they were overwhelmed before they had time to reload.

Four marines fell dead; the rest scrambled into the sea and swam to the pinnace. Phillips was the last to climb in, and then, despite a stab in the shoulder from an iron *pahoa*, he went overboard again to haul in a struggling older man.

Once more Captain Cook was alone on the soil of the island he had discovered. He turned his back to the throng and shouted an order for the boats to cease firing and come closer to the rocks.

A club struck him down. As he tried to rise, a dagger plunged into his back. The blood ran; he groaned. A god does not groan. A shout rose: "This is not Lono!" He fell forward into the water.

Did he die of his wounds, or did he drown? The great sailor had never learned to swim.

There was an instant when Cook might have been saved. The pinnace was too crowded to be of help; but the armed launch was not twenty yards away. Prompt action might have rescued the wounded man, or at least taken off his body. But Williamson ordered the boat to pull offshore. Cook's body disappeared under the howling mass of natives, "who, snatching the dagger from each others' hands, displayed a savage eagerness to join in his destruction."

The Rise of a Conqueror

THE HAWAIIANS RETREATED UNDER A LIVELY FIRE FROM THE BOATS, leaving many of their own warriors dead but carrying the bodies of the slain Englishmen. Lono was dead; in death his remains would be treated like those of a god.

Lieutenant King, in charge of the camp a mile down the bay, had heard the firing. Now he tried to reassure the natives who crowded around, but several cannon balls from the *Discovery* scattered the group and raised greater alarm. King sent off a boat to say that all was well with him. The boat returned in charge of the efficient, stubborn young sailing-master of the *Resolution*, who brought the sad news of Cook's death and orders to strike the tents and bring the equipment aboard.

Leaving the sailing-master in charge of the marine guard at the heiau, King went to consult with Captain Clerke, now left in command of the expedition. The Hawaiians at the heiau had heard rumors of Cook's death, and they began to heave stones at the sailors. The sailing-master was a man with a temper. His name was William Bligh, and in later years he was to encounter troubles again in the Pacific, in command of a ship named the *Bounty*. He promptly ordered the marines to open fire, and eight natives fell.

King turned back at the sound, but he was too late to stop the fighting. Reinforced by marines from the *Discovery*, the shore party took heavy toll. Finally the priests managed to make a truce, for the organized musket-fire had a chastening effect. King managed to get the sails and other equipment into the boats and haul the mast back to the *Resolution*.

That afternoon, after consulting with Clerke, King pulled again near the shore, and opened negotiations with old Kuaha. The Hawaiians must return the bodies immediately, or the ships would open fire on the village. The priest said he would try, but it would take time. The bodies of the marines had been burned. Cook's body had been divided into many pieces and each high chief around the countryside had been given a piece. The head had gone to Kahuopeonu, the hair to Kamehameha, and the legs, thigh bones, and arms to Kalaniopuu. . . . The stolen boat could not be returned — it had been broken up to get the nails that had held it together.

That night two young priests secretly brought off to King and

Clerke a bundle wrapped in native cloth. It contained several pounds of flesh hacked from a thigh, which had been given to the priests for ceremonial use. They explained that the rest of the flesh had been stripped and burned, as was the custom.

The Englishmen had been convinced, during their stay at Niihau the previous year, that cannibalism was practiced there. King now turned to one of the priests. Perhaps the rest of the body had been . . . eaten? The priest goggled in horror. "Is that the custom among the haoles?" he asked. The two officers were somewhat reassured.

In spite of the efforts of the priests, desultory fighting went on for several days. While the carpenters hastily repaired the *Resolution*'s mast, cannon shots were fired into Kaawaloa, and in return the Hawaiians bombarded the watering parties with rocks. Ordered to burn a few houses to clear the line of fire, the men from the ships went further, and shortly the whole village of thatched huts was in flames, while the sailors shot at the natives fleeing from their burning homes. The houses of the conciliatory priests were the first to burn.

On Saturday the twentieth, just a week after the first trouble, the Hawaiians brought back more bones and fragments of Cook's body, all charred by fire except the hands, which had been rudely preserved by salt. Next morning the jawbone and feet were restored, as well as the captain's shoes and the flattened barrel of his gun. The remorseful chiefs placed a *kapu* on the bay. The sad relics were nailed in a wooden coffin that was draped with the British flag. With both ships' companies standing in silence, drums rolled, cannons boomed, and the mortal part of Captain James Cook, R.N., was consigned to the waters of the archipelago that was his last and greatest discovery.

The ships of Lono left Kealakekua on the night of February 22 and sailed north, past Maui, Lanai, and Molokai. After a visit at Waimea, Oahu, they crossed to Waimea, Kauai, and then stopped for water and provisions at Niihau. A civil war was in progress on these leeward islands, and the goats and pigs left there the previous year had probably been eaten. On March 15 the *Resolution* and the *Discovery* took their final departure from the Sandwich Islands to continue their explorations in the north.

More than six years were to pass before another "floating island" would visit the Hawaiians — not so much because the death of Cook had given them a reputation for ferocity as because no commercial need arose until then for visiting these waters. During the interim, one of the chiefs who had spent many hours on Cook's ships was to begin his march to the dominance of the entire chain of islands. So nearly equal had been the powers of the local chiefs, and so great their jealousies, that the odds against success had always been formidable. Now, with the aid of the weapons and skill of the white men, that task was to be achieved by a great warrior. The united kingdom that he built was finally to be inherited by the American nation.

This chief was Kamehameha, who became the national hero of the Hawaiian people. He had observed the haole methods of warfare and had himself been wounded during the bombardment of Kaʻawaloa. He decided that these new methods were what was needed to end the centuries of tribal war that had lacerated the isles. Early in his warlike career he earned for himself a name that means "The Lonely One." (Kamehameha's name was spelled by the early voyagers in a dozen different ways; the Russians even wrote it as "Tomi-Omi.") The story of his rise to power is one of drama and battle and romance.

That story starts at the court of Alapai, king of Kohala, northern province of the Big Island. He brought up two stepsons: Kalaniopuu, who later welcomed Cook at Kona, and Keoua Kalanikupuapaikalaninui. This Keoua married Kekuiapoiwa, niece of Kahekili, king of Maui.

On a November night of storm — the year is not known, but 1758 is a good guess, for the portentous star that blazed at the birth was probably Halley's comet — a son was born to Kekuiapoiwa. The soothsayers of Alapai had reported that the baby would be a rebel who would "slay the chiefs." The king therefore gave orders, Herod-like, that the child should be killed as soon as it was born. The mother had made a plan, however, and at birth the little chief was spirited away by a man named Naeole and reared in the mountains by foster parents.

There is a strong tradition that the father of the child was actually his mother's uncle, at whose court on Maui she had recently visited her relatives. Kahekili sent his twin stepbrothers, Kameeiamoku and Kamanawa, to serve the boy that was born, and they fought by his side all their lives. If the tradition is true, the child was destined to spend many years carrying on war against his true father, Kahekili.

After five years, Naeole brought the boy back to the court, where he was reared as a prince and taught the profession of arms by a celebrated fighter named Kekuhaupio. When Kamehameha's uncle, Kalaniopuu, became king of the region, his chunky nephew was a seasoned knight-at-arms, and in 1775, in one of the battles against Kahekili's forces on Maui, he saved the life of his former tutor Kekuhaupio. Kamehameha was so strong, according to an account given by his Maui enemies, "that he could break the body of his opponent in twain, while poised on his spear in mid-air. This little man was of a hard, thickset build, with large lips."

When the ships of Cook arrived, Kamehameha's prowess had already made him a leader. Lieutenant King wrote that among those who went aboard the *Discovery* with Kalaniopuu was Kamehameha, "whose hair was now plastered over with a brown dirty sort of paste or powder, and which added to as savage a looking face as I ever saw; it however by no means seemed an emblem of his disposition, which was good-natured and humorous, though his manner showed somewhat of an overbearing spirit, and he seemed to be the principal director in this interview." The young chief, now about twenty-five, had already assumed a leading role among the Hawaiian *alii*, or nobility.

The year after the departure of the two English ships, the aged

Kalaniopuu called a council in the sacred valley of Waipio, a green, mile-wide gash in the Hamakua Coast. There he proclaimed his son Kiwalao as his successor; but he gave to Kamehameha, next in line of succession, the special office of guardian of the terrible war god Kukailimoku.

Kamehameha took his duties seriously. Not long afterward a captured chief was to be sacrificed, and while Kiwalao was getting ready to perform the ceremonial act, Kamehameha stepped in and took over the ritual. Naturally the prince was irritated, and following the friendly advice of the old king, Kamehameha retired for a while to his estates at Halawa, to live as a farmer, fisherman, and sportsman.

The death of Kalaniopuu in 1782 brought Kamehameha back once more into politics. The new ruler, Kiwalao, was under the thumb of an uncle, Keawe, who hoped that the redistribution of lands that always inaugurated a new reign would favor him and his friends. Four high chiefs — Keeaumoku, Keaweaheulu, and the twins Kameeiamoku and Kamanawa — feared that Keawe's gain would be their loss, and sent the warrior Kekuhaupio to persuade Kamehameha to join them. When the issue came to open conflict later in the year, at the battle of Mokuohai near the City of Refuge at Honaunau, Kiwalao was killed and a long civil war began on the Big Island.

One of the three warring factions was led by Kamehameha and his five friends, who remained his loyal henchmen as long as they lived. This party held Kona and the northern districts. Keawe held Hilo and the eastern side. The south was held by Keoua, a handsome stepbrother of Kiwalao, a tall youth of about twenty, with fair skin and long reddish hair; he was one of the two princes that had been with Kalaniopuu at the death of Cook. King Kahekili of Maui, ancient enemy of the chiefs of Kohala, often sent aid to Keawe and Kiwalao. Thus the men of Kamehameha were pitted against the rest of the island world during much of the decade of baronial warfare that followed.

Soothsayers and Gunpowder

ONE INCIDENT OF THE EARLY PART OF THIS PERIOD HAS PASSED INTO Hawaiian lore. During a raid on the coast of Puna, Kamehameha leaped ashore to attack some unarmed fishermen on the beach. His foot caught in a crack in the lava and, when he was thus held in a trap, one of the fishermen boldly struck him on the head with a canoe paddle, which shattered against his skull. Kamehameha's companion arrived and freed him, but the fishermen escaped for that time. Later they were caught, however, and brought before Kamehameha for punishment. Then the chief admitted his error in attacking innocent workers, and set them free with gifts. To the most celebrated edict of Kamehameha's reign he gave the name of *Mamalahoe Kanawai* (The Law of the Splintered Paddle). It proclaimed: "Let the aged men and women and little children lie down in safety in the road." Henceforth, an attack on defenseless people would be punished by death.

Just as Kamehameha had once traded his feather cloak for seven iron daggers made by Cook's armorers, so he now began collecting haole guns and haole gunners to fire them. The early trading vessels to the islands were always asked to supply cannons, muskets, and ammunition. Captain William Douglas of the *Iphigenia Nubiana* in the spring of 1789 presented Kamehameha with arms and powder, including a swivel gun that was mounted on the platform of a large double canoe.

Douglas described the chief at this time as "rather an object of fear among his people," "of tyrannic disposition," and possessing "few of those qualities which gain a sovereign that first of all titles, father of his people." The following year, Captain George Mortimer, who also supplied Kamehameha with armaments, put him down as "one of the most savage-looking men I ever beheld, and very wild and extravagant in his actions and behavior."

At this time Kamehameha won a husky ally named Kaiana, six

and a half feet tall, who had earned great prestige because he was the first Hawaiian to travel to foreign lands. Kaiana, a half-brother of Kahekili, had sailed in the *Nootka* to China in 1787 with Captain John Meares, a fur trader. He had been given many presents by the admiring Chinese before sailing with Meares to the northwest coast of America; after seeing those shores from Alaska to Vancouver Island he returned in the *Iphigenia* to his native land, a man of wealth (in trade goods) and worldly experience. He joined Kamehameha's council and for several years was his ardent supporter.

Kamehameha was now ready to start broader operations. He patched up an alliance with Keawe of Hilo and then rallied his troops for an attack on Kahekili, who with the aid of his brother Kaeo had now extended his rule over Oahu and had set up court at Waikiki, leaving his son Kalanikupule to rule Maui. In the spring of 1790, the forces of Kamehameha invaded the old battlegrounds of east Maui, and were victorious in a great conflict beneath the spiring Iao Needle in the valley behind Wailuku. The dead bodies filled the stream in such heaps that the battle was given the name of Kepaniwai (The Damming of the Waters).

After ravaging Maui and Lanai, Kamehameha went on to Molokai. Here he made a reconciliation with a high-born old lady, Kalola, a sister of Kahekili and widow of Kalaniopuu. Later, when Kalola died, he took over the protection of her granddaughter, a child of Kiwalao; and when the girl, Keopuolani, was old enough, he took her as his "sacred wife" and thus allied himself with the highest blood in the land. She became the mother of the two princes that were to follow Kamehameha on the throne.

From Molokai, Kamehameha sent a message to Kahekili offering him the white stone of peace or the black stone of war. The reply came that after Kahekili's death, Kamehameha could take over his kingdom — but not before. "The Lonely One" also sent to a famous oracle of Kauai, who predicted that if Kamehameha wanted to make himself master of the whole island of Hawaii, he should build a big new heiau at Puukohola near Kawaihae in honor of the war god Kukailimoku.

Meanwhile Keoua, angered at Keawe, invaded the domains of his uncle at Hilo and killed him. Kamehameha was thus drawn back to protect his home island. Two indecisive battles were fought at Hamakua. Then, as Keoua was returning to his base at Kau after setting up his regime at Hilo, a terrifying blow hit him that was taken to be highly prophetic.

Keoua's army took a route that led by the volcanic crater of Kilauea, and while they were camped nearby, a terrible eruption began, filling the air with smoke, ashes, rocks, and poisonous gas. Although safe enough in their camp, the warriors and their train of women and children were anxious to leave the region. They divided into three parties, and when the middle party was just beyond the mouth of the crater, a frightful explosive eruption began. The entire group, about four hundred people, perished in their tracks — some by burns, some by falling stones, but most by suffocation. This event was taken as an omen that Pele, the revered volcano goddess, was on the side of Kamehameha.

Further expeditions against Keoua were routed, however, and then Kamehameha bethought himself of the soothsayer's words and began building the immense heiau near Kawaihae. The priests busily directed the thousands of commoners who thronged from all parts of Kamehameha's domains to carry stones for the temple, and the nobles and even their ruler hauled rocks for the edifice.

Kahekili had taken advantage of the struggle with Keoua to recapture Molokai and Maui, and now began an invasion of northern Hawaii with a large fleet of canoes. Kamehameha's policy of collecting foreign guns and gunners at last paid off. Swivel guns were mounted on some of his double canoes, manned by crews under the direction of two Englishmen, John Young and Isaac

Davis, who had been persuaded to enter his service. He probably also used a little Yankee sloop, the *Fair American*, that had come into his hands.

But the opposing fleet also had guns and foreigners (including one "Mare Amara," which could be translated as "Murray the armorer"), and this first Hawaiian naval engagement making use of cannon was so long and bloody that it became known as Kepuwahaulaula (The Red-mouthed Gun). It was fought off Waipio in April or May, 1791. The guns of Kamehameha were fired with better effect, however, and finally the enemy fleet was driven back to Maui.

Now only one chief — his cousin Keoua — stood in the way of Kamehameha's domination of the Big Island. The great heiau was finished in the summer of 1791, and messengers were sent to Keoua to come to this temple and talk of peace face to face. Unless Keoua was willing to acknowledge Kamehameha as his overlord, such a talk could lead to little more than a truce. But Keoua fatalistically agreed and with his supporters made the canoe journey to Kawaihae. He must have had premonitions of what he would meet there, for shortly before arriving he put in his own canoe the men that would be suitable death companions for him.

Entering the bay, Keoua saw the big new heiau on the hill. Beside it stood Kamehameha, grim in feather cloak and helmet, hailing him: "Rise and come here, that we may know each other." Keoua returned the greeting and was about to step out of his canoe when Keeaumoku, one of Kamehameha's paladins, hurled his spear. Keoua fell after a brief struggle, along with his companions in the canoe, and his body was the first sacrifice on the new altar of Kamehameha's war god.

Thereafter for several years Kamehameha ruled wisely the island of Hawaii, all now a part of his kingdom. Captain George Vancouver, who made three visits to the islands between 1792 and 1794, found that Kamehameha had mellowed since he had first seen him when a midshipman with Cook fourteen years before. "I was agreeably surprised," Vancouver wrote, "in finding that his riper years had softened that stern ferocity which his younger days had exhibited, and had changed his general deportment to an address characteristic of an open, cheerful, and sensible mind, combined with great generosity and goodness of disposition." He concluded that Kamehameha's conduct had been "of the most princely nature."

Vancouver in 1793 fitted out one of the king's double canoes with a full set of sails, sloop-fashion, and gave him a Union Jack to fly before his house. The following year he found the king's carpenter, James Boyd, trying to build a sailing ship, and ordered his men to supply ironwork, masts, and sails to finish the vessel, which was christened the *Britannia*. Vancouver spoke out violently against the trade in arms and ammunition that was going on. Soulless captains were selling defective guns and adulterated powder to the chiefs. Vancouver's surgeons saved the life of a young chief at Kealakekua whose right arm had been taken off when a worthless gun exploded. But despite the British commander's advice, Kamehameha continued to invest in haole armaments. The wars were not yet over.

In the spring or summer of 1794, not long after Vancouver's final departure, old King Kahekili, ruler of all the islands except Hawaii, died at Waikiki. His dominions were divided between his younger brother Kaeo and his son Kalanikupule, who soon disagreed and fell into a struggle that was to prove fatal to both.

Kaeo was at Waianae on Oahu in mid-November, on his way back to his island of Kauai, when he learned that some of his chiefs were plotting against him. To divert their restless spirits with ideas of plunder, he proposed an attack on his nephew Kalanikupule. His eager troops marched to the campaign, and in several weeks advanced through the Ewa district and defeated the Oahu forces at Aiea.

Things looked black for Kalanikupule, and he conceived the idea of enlisting foreign aid. Three trading ships were then on his shores. One was the American ship *Lady Washington*, under Captain John Kendrick. The other two, the *Jackall* and the *Prince Lee Boo*, were under the command of an Englishman, Captain William Brown. This was Brown's third trip to the islands, and a year or two before, in the London ship *Butterworth*, he had entered the harbor of Honolulu — probably the first foreigner to do so. He had previously sold guns and ammunition to any chiefs who could buy them, and he now readily supplied them to Kalanikupule, while the mate of the *Jackall*, George Lamport, and eight sailors volunteered to fight for the defenders of Oahu. They were stationed in boats, along the eastern arm of what is now called Pearl Harbor. Their flanking fire helped to bring victory in the battle, in which Kaeo, singled out by his yellow feather cloak, was killed.

Captain Brown decided to celebrate the occasion by firing a salute from his ship. By mistake, one of the guns was loaded with grapeshot, and the salute crashed through the side of the *Lady Washington*, anchored nearby, killing Kendrick and several officers who were at dinner with him.

Under another captain, the *Lady Washington* soon sailed for Canton, but the other two ships remained in the harbor for several weeks, butchering and salting the four hundred hogs paid them for their help. Kalanikupule began to get ambitious ideas about conquering Kamehameha with the aid of these fine ships. He formed a murderous plot, and on New Year's Day, 1795, his warriors captured the *Jackall* and the *Prince Lee Boo*. Both captains, Brown and Gordon, were killed, and the members of the crew, who were ashore, were made prisoners.

The sailors were forced to fit out their ships for war and store them with ammunition. On January 12 they were anchored off Waikiki and the king, his chiefs, and some warriors came aboard, ready to sail against Kamehameha. But the two mates, George Lamport and William Bonallack, had also made a plan. At midnight they led a desperate uprising. The natives on board were killed or driven away, with the exception of the king and queen and their servants, and the triumphant Britishers put to sea. At dawn they went inshore again, dumped the discomfited royal family into a canoe, and then sailed for Hawaii. There they left the armament as a gift for Kamehameha, with a letter telling him of the plot. Then they departed for Canton, having had more than enough of a taste of partaking in civil war in the Sandwich Islands.

Kamehameha was ready to act. He had built up a well-drilled army of sixteen thousand men — the largest ever seen in the islands — and a fleet of canoes to transport them. Sixteen white men were in his service; Young and Davis were again in charge of the artillery.

First Maui and then Molokai fell before him. Then he crossed to Oahu. Here Kaiana, the much-traveled chief, decided to leave him and fight on the other side; but the loss was not fatal to Kamehameha.

The invading fleet of canoes stretched from Waialae Bay to Waikiki. The warriors poured ashore and fought their way up to the Nuuanu Valley behind Honolulu. There the defenders of Oahu, battling desperately, were slowly driven up the slope, until the retreat turned into a rout. Some of the fleeing soldiers escaped over the knife-edged ridges on either side of the valley, some scrambled down the hazardous Pali trail toward Koolau. But many, driven before the artillery of Kamehameha, were forced to leap to destruction over the thousand-foot precipice of the Pali.

In this decisive battle of Nuuanu, in the spring or summer of 1795, Kaiana was killed and the defeated Kalanikupule, after wandering in the mountains for several months, was captured and sacrificed to Kamehameha's war god. A period of relative peace was to follow, for except for the leeward islands of Kauai and Niihau, all the territories of the Hawaiian group were now under the sway of the conquering Kamehameha.

Kamehameha's Kingdom

A Scots sailor named Archibald Campbell, seeking refuge in the Sandwich Islands after losing his feet from frostbite in Alaska, had been kindly treated by Kamehameha I, who had made the white man a chief. Now, in 1810, Campbell was ready to leave for England on the sealer *Duke of Portland*, and was given the king's permission to depart. "He then desired me," wrote Campbell, "to give his compliments to King George. I told him that, though born in his dominions, I had never seen King George; and that, even in the city where he lived, there were thousands who had never seen him. He expressed much surprise at this, and asked if he did not go about amongst his people, to learn their wants, as he did? I answered that he did not do it himself, but that he had men who did it for him. Kamehameha shook his head at this, and said that other people could never do it as well as he could himself."

Founder of the Dynasty

KAMEHAMEHA DID INDEED GIVE PERSONAL ATTENTION TO THE NEEDS of his people and of the visitors from the world beyond his islands. He was to live into his sixties and to reign over the united group for a quarter of a century. His strong mind was well able to deal with problems of government, and he rigidly put down disorder and crime. He was ruthless in war — especially during his earlier career, when the task of winning the kingdom might have seemed insuperable — but when the fighting was over, he was capable of forgiveness and statesmanship. He was faithful to the traditions of his race; yet he was curious about the new things the foreigners brought into his realm, and adopted new ideas when they seemed good to him. Perhaps his strongest trait was the capacity to inspire devotion in his followers. He was the foremost of the chiefs to appreciate the advantages of friendly relations with the foreigners, and took many of them into his service; but they were his advisers only, and never his masters.

During his reign over the united islands, Kamehameha still bore traces of the savage-looking face that Lieutenant King had described in 1779. "He is of large stature and very athletic," wrote Thomas Manby in 1793; "his countenance is truly savage, as all his fore-teeth are out." (Kamehameha had knocked out several of his teeth between 1789 and 1791, probably as a sign of mourning.) Richard Cleveland, supercargo of the *Lelia Byrd*, described him in 1803 as "a perfect savage, but evidently destined by nature, both physically and mentally, to be a chief." Samuel Patterson, who stopped at Oahu in 1805, remarked on the king's desire to own foreign goods by terming him "an artful and sagacious man, and extremely avaricious. He wants everything he sees." Amasa Delano, on the other hand, put him down in 1809 as "a man of very good natural abilities, of tender feelings, and aiming to be just, making a very good ruler."

Peter Corney in 1815 described the king thus: "He is a tall, stout, athletic man, nose rather flat, thick lips, the upper one turned up; an open countenance, with three of his lower front teeth gone." One of the best descriptions of Kamehameha was given by Campbell, who wrote: "In 1809 the king seemed about fifty years of age; he is a stout, well-made man, rather darker in the complexion than the natives usually are, and wants two of his front teeth. The expression of his countenance is agreeable, and he is mild and affable in his manners, and possesses great warmth of feeling; for I have seen him shed tears upon the departure of those to whom he was attached, and has the art of attaching others to himself. Although a conqueror, he is extremely popular among his subjects; and not without reason, for since he attained the supreme power, they have enjoyed repose and prosperity."

The only portrait of Kamehameha made during his lifetime is the one by Louis Choris; this likeness was good enough to be recognized and approved by some of the king's subjects. The statues of him erected in the islands are idealized images of the Hawaiian warrior, robed in a feather cloak and bearing the *pololu*, a barbed spear signifying peace. The statue that stands in front of the Judiciary Building in downtown Honolulu — a striking sight on Kamehameha Day, when it is draped with dozens of long and fragrant strands of flowers — is a replica. By a quirk of fate, the original statue was erected in Kohala, Kamehameha's birthplace on the Big Island. This is the story:

The legislature of 1878, to commemorate the centennial of the discovery of the islands, appropriated money for the original statue. When it was being molded by Thomas R. Gould in Florence, Italy, the residents of Kohala argued that it should be erected in Kamehameha's homeland, rather than in Honolulu as the legislative act provided. "You will see," they predicted; "the statue will still come to Kohala."

The statue was shipped on the German bark *G. F. Haendel* of Bremen in September, 1880. This ship caught fire and sank off the

Falkland Islands at the tip of South America. The statue was salvaged by a junk dealer and set up for sale on the beach at Port Stanley, but it found no buyer until the *Earl of Dalhousie* touched there on its way to Honolulu with a shipload of Portuguese laborers. Captain Jarvis risked £100 of his money and bought the statue. When he arrived in Honolulu, he sold it to the government for £175. A replica had been bought with insurance money and set up in Honolulu, and so the original was erected in Kohala. Thus the king returned to his birthplace after all.

Kamehameha led his people in practicing the arts of peace. After the civil wars were over in 1795, the land was untilled and starvation was rife. The king urged his people to raise food, and he himself took the lead. His subjects said of him: "He is a farmer, a fisherman, a maker of cloth, a provider for the needy, and a father to the fatherless." He ordered the cultivation of the soil and himself worked in the communal fields, first divesting himself temporarily of the sacred *kapu*, so that the workers around him would not have to prostrate themselves every few minutes when he walked by, digging stick in hand. Campbell observed that, although the cultivation of taro is laborious and the workers are almost continually up to the middle in mud, he had often seen Kamehameha working in a taro patch. "I know not whether this was done with a view to setting an example of industry to his subjects. Such exertion could scarcely be thought necessary amongst these islanders, who are certainly the most industrious people I ever saw." (High praise, indeed, from a Scotsman!)

Kamehameha could be imposing in his dress, whether he wore a priceless cloak of yellow feathers or the full uniform of an officer of the British Navy. His favorite attire was a large Chinese dressing gown which he had inherited from King Kalaniopuu, to whom it had been given by Captain Cook a few days before his death. But when the ceremonies were over, Kamehameha would doff his foreign garments and slip into a loincloth in which he could relax with his friends, or engage in surfboard-riding or other strenuous feats. During the *makahiki* festival, he was required to take part by proving his skill at self-defense. "He is obliged," wrote Campbell, "to stand till three spears are darted at him; he must catch the first with his hand, and with it ward off the other two. This is not a mere formality. The spear is thrown with the utmost force, and should the king lose his life, there is no help for it." Captain George Vancouver also reported that in such an attack he saw the king ward off six spears hurled at him at almost the same instant. Three he caught in the air with one hand; two more he broke by parrying them with his own spear; and the sixth he dodged, so that it fell harmlessly.

Kamehameha's mind, stored with the lore of his race, was faithful until his death to the religion in which he had been brought up, and to the grim war god that had brought him to power. He told Captain von Kotzebue in 1816: "These are our gods, which I worship; whether I do right or wrong in thus worshiping them, I know not, but I follow my religion, which cannot be bad, since it teaches me to do no wrong." The death penalty for violating a *kapu* was invoked by him as late as 1817. Campbell once saw one of the queens partaking of the forbidden delicacy of shark's flesh, and was pledged to secrecy, since it would be as much as her life was worth if she were found out. When one of the other wives of Kamehameha fell ill in 1807, a priest claimed that the illness arose because somebody had eaten ten *kapu* coconuts; luckily, she recovered rapidly, so that only three of the ten men seized for sacrifice were actually executed.

Kamehameha believed in his gods. One of the large craters on the top of Mount Hualalai in Kona erupted in 1801. The lava poured down, flattening stone walls, trees, and houses before it; it covered several villages, destroyed plantations and fishponds, and filled up a deep bay along the coast. The priests tried to appease the anger of the gods by offering many sacrifices, and numerous hogs were thrown alive into the burning stream; but all to no avail. Then one day Kamehameha went to the river of lava with his retinue. As the most valuable offering he could make, he cut off part of his hair and threw it into the torrent. A day or two later the lava ceased to flow, and the king obtained further influence for thus saving his people from the anger of the volcano gods.

At other times, the judgment of Kamehameha might seem to us harsher than that of Solomon. Before the king moved to Honolulu, he had his eldest son executed for tampering with one of his father's wives. Again, around 1810, a native couple, tenants of John Young, quarreled over their little boy, and in wrath the husband picked up the child and killed it before the eyes of his horrified wife. When the man was brought by Young to be punished, Kamehameha asked: "To whom did this child belong?" It was the murderer's own son, said Young. "Then," came the king's edict, "neither you nor I have any right to interfere."

Like too many of his chiefs, Kamehameha at first fell under the sway of the white man's firewater, and for a time kept a bottle always handy. But gradually, seeing the evil that drunkenness was working among his people, he restricted his grog to a small allowance a day, and later on, strengthened by the advice of John Young, he abandoned liquor entirely and prohibited its manufacture in his kingdom. His antipathy became so great that when he was stricken with a bad cold and Marín the Spaniard tried to get him to take a cup of eggnog laced with gin, Kamehameha violently dashed the drink into the face of the faithful physician.

The king was fond of entertainment, and the earliest theatrical performance in the islands was given under his sponsorship. "A theater was erected," wrote Campbell, "under the direction of James Beattie, the king's block-maker, who had been at one time on the stage in England. The scenes representing a castle and a forest were constructed of different-colored pieces of tapa, cut out and pasted together.

"I was present on one occasion, at the performance of *Oscar and Malvina*. This piece was originally a pantomime, but here it had words written for it by Beattie. The part of Malvina was performed by the wife of Isaac Davis. As her knowledge of the English language was very limited, extending only to the words 'yes' and 'no,' her speeches were confined to these monosyllables. She, however, acted her part with great applause. The Fingalian heroes were represented by natives clothed in the Highland garb, also made out of tapa, and armed with muskets.

"The audience did not seem to understand the play well, but were greatly delighted with the after-piece, representing a naval engagement. The ships were armed with bamboo cannon, and each of them fired a broadside, by means of a train of thread dipped in saltpeter, which communicated with each gun, after which one of the vessels blew up. Unfortunately, the explosion set fire to the forest, and nearly consumed the theater."

Bright Flags from Afar

THE ERA OF KAMEHAMEHA WAS AS CLOSE AS THE HAWAIIAN PEOPLE ever came to a golden age. The temperate climate of the islands allowed a healthy outdoor existence, and in spite of the frequent wars — which often provided the chiefs with an outlet for their proud exuberance — the population was well adjusted to its environment. The rigors of primitive living and a system of infanticide kept the people from crowding the food supply. The common man, it is true, worked hard most of the time and gave much of his produce to the taxgatherer; but he could move about somewhat and find a less exacting chief, and on the whole his lot was certainly better than that of many a European peasant in 1778.

In many ways, the islands were truly a paradise. There were no mosquitoes, cockroaches, scorpions, centipedes, house rats, spirochetes, or measles viruses. All these were introduced — usually by accident — by the white men. Mosquitoes were planted in island waters deliberately, it is said, when the crew of the *Wellington*, angered when they arrived in 1826 from San Blas, Mexico, and found that women were not permitted to swim out to them, let loose the larvae found in the water casks.

The foreigners, of course, did bring in many useful plants and animals to supplement the meager diet of fish, dog, pork, and poi; but the arrival of Cook and the throng of visitors who followed him in later years was certainly not an unmixed blessing. The introduction of new diseases accounted in large part — along with civil war, famine, intermarriage with the foreigners, and the hazards of a new way of life — for the great decline in native population not long after. In Cook's time, it is estimated, the Hawaiians numbered some three hundred thousand; today, there are about twelve thousand pure-blooded Hawaiians in their native isles, or less than three per cent of the population. About seventeen per cent are listed as part Hawaiians; the mingling of the races began as soon as Cook's ships dropped anchor, and caused a new and increasing element in the islands — the *hapa-haole*, or those of mixed blood.

Did any foreigners reach the Hawaiian Islands before Cook? It does seem hardly possible that the Spaniards, who voyaged in these latitudes for two centuries, never sighted the islands whose towering mountains are visible for many miles at sea. Stories grew up after 1779 that the Spanish had really found the isles and put them on some of their maps. In particular, a voyager named Juan Gaetano was supposed to have discovered them in 1555 and reported their location to his Colonial Office. But careful studies, such as that by E. W. Dahlgren, have pretty well exploded the theory that the Spanish knew about Hawaii and kept it a secret.

It is barely possible that a few foreigners, either Spanish or Japanese, were shipwrecked on Hawaii. William Ellis, who made a famous tour around the Big Island in 1823, mentioned that he found a number of natives with lighter skins and curly brown hair who called themselves *ehu* and proudly considered that they were descended from foreigners landing on their shores. But even though it is conceivable that castaways might have reached the islands earlier than Cook, the event was of little consequence to history, for nobody before him brought authentic knowledge of Hawaii to the outside world.

The first ships to arrive after the days of Cook were brought by news that a few skins of the sea otter collected by his men on the Northwest Coast had sold in China for high prices. Ten years after Cook left Nootka Sound, ships of England, Spain, Russia, and the United States were combing that region for these precious furs. They soon discovered the advantages of stopping at the Sandwich Islands to obtain provisions, news, rest, and female companionship. Here was a providential way station between America and China, and the pork and yams of the islands became a mainstay of diet for the fur hunters. When furs became scarcer and two seasons were needed to obtain a cargo, the custom of wintering in the islands became popular. After about 1792 hardly a ship in the trade failed to stop at some time in Hawaiian ports.

The first merchant ship to reach the islands was a 60-ton brig (name unknown) under Captain James Hanna which, in the autumn of 1785, touched there on the way to China with a valuable cargo of otter furs. The following spring, two English traders — Nathaniel Portlock in the *King George* and George Dixon in the *Queen Charlotte,* both of whom had been with Cook at the time of his death — spent twenty days in the islands on their way to Nootka. The two ships had been sent out by a group of Englishmen who, under the name of King George's Sound Company, had been given an exclusive trading privilege on the Northwest Coast. These ships returned later in the year and wintered at the islands.

An ill-fated French exploring expedition spent one day ashore in the group. King Louis XVI, dreaming that one of his subjects might emulate the exploits of Cook, had sent out two frigates, *La Boussole* and *L'Astrolabe,* under the command of the gallant Jean François de Galoup, Count de la Pérouse. On May 28, 1786, he and his officers visited the village on the bay of Keoneoio, Maui, traded for hogs and vegetables, and obtained some feather cloaks and helmets. Pleased with the friendliness of the people, they might have stayed longer, but their ships began dragging anchor in the wind and they sailed for Alaska. Later La Pérouse discovered Necker Island and French Frigate Shoal, both belonging to the Hawaiian chain. The loss of his ships in the Solomon Islands was to be a sea mystery for nearly forty years.

The *Imperial Eagle,* under the flag of the Austrian East India Company, stopped at the islands in 1787 on the way to Canton with a cargo of furs. Captain Barclay put ashore a passenger, John Mackay, who had been a surgeon's mate on a trading ship and by his own wish had spent a year among the Indians of the Nootka Sound country as the first European resident of that region. This Irish "doctor" was to become as well the first white resident of the Hawaiian Islands. The *Imperial Eagle* took away the first Hawaiian to sail for foreign lands. Strangely, this native was a woman, whom the captain's wife hired as her maid. (The girl's name was put down as "Wynee"; possibly this was a misunderstanding of "wahine," the Hawaiian word for "woman.")

Captain John Meares arrived in 1787, after a year of hardships on the coast near Prince William's Sound, in the 200-ton snow *Nootka,* in which he took Chief Kaiana to China. In the same year two other British merchantmen wintered in the islands: the *Prince of Wales* under James Colnett and the *Princess Royal* under Charles Duncan. The next year William Douglas arrived in the *Iphigenia Nubiana,* Robert Funter came in the *North West America,* and Meares returned to the islands, this time in the *Felice Adventurer.* The British ship *Mercury* arrived in 1789 under Captain T. H. Cox, who occasionally sailed under Swedish colors, at those times calling his vessel the *Gustavus III.* The *Grace,* commanded by William Douglas, came in 1790.

The first American ship to arrive in the islands touched there in the fall of 1789; it went on and earned the further distinction of being the first American ship to circumnavigate the globe. It was the *Columbia Rediviva,* a 220-ton, two-decked, full-rigged ship armed with ten guns and commanded by Robert Gray, who later discovered the Columbia River. This ship was probably accompanied by the 90-ton sloop *Lady Washington* under John Kendrick, who certainly came to the islands in the same ship in 1791 and there was killed by a salute gun. In 1791 Captain Samuel Crowell arrived in the brig *Hancock*. Within a decade thereafter, the transpacific fur trade, because of the preoccupation of Europeans with the Napoleonic wars, was to become almost an American monopoly.

The first Hawaiian to visit the United States was a young native of Kauai named Opai, who was taken aboard by Gray and sailed in the *Columbia* on its voyage of circumnavigation. Opai, returning from his round-the-world tour, came back to the islands in 1791 in the Boston brigantine *Hope*, commanded by Joseph Ingraham, who had also sailed with Gray. Opai, in true Hawaiian fashion, had swapped names with the captain of the *Hope*, and thereafter called himself "Joseph Ingraham." When the flagship of George Vancouver arrived off Oahu in 1792, it was hailed in English by this wandering Joseph, who soon decided to take another voyage and joined the ship's complement on its round trip to the Northwest Coast.

The first stowaways to leave Paradise were two native women, Laheina and Kaimalo, who hid aboard the Bristol ship *Jenny* off Niihau. They worked their passage to Nootka, washing dishes in the galley, and were brought back by Captain Vancouver when he returned to the islands in 1793.

Two Britishers who became the most celebrated early white residents of the islands arrived in 1790. In February of that year, Captain Simon Metcalfe of the Boston snow *Eleanora* was trading off Honuaula, Maui, when one of his boats was stolen and the sailor in it was killed. The captain retaliated by firing some shots into the village. Hearing that the thieves came from Olowalu, up the coast, he sailed there and encouraged the people to come to the ship and start trading. Then the crafty Yankee had his revenge. He placed a *kapu* on one side of the vessel; from the other side protruded all his cannon, loaded with musket balls and langrage. When scores of canoes were floating within range, he let off the deadly broadside, under which at least a hundred natives were killed outright.

Leaving behind the victims of this "Olowalu massacre," Metcalfe sailed to the Big Island. But he had forgotten the rule about the sins of the fathers, and fate was planning its own ironic revenge. When Kameeiamoku, one of Kamehameha's councillors, came aboard, Metcalfe gave him a taste of a rope's end, and the chief decided that the next foreign ship on that coast would pay for the insult.

Some weeks later, Metcalfe's eighteen-year-old son Thomas arrived off Kawaihae in the little schooner *Fair American*, to make a rendezvous with his father. Kameeiamoku took the craft by surprise on March 16, threw Thomas overboard (although he was unaware that the lad was the son of his enemy), and killed all five members of the crew except one man named Isaac Davis.

The *Eleanora* was at that time anchored off Kailua, down the coast, and on the very day of the attack Simon sent ashore his boatswain, John Young, to seek news of Tom from several white men living in Kamehameha's domains. These men were the Irishman Mackay and three Americans: S. I. Thomas, who had arrived in the *Columbia* in 1791; Isaac Ridler, carpenter's mate of the *Columbia*, who may have been left ashore to collect sandalwood; and a third American who had come in the *Grace* and who, by coincidence, was also named John Young. From these men the boatswain heard of the attack on the *Fair American*, but Kamehameha — who had rebuked Kameeiamoku and taken charge of the small schooner — feared retaliation, and kept the boatswain from sending the news to the *Eleanora*. Metcalfe wrote a letter to the white men ashore, threatening vengeance if his boatswain was not returned, but soon gave up and left the islands without him and without having learned the fate of his son.

The American John Young and Isaac Ridler could not get along with Kamehameha and escaped to Maui to join his enemy Kahekili; there they were picked up by Ingraham and taken to China. The British John Young stayed — at first as a captive, and later of his own free will. He soon became a friend of Isaac Davis, the lone survivor of the *Fair American*. Davis had been spared because he had fought bravely. He was found tied in a canoe, half blind and half dead, by Ridler, who interceded for his life and nursed him back to health.

Both Young and Davis were simple and uneducated, but they were men of integrity and common sense, and they soon became Kamehameha's most trusted advisers. Young, best known by his nickname of "Olohana" (a Hawaiian version of his boatswain's cry of "All hands!"), aided Kamehameha in the wars, and later became governor of several of the islands. He died in Honolulu in 1835. His descendants were prominent in Hawaiian history, and one of his granddaughters became the good Queen Emma, wife of Kamehameha IV. Davis, a Welshman known as "Aikake" (Isaac), also became a high chief, was married twice, and founded the oldest foreign family in the islands. One reason for the high prestige of the British Empire in the reign of Kamehameha I was the sterling character of these two castaways.

The first French trader, Etienne Marchand, touched Hawaii in the *Solide* in October, 1791. In that year the Spanish flag was first flown in these waters by Lieutenant Manuel Quimper on the *Princess Royal*, which had been captured from James Colnett at Nootka. Quimper was now taking this ship to Macao to return it to the English. Strangely enough, Colnett happened to be off the Big Island at this same time, in command of the trader *Argonaut*. Colnett became at once fearful that Spain was plotting to settle the islands. The sight of his old ship under the Spanish banner was nearly too much for him, and after a talk with Quimper he almost came to an exchange of broadsides with the Spaniards. But Quimper departed peacefully, and thereafter Spain, which had once laid claim to all the rolling South Sea, took little part in the history of Hawaii.

A Visitor Named Vancouver

THE MOST IMPORTANT VISITOR DURING THE REIGN OF KAMEHAMEHA was Captain George Vancouver, and the record of his visits makes a happy page in island annals. The captain was then thirty-four — almost twice as old as he had been when as one of Cook's midshipmen he had first sighted Kealakekua. Now he had a double chin and an air of authority, but his face still bore traces of youthful candor. Vancouver had been sent from England to settle certain disputes with the Spanish about land rights at Nootka Sound, and to complete the explorations of Cook on the Northwest Coast. He had two vessels under his command: the sloop *Discovery* (not the same *Discovery* in which he had sailed with Cook), and the *Chatham* (commanded at first by Lieutenant William Robert Broughton, and later by Lieutenant Peter Puget). A supply vessel, the *Daedalus*, met the squadron twice.

Vancouver's first stop in the islands, in March, 1792, was so brief that he met none of the important chiefs except Kaiana and the young prince of Kauai, Kaumualii; but on his successive visits, in the spring of 1793 and the spring of 1794, he saw all the islands and became well acquainted with the people. Kamehameha in particular aroused his interest and support, and the success of the conqueror was due in no small part to his friendship with the Englishman.

Cattle and sheep were introduced into the islands by Vancouver on his second visit; and these animals, brought from California, were used to start an industry that became highly valuable through the years. At first view of the cows aboard ship, Kamehameha feared that these "big hogs" might attack him, but later he began asking all sorts of questions about their care and feeding. When the first cow was taken ashore at Kealakekua she dashed wildly down the beach, leaving in her wake a throng of scared Hawaiians. On his final trip, Vancouver gave Kamehameha three young bulls, two cows, five rams, and five ewes. Asking about the health of the cows that had been left there the previous year, Vancouver was told the story of the bull calf. It had been born when the king was at Hilo, and Keeaumoku was so anxious to show him the bovine offspring that the calf was carried overland on the backs of runners. The infant was fed en route on fish, but in three days it arrived at Hilo, healthy and lively, for Kamehameha to admire.

Vancouver also brought in goats and geese, and gave orange and almond trees to the chiefs of the various islands. He found that the natives were already growing delicious muskmelons, from seeds given them by Portlock in 1786. Next to Vancouver himself, the most helpful member of the expedition was the naturalist Archibald Menzies, a clever and energetic Scotsman who had been among the islands in 1787 as surgeon of the *Prince of Wales*. He collected and classified the flora of the regions he visited, and led an expedition up the sides of Mauna Loa to study that volcanic region. Menzies also introduced many new fruits and vegetables, including a number of young orange trees which he had raised on shipboard from seeds obtained at the Cape of Good Hope. Sixty years later, the oranges of Kona were one of the important island products for export.

On his second trip Vancouver was warmly welcomed by Kamehameha on the Big Island. He also met the favorite wife of the king. She was Kaahumanu, a daughter of Keeaumoku, and had been "born with a yellow feather in her mouth" — the Hawaiian equivalent of a silver spoon. She was to become, after Kamehameha's death, the most important person in the kingdom. At this time she was about twenty-five, but appeared to the English captain to be "about sixteen, and undoubtedly did credit to the choice and taste of Kamehameha, being one of the finest women we had yet seen on any of the islands." When he returned a year later, Vancouver was saddened to learn that she had separated from the king, who suspected her of dalliance with the handsome Kaiana.

By a happy strategem Vancouver was able to reunite the estranged pair.

On his second visit Vancouver had a gloomy matter to settle with Kahekili, then king of Oahu and Kauai. His supply ship, the *Daedalus*, had anchored in May, 1792, off the mouth of Waimea Stream on the windward shore of Oahu. Lieutenant Hergest, in charge of the vessel, had led a watering party up the stream without taking proper precautions against attack. Accompanied only by the astronomer, Mr. Gooch, and two seamen, he had been trapped by a group of natives and all were killed except one of the sailors. The Hawaiians may have been after firearms; orders had been given not to tempt them by taking guns ashore, but, unknown to Hergest, some muskets had been put in the boat.

Vancouver was determined to have the offenders punished as an object lesson. Three natives who might have been implicated were brought in a canoe to the side of the *Discovery* off Waikiki and shot to death by a pistol in the hands of a native executioner.

Vancouver made active efforts during his visits to reconcile the warring chieftains, and time and again he inveighed against the wicked traders who sold firearms. Just before his final departure, Vancouver obtained from Kamehameha on February 25, 1794, what the Englishman called a "cession" of the island of Hawaii to Great Britain. This pact was celebrated by the raising of the British flag over the same Bay of Kealakekua where Cook had fallen fourteen years before. The British government never ratified the agreement, and Kamehameha probably did not feel that he was putting his island under the protection of the nation that had sent his friend Vancouver to visit him. None the less, England's influence was foremost in the islands in the early years.

Narratives of the Vancouver visits have a lighter side. One of Vancouver's officers was a gay young blade named Thomas Manby, whose journal reveals that his main interest in the islands was amorous. "The girls were by no means equal in beauty to the Otahiteans," he wrote; "they are of darker complexion and not so prettily featured. Instead of graceful ringlets to gratify the eye, the hair is cropped close to the head except in the fore part, where it is plastered up with lime, which gives it a dirty red color." Manby was here remarking on the old Polynesian beauty hint of bleaching the hair. He was also unaware that a Hawaiian sign of mourning was to knock out a few teeth. "Some abominable custom has deprived every woman of her foreteeth. The deuce take the inventor of such a fashion!" None the less, young Tom was always ready to welcome a canoeload of "good-natured brunettes," and proudly records that after he spent the night ashore with two beauteous nymphs, each one presented him with a small packet containing six pearls.

The Melting Pot Begins to Bubble

ONE OF KAMEHAMEHA'S GREATEST QUALITIES WAS HIS ABILITY TO attract many white men to his service and retain their loyalty for years or even a lifetime. Right from the beginning, foreigners were welcomed by the Hawaiians, and it was fashionable for each chief to have at least one of them as an adviser.

The island melting pot began to simmer early. There were at least eleven foreigners on Hawaii in 1794, including American, English, Irish, Portuguese, Genoese, and Chinese. Twenty-five years later, between one and two hundred foreigners lived on the islands. Hardly a ship touched without leaving a deserter or two behind to enjoy the charms of the tropics, and escaped convicts from European colonies were not unknown. The beachcomber's lot was not always a happy one. Alexander Ross, who stopped at Oahu for a few days in 1811, later recalled that he had seen there "eight or ten white men comfortably settled; and upwards of thirty others naked and wild among the natives, wretched unprincipled vagabonds of almost every nation in Europe, without clothing and without either house or home."

Many of the white men, however, became solid citizens, and their skill and knowledge of civilized arts were invaluable during Kamehameha's rise and reign. The king found jobs for them to do, and most of them worked faithfully as experts in one or another post of importance. A white man automatically ranked as a chief, although he could not own land in fee simple or build a permanent house. Many of them settled in the kingdom and took native wives, and the origin of more than one family important in the story of Hawaii derives from these early foreign residents.

They came from several lands. Oliver Holmes was a blueblood from Massachusetts. John Palmer Parker also came from that state; he was put in charge of the king's cattle herds, an assignment that led to the founding of the great Parker Ranch. George McClay, another Yankee, had been a carpenter in English vessels; he was a good-natured, honest fellow who built some twenty small craft for the king's fleet. William Moxley was a young Virginian. John Young and Isaac Davis were British, as was George Beckley, a sea captain who commanded Kamehameha's fort in Honolulu. James Boyd, shipbuilder, was an Englishman who had been mate of the American sloop *Washington*. Another British tar, Alexander Adams, was captain of the king's most valuable ship. John Harbottle, Honolulu pilot, had been mate of the *Jackall* of London. Another Englishman, with the prosaic name of John Smith, had become one of Kamehameha's chiefs after leaving an American fur ship because of ill treatment. James Beattie, Kamahameha's "blockmaker," had been a London actor. William Davis was a hardworking Welshman. Captain Alexander Stewart, born in the Orkneys, who had sailed with Duncan and with Brown, had settled at Kealakekua in 1795. Archibald Campbell, who found no less than sixty white men living on Oahu when he arrived there in 1809, was a Scot whom the king set up in business as a weaver of cloth. He discovered a compatriot on Maui who went by the name of Joseph Wynn but was actually Angus McCallum of Renfrewshire. Another Scot, named Law, was the king's physician. William

Stevenson was a Scotsman who had escaped from Botany Bay; he was noted for having been the first to distill a fiery liquor from the root of the ti plant, but had restricted his drinking to New Year's Day, and for the rest of the year labored from dawn to dark raising European vegetables in his garden.

A zealous Englishman named John Howel, who arrived as a clerk on the *Lady Washington*, decided to settle on Hawaii. He had once been a clergyman of the Church of England, and liked to be called "Padre" Howel. He tried several times to convert Kamehameha, who finally responded: "You say that your God will shield those who truly believe in Him. Give me proof of this by jumping off the Kealakekua cliffs. If you are unharmed, then I will embrace your religion." After one look at the jagged precipice, Padre Howel's missionary zeal departed from him.

An American Negro named Anthony Allen, who had been a slave in Schenectady, New York, arrived in 1810 and soon became one of the most respected citizens of Honolulu. On his farm on the plain toward Waikiki he supported his native wife and three children by selling milk from his cows and goats, and by running a sort of sailor's boardinghouse.

An amusing adventurer who spent some years at the court of Kamehameha was John Elliot de Castro, of English and Portuguese blood. Chamisso jokingly described him as being so small that he did not even reach to his own knees. Elliot's quest for fortune had led him to many parts of the globe, including Rio de Janeiro and Buenos Aires (where he had been imprisoned for smuggling tobacco). Around 1814 he acted as Kamehameha's physician, but after a while, still searching for easy money, he went to Sitka and later wound up in a San Francisco jail. There Captain Otto von Kotzebue rescued him in 1816 and brought him back to Hawaii, where he was of much use to the Russians as an interpreter. When Golovnin, captain of another Russian ship, arrived there in 1818, he was given to understand that Elliot was Kamehameha's secretary of state, and spent much time in his charming company.

One of the earliest foreign residents of Honolulu was Don Francisco de Paula Marín, whom the Hawaiians called "Manini." He served as Kamehameha's interpreter, his business manager, and, on occasion, his tailor. He cultivated large stretches of garden land and pasture, and was responsible for introducing dozens of useful plants into the islands. He had some knowledge of medicine, and was to attend Kamehameha on his deathbed.

Marín was a native of Jerez in Andalusia, where the sherry comes from, and went to California with a Spanish expedition under Captain Juan Francisco Bodega y Quadra. He was still very young when, according to a story in Chamisso's journal, he made a "Shanghai passage" to Hawaii. In San Francisco, Marín was sent with fruit and vegetables on board a ship that was about to leave port. (This ship was probably the *Princess Royal*, which arrived in the islands in 1791, the first vessel to sail those waters under the Spanish banner.) The sailors gave him a few drinks, the boy fell asleep, and when he awoke he was on his way to the Sandwich Islands.

He went ashore and wandered from island to island until he met Kamehameha, and thereafter followed the fortunes of the conqueror. The Spaniard remained in Honolulu until his death, more than forty-five years after he landed. He was to have more than thirty children, some of whose descendants still live in that city today.

Most of the early plant wealth of the islands derived from seeds, roots, and cuttings introduced by Marín. From his diary (which fortunately was translated into English by Robert C. Wyllie before the original was lost), one can learn that Marín was a one-man agricultural experiment station. Through friends in Spanish America and other parts of the world, he obtained plants to supplement the native flora, and successfully adapted them to the Hawaiian soil. Early in his career he cultivated pineapples, oranges, grapes, peaches, cherimoyas, melons, figs, lemons, beans, cabbages, potatoes, horseradish, carrots, asparagus, corn, lettuce, roses, and tobacco. Later he grew coffee, cotton, clover, tomatoes, turnips, peppers, wheat, and barley. He experimented in making coconut oil, candlenut oil, castor oil, soap, sugar, molasses, pickles, and lemon syrup, and manufactured lime, tiles, hay, nails, cigars, candles, beer, wine, and brandy.

"Manini" was less than generous with his imported stocks. "I am sorry to add," wrote Laura Fish Judd, an early missionary, "that he was very selfish about his plants, never parting with a seed or slip, if he could avoid it. When he trimmed his vines and roses, he would make bonfires, instead of distributing among others what he prized so highly himself. When we arrived at Honolulu, in 1826, there was not a vine or fig tree to be found outside of his garden, except a few obtained from other sources."

His house was a two-story adobe on Nuuanu Stream near Vineyard Street, and he owned an extensive garden running up Nuuanu Valley. He kept a large herd of dairy cattle, from which he got butter and cheese. He owned what later came to be called Ford Island in Pearl Harbor, and on it raised hogs, goats, and rabbits. Hiram Paulding was told in 1828 that Marín owned nearly all the cattle on Oahu, a number of horses, flocks of goats and sheep, extensive tracts of land, and a great many houses.

Marín's first wife died after a few years, leaving him several children; his second wife, a high-ranking lady, gave him many more offspring. He seemed fond of his family, but often his diary bears the simple entry: "This day I beat my wife."

Marín's mind was a strange mixture of scientific pragmatism and blind superstition. Peter Corney, who was shown around Oahu by Marín (whom he calls "Manning") and who spent two days with him on the island in Pearl Harbor, describes the terror the Spaniard showed when he thought he had seen the ghost of a Hawaiian chief. The Catholic priests who arrived in the islands in 1827 found Marín to be useful but they despised his religious weakness. He had taught his wives the faith in which he had been born, but had not forbidden them to take part in "heathen" ceremonies, and even he himself had found it expedient to join in the *makahiki* celebrations and other Hawaiian observances. Yet Marín told Jacques Arago that he had secretly saved many native souls from damnation; under the pretext of giving medical attention, he had visited more than three hundred natives and baptized them before they died.

When Marín himself, a man in his sixties, died in 1837, he had seen many startling changes in the isles of his adoption. And he will always be remembered as the man who enriched the Hawaiian landscape with dozens of exotic trees, shrubs, and flowers.

Trading Post in the Pacific

ONE DAY KAMEHAMEHA PLAYED A LITTLE GAME WITH A YANKEE trader who offered twenty quarts of rum in exchange for some hogs. The king stood by while the man ladled out the amount in a quart measure. When the count was finished, Kamehameha objected that there were only nineteen. Confident that he had not erred, the Yankee offered to count over again. "Never mind — let's split the difference," the king suggested. The trader refused and started to measure the rum a second time. The monarch chuckled and said he would take the man's word for it. Kamehameha was not trying to cheat; he was merely having some sport by haggling in the fashion of the visiting Yankees.

"As Safe as London Docks"

KAMEHAMEHA CONTINUED THROUGHOUT HIS REIGN HIS EARLY IN-
terest in cultivating foreign trade, and himself built up a fortune in
goods and specie by dealing in commerce. "He has amassed a
considerable treasure in dollars," wrote Archibald Campbell, "and
possesses a large stock of European articles of every description,
particularly arms and ammunition; these he has acquired by trading
with the ships that call at the islands." Because of its harbor, Honolulu soon became the foremost seaport of the eastern Pacific — a
title it still retains. In 1804 Kamehameha moved his court to Honolulu, which with Lahaina, Maui, had grown to be one of the two
principal centers for foreign shipping.

The harbor of Honolulu was first surveyed in 1796 by Captain
Broughton of the 400-ton British sloop of war *Providence*. Broughton, who had left the command of the *Chatham* to return to
England with dispatches from Vancouver, had come back to the
islands in the *Providence* and, touching at Kealakekua in January,
had left there the first grapevines in the islands. In July, when the
Providence had come back from the Northwest Coast and was
pausing at Niihau on the way to Asia, two of its marines were
killed by the natives, in the last of such attacks on foreign ships.

Captain Henry Barber was trading at Oahu in the same year. He
left Honolulu on Halloween in the snow *Arthur* with a cargo of
sea-otter skins, and at once piled up his ship on a reef near Pearl
Harbor. Six men were lost, and the rest reached shore at the spot
known ever since as Barber's Point. John Young salvaged the cargo
and Barber later recovered it, but Kamehameha mounted ten guns
from the *Arthur* in front of his palace and refused to give them
back.

Kamehameha was still collecting weapons; for although he had
conquered all the rest of the chain by 1795, one island, Kauai, still
refused to acknowledge his sway. At once he began assembling an

invading force. His carpenters were set to work building a 40-ton ship, but it was not finished when, in April, 1796, he decided to make the ninety-mile voyage with a fleet of canoes.

So that Oahu would not be able to rise at his back, he took the drastic measure of killing all the hogs on the island and destroying other provisions, and thereby caused a famine. But before his fleet was halfway across the Kauai Channel, a heavy storm arose and capsized many of the canoes. When he put back to Oahu, he got the news that Namakeha, a brother of Kaiana, was leading a rebellion on Hawaii. Kamehameha was forced to direct his fleet to Hilo, where his men hunted down Namakeha's forces and sacrificed the leader.

Learning by experience that the invasion of Kauai would not be easy, Kamehameha spent several years building up a fleet of hundreds of double canoes of the sort called *peleleu*, with long, deep hulls joined by a platform and driven by foreign-type sails. He also had his men build some small schooners, and accumulated six hundred muskets, fourteen small cannon, and forty swivel guns. Early in 1804 he was once again prepared to launch an attack from Oahu; but again disaster held him back. This time it was an epidemic of a disease called *mai okuu*, which was either cholera or bubonic plague. Many of the king's veterans were struck down, and he himself caught the disease and recovered only with difficulty.

At this time Kauai was ruled by a young king who was about fifteen years old. He was Kaumualii, "Oven of the Nobility," a son of Kahekili's brother Kaeo, and had been brought up under the guidance of an old councillor, Inamoo. Kaumualii was a handsome lad who looked more English than Hawaiian, and was one of the best swimmers in all the islands. He had picked up some English and was a fervent admirer of King George of Beretania. In fact, he had adopted the name of George for himself and was to name his children for various members of the British royal family, not always managing to keep the sexes straight.

Kaumualii had gathered some foreigners around him, including

three Americans named Rowbottom, Williams, and Coleman, who
had been left behind by Kendrick. They were helping to build a
ship in which they and the young king might escape to some other
Pacific island should the conqueror land on Kauai. But luck was
with Kaumualii, and his defensive game was so successful that
Kamehameha had to resort to diplomacy instead of invasion. After
several embassies had failed to get Kaumualii to come to Oahu
and talk peace, he was persuaded to come in April, 1810. Captain
Nathan Winship, an American trader, agreed to take Kaumualii
in his ship, the *O'Cain*, leaving his first mate ashore on Kauai as a
hostage.

The *O'Cain* anchored off Oahu, and Kamehameha and his entourage came aboard and greeted Kaumualii with honors. On deck a
pact was made whereby Kauai should become a tributary kingdom
in which the young king should continue to govern, returning a
nominal tribute as a sign of suzerainty. It is quite possible that
Kaumualii was overawed by a view of Kamehameha's fleet. Thirty
small sloops and schooners were hauled up on shore at Waikiki, and
about a dozen more were moored in the harbor of Honolulu, besides
the 175-ton flagship *Lelia Byrd*.

Afterward Kaumualii was persuaded to go ashore and attend a
feast to celebrate the new alliance. Several courtiers led by a
priest named Kaumiumi plotted to put the young man out of the
way, but when Kamehameha heard about the plan he disdained
assassination, saying: "This is not a time of open war, when a
prince can be slain like a robber!" But the plot still might have
come off had not the conqueror's faithful adviser, Isaac Davis,
heard of it and warned Kaumualii. The young king hurried back
home to Kauai in safety; but soon afterward Davis died of poison,
victim of the plotters' grudge.

The subjugation of Kauai allowed Kamehameha, now lacking
more worlds to conquer, to bend his efforts further toward building
a fortune in foreign trade. He had obtained the *Lelia Byrd* from a
trader named William Shaler, who first came in 1803. In the summer

of that year Shaler landed at Kawaihae the first horses ever seen in the islands. Thus was fulfilled a prophecy of the old sage Kekiopilo: "White people shall come here; they shall bring dogs with very long ears, and men shall ride upon them." Kamehameha himself was the first to learn horsemanship. He was the earliest of a long line of Hawaiian riders, who thereafter found their wildest delight in careering along the beaches or dusty trails. The parade of *pa-u* riders — lovely girls in trailing garments astride prancing steeds — is still today a feature of the Kamehameha Day celebrations.

The *Lelia Byrd* came again in 1805, and when she began leaking badly, Shaler exchanged her for the *Tamana*, a ship built at Oahu in that year, and thus the *Byrd* joined Kamehameha's growing fleet.

Foreign ships continued to touch at the islands. Campbell, who spent thirteen months in Honolulu in 1809 and 1810, noted that at least a dozen ships called there in that time — two British, one Russian, and the rest American. Yankee ships were indeed moving into the Pacific. The first celebration of the Fourth of July in the islands of which there is a record was held aboard the *New Hazard* in 1811. Since the fourth fell on Sunday, the festivities were held over until the fifth. The following year, Kamehameha spent the Fourth of July aboard Nathan Winship's vessel, the *Albatross*, where he was given three salutes and took part in a "grand feast." The *Albatross* was purchased by the king a few years later, along with several other American vessels.

John Jacob Astor's annual supply ships for his Astoria fur trade always touched at Kamehameha's kingdom. The first of them, the *Tonquin*, under Jonathan Thorn, came in February, 1811. The captain recruited twelve Hawaiians for labor in Oregon, but along with the crew they were all massacred by Indians off Vancouver Island in July. The *Beaver*, which came the next year, also took away Hawaiian laborers to work in the Northwest. The third and last of these supply ships, the *Lark*, was caught near the islands in a heavy storm in 1813 and was dismasted. The crew worked the ship as far as the inhospitable isle of Kahoolawe, where they beached it.

Kamehameha rescued the frightened seamen but asked in return the right to salvage the vessel and its cargo — which consisted mainly of rum for the Russian trade. Chief Keeaumoku, in charge of salvage work, refused, it is said, to leave the scene until all the rum was gone.

The War of 1812 extended to the far Pacific, and the growing Yankee commerce was alarmed at the prospect of raids on their shipping. One British letter-of-marque ship, the *Sir Andrew Hammond*, was captured by the Americans, and arrived at Honolulu on May 23, 1814, commanded by Lieutenant John Gamble of the Marine Corps. This was the first war vessel flying the United States flag to enter that harbor. The ship departed June 11 and two days later was retaken by the British ship *Cherub* and brought back to Honolulu. Gamble was taken away on the *Cherub* as a prisoner of war. In July, 1813, the armed schooner *Tamaahmaah* — one of several vessels to be named for Kamehameha — arrived in Honolulu, sent out by a group of Boston merchants. Its captain, Porter, found in the harbor a number of American ships that had sought refuge there, and he took on to China a part of the valuable cargoes of furs that they had collected; the remainder were stored on Kauai until the war was over.

The origin of the distinctive Hawaiian flag probably goes back to the War of 1812. Since Vancouver's time, Kamehameha had flown the British colors in front of his residence. But during the War of 1812, an American remarked to the king that showing this flag might cause complications, and Kamehameha thereupon decided to design a new banner for his kingdom. This Hawaiian flag, which at least as early as 1816 was flown over the fort at Honolulu, was a flattering combination of both the American and the British ensigns. It retained the Union Jack in the upper quarter, but the rest of the field was spangled with seven to nine stripes alternately white, red, and blue, and, as one observer noted, the stripes were "like those of the American flag, in allusion probably to the number of islands." The Hawaiian colors were first shown in foreign waters when Captain Alexander Adams in the brig *Taamano* arrived at Macao in 1817 and baffled the harbormaster with the new ensign.

The bay of Waikiki was a popular spot for trading ships to anchor, but the harbor of Honolulu was gradually becoming the center of trade. It was protected by the fort, with its battery of sixty guns mounted in embrasures on top of an eighteen-foot parapet of coral blocks. Inside were houses and barracks for the soldiers, who lived under strict discipline. At night the guards were relieved regularly, and they sang out every ten minutes, in English, "All is well!" Honolulu was a center for transshipping goods from and to the other islands of the group. Storehouses of stone were built near the docks to hold the royal property. After a few years the traders were allowed to store their goods in houses on shore, from which they might sell to the people; but while Kamehameha lived, no permanent trading houses were allowed to operate.

The harbor of Honolulu around 1815 was graphically described by Peter Corney. "The best time to get into the harbor," he wrote, "is early in the morning, before the wind sets violently in a contrary direction; the chief generally sends a number of large double canoes to tow the ship in, as the entrance of the harbor is not more than a quarter of a mile wide. Small vessels, when about to enter, run close to the east side of the reef, where hundreds of the natives are collected, and, by throwing a rope to them, the ship is pulled up to the anchorage. Ships can moor close to the shore, so as to have a stage from thence, and be as safe as if they were in the London Docks."

Sandalwood for Sale

KAMEHAMEHA BEGAN EARLY TO SEEK A PRODUCT WHICH COULD bring him a fortune from world trade. It was all well and good to sell visiting ships a supply of fresh fruits and vegetables, but even though pork was made a royal monopoly, little cash could be obtained from the provision business. The rise of the whaling industry brought many ships to the islands (in the year Kamehameha died the first whale was killed in Hawaiian waters), but little profit came to the crown from this source. Kamehameha cultivated the oyster beds at the mouth of the Pearl River and employed divers to harvest pearls and shell (he was delighted by Peter Corney's gift of an oyster dredge), but the pearl trade never amounted to much. At one time the king, on the basis of a report by ignorant sailors that gleaming crystals found on Leahi Hill overlooking Waikiki were diamonds, felt that he was the proprietor of a thriving jewel mine, but the crystals turned out to be worthless and the chief result of the boom was to change the name of the hill to Diamond Head.

The local product that finally turned out to be a treasure was a tree growing in the hills, whose fragrant wood brought high prices in the Orient. There it was used for making idols and sacred utensils, for fancy boxes and carvings, for incense sticks, and for fuel at funeral pyres. The distilled oil was used in medicines, perfumes, and cosmetics.

This was the sandalwood tree, of which about seven species are found in the Hawaiian Islands. The natives had long been familiar with this agreeable wood, which they called *iliahi*. No one knows how the haoles first discovered that the *iliahi* was the same as the wood valued so highly in the Orient. Perhaps some sea captain in the China trade, using firewood collected in the islands, recognized the sweet aroma of sandalwood oil coming from the galley stove. The first mention of the trade is the statement of Isaac Ridler to Ingraham in 1791 that Simon Metcalfe had been taking in sandalwood at Kealakekua, and thus the vengeful captain of the *Eleanora* may have been the first to carry this wood to China for sale. Ridler himself may have been left ashore to collect the wood, for his captain, John Kendrick, in 1790 left two men on Kauai to do the same thing. Early shipments were not profitable, however, and may not have been of the best variety. Captain Amasa Delano remarked in 1801 that the first loads shipped were so inferior in quality that the Chinese would not buy, and thus for twenty years this rich source of wealth was overlooked in the islands.

The story of sandalwood as a commercial jackpot began on New Year's Day, 1812, when three Americans picked up a shipment of logs on their way to Canton with furs. On the return they were able to pay Kamehameha a good profit from its sale. The three were Nathan Winship of the *Albatross*, his brother Jonathan Winship Jr. of the *O'Cain*, and William Heath Davis of the *Isabella*. These men on July 12, 1812, signed a contract with the king that gave them a ten-year monopoly of the trade, and they sailed back to China with five shiploads which brought a high price. But in China they got news of the outbreak of the War of 1812, and British influence put a damper on the trade for several years. After the war, however, sandalwood boomed, and for fifteen years thereafter was the main source of revenue for the rulers of the Sandwich Islands.

At first Kamehameha tried to carry on the business without the aid of the middleman. He bought in 1816 one of Astor's ships, the *Forester*, which had sailed under British colors, and renamed her the *Taamano* after his favorite queen, Kaahumanu. Loaded with sandalwood, the vessel sailed for Canton on February 22, 1817. The inexperienced crew was fleeced right and left, and the cost of the voyage left the king with a deficit of $3000. Where had the money gone? Well, port fees were high in Macao and Canton. Kamehameha had never heard of port fees, but he got the point at once. From now on, foreign ships entering Honolulu would have to pay the king a harbor fee of $80, besides $12 for the services of Harbottle, the pilot. But thereafter Kamehameha traded in sandalwood on an f.o.b. basis.

The king shrewdly kept the trade as a royal monopoly, and encouraged conservation by placing a *kapu* on the cutting of young trees. He heaped up foreign coin in his treasury, and between 1816 and 1818 added six ships to his fleet, all of them paid for with sandalwood. Corney's vessel, the *Columbia*, was bought for twice its volume in fragrant logs. A pit was dug in the ground the size of the greatest dimensions of the hull, and filled with sandalwood brought down from the hills by toiling natives. The sites of a number of such pits are still to be found in the islands — holes in the ground which once were used to measure off the price of a sailing ship.

King Kaumualii of Kauai shared the wealth of the sandalwood trade, and on at least one occasion suffered delusions about his buying power. The traders often took orders from the king for goods to be obtained in China. As one trader was getting ready to sail, Kaumualii gave him the usual list of dry goods, hardware, furniture, and weapons, and then said: "I hear that other kings have jewels of great beauty, and I have none. What are these jewels?" The trader said there were various kinds, and allowed that diamonds were considered the topnotch thing in that line. "Then bring me back a diamond." The trader said he would do the best he could. How big a diamond would His Majesty like? "Well, say one about as big as a coconut!"

After the death of Kamehameha, his successors felt that the sandalwood trade was an inexhaustible bonanza, which they soon shared with the more influential chiefs. The wood was sold by weight, an odd measure being used called the picul — a Malayan word, pronounced "pickle," which meant a weight equal to 133 1/3 pounds, or about what a strong man could carry on his back. The traders paid $7 to $10 a picul for wood which they sold in Canton at a profit of $3 or $4 a picul. American traders handled sandalwood worth some $400,000 during the four years 1817-1821. But before 1830 the price dropped somewhat, and after that year the trade collapsed completely. The quality had degenerated, and reckless exploitation shut off the supply. The natives would set fire to the central plain of Oahu so as to detect the logs by their sweet smoke, and the flames killed new seedlings. It is not true that all sandalwood trees in the islands were destroyed in the boom, for a number of them still survive on the less accessible slopes of the mountains; but by 1830 the bonanza had petered out.

While it lasted, the chiefs thought it was wonderful. They went on a buying spree, and the traders whose warehouses sprang up in Honolulu stood ready to take orders for all the products of the civilized world. The heirs of Kamehameha paid $90,000 in sandalwood for the Salem-built yacht called *Cleopatra's Barge*. Some chiefs bought frame houses to be shipped to Hawaii in prefabricated form. Grass shacks were filled with silks and other rich fabrics, foreign suits and dresses, imported liquors, cut-glass vessels and blue willowware dinner sets, and carved furniture. Carriages and billiard tables were much in demand. One chief paid $800 for a looking-glass, and another paid $10,000 for a brass cannon. Sandalwood became the local standard of exchange, and piculs of wood were used in place of money.

Taxes were soon being paid in sandalwood (Don Francisco Marín was one of the collectors, as his journal entries about "sanlegud" indicate). Soon the chiefs forced the inhabitants to go into the wet and windy mountains to drag down their share of logs. At first the gathering of sandalwood might have been the occasion for a gay outing; the picture of collecting at night in the hills of Oahu given by a British sailor who signed himself "Old Quartermaster" seems idyllic: "There stood a vast number of men assembled, each with a torch made from sandalwood, which burns bright and clear. At a certain signal they dispersed, each taking his own way to cut his load, accompanying his labor with a song, to which the whole band within hearing joined in chorus; the song we understood not, but in the calm of a beautiful night it was calculated to inspire delight."

Later on, the singing stopped, and the labor became harder. Men and women tied six-foot logs to their backs and climbed to and fro between the woods and the measuring pits, both by day and by night. Collecting on Kauai in 1830 in very cold weather, the natives were often driven by hunger to eat moss or wild, bitter herbs. Near Waipio, Hawaii, two or three thousand people were hauling wood at one time. Years of such labor, added to their daily toil, caused the people to neglect their food growing, and malnutrition set in. Working in damp forests, where the good trees were farther away and smaller in size, did much to wear down the stamina of the natives, and contributed to the gradual decline of the Hawaiian population.

The common folk gained little from the trade, and the chiefs soon tired of the showy goods that were sold them. The traders were the main ones to profit by the sandalwood boom; and they made a double income. They paid the chiefs in merchandise rather than in cash — merchandise on which they made an exorbitant profit — and they also made a profit on the sale of the wood in the Orient. Naturally they were happy to extend unlimited credit, and when the supply dwindled, the traders developed a habit of asking their home governments to send around a warship to collect.

Most of the trade was in the hands of Americans, and by 1824 the chiefs owed the traders about $300,000. Early in 1826 Lieutenant John Percival, commander of the United States ship-of-war *Dolphin*, obtained an acknowledgment that the trading debts would be recognized as government obligations. This was the origin of the Hawaiian national debt. In the fall of the same year, Captain Thomas ap Catesby Jones of the sloop-of-war *Peacock* obtained a renewal of this pledge, and in December the rulers passed the earliest written tax law of the kingdom, requiring every able-bodied man to deliver half a picul of good sandalwood or to pay four Spanish dollars. Each man was allowed to cut half a picul for his own account, and the decline of the forests was thus hastened. The tax was not spent to pay off the debt, however, and the claims of the traders were not fully settled until 1843 — long after the sandalwood boom had finally collapsed.

The sandalwood era in the islands was marked by the incursion of a hardened gang of pirates. In April or May, 1818, a mysterious vessel appeared off the Big Island. Its captain, who called himself Turner, said that she was the corvette *Santa Rosa* of the United Provinces of Río de la Plata, then in revolt against Spain. He offered the ship to Kamehameha for six thousand piculs of sandal-wood — a bargain, considering that she was an American-built vessel of 300 tons, carrying eighteen guns and loaded with a cargo of dry goods. The crew, who settled ashore, seemed to have plenty of cash, and some of them owned gold and silver ornaments of the sort usually found in Catholic churches.

Three of the crew came to Oahu, where Peter Corney, mate of the *Columbia*, was guarding the heap of sandalwood which had been paid by Kamehameha for that ship, on which Corney had sailed in the Pacific for five years. One of the strangers, babbling in his cups, aroused Corney's suspicions, and soon the man was brought for examination before Governor Boki. The true story then came out. The *Santa Rosa*, alias *Chacabuco*, alias *Liberty*, had been fitted out at the River Plate to cruise against the Spaniards. Beyond the Horn, the crew had mutinied and taken over the ship on July 27, 1817, when a master's mate named McDonald took command and assumed the captain's name, Turner. The real Turner and thirteen loyal men were set ashore off Valparaiso, and the ship then attacked other vessels and raided towns on the South American coast, now and then robbing and burning a church.

When the first lieutenant, Griffiths, and forty men were sent to cut off some ships at one port, their faithless fellow pirates abandoned them and sailed away to Hawaii. But Griffiths, in a captured brig, also headed for Hawaii, where he soon arrived with his forty men and settled ashore. McDonald, perhaps fearing his vengeance, somehow seized the brig and departed from the realm of Kamehameha.

He was wise, for nemesis was on the pirates' track. At the end of September, a 44-gun frigate of war from the United Provinces, the *Argentina*, came to the Big Island. Her crew were so sickly that out of 260 men there were hardly enough able to work the ship.

Captain Hipolito Bouchard, a dashing young man born in Marseilles, demanded the delivery of the *Santa Rosa* and her crew as pirates, and Kamehameha immediately complied. (It is not clear that he got his payment back.)

Bouchard pardoned most of the gang and added them to the crews of his squadron, which sailed for Honolulu to refit. Here the captain took a liking to Corney, and offered him the command of the *Santa Rosa*, which Corney accepted.

The ships sailed for Kauai in October, to round up more of the mutineers. Four of them were handed over, but the ringleader, Griffiths, had fled to King Kaumualii, who for some reason was determined to protect him. Bouchard was even more determined to shoot Griffiths, and told the king that unless he was delivered, the fort and village of Waimea would be destroyed by the frigate's guns. Three days later Griffiths was handed over, tried by court-martial, and in two hours was brought to the beach, blindfolded, and shot by four marines, while hundreds of natives witnessed the execution.

After capturing two more pirates in the mountains of Maui, the two "patriot" ships departed, carrying eighty Sandwich Islanders among their motley crews. Corney soon became sickened with the campaign that was made against the Spanish on the West Coast — one act of Bouchard was to sack and burn the California town of Monterey — and left the ship in Valparaiso without his pay or prize money, fearing that, for a respectable British trader of the Pacific, he had become little better than a pirate himself.

The Russians Build Some Forts

KAMEHAMEHA'S FIRST MEETING WITH THE COMMANDER OF A Russian ship was friendly. Off Honolulu early in 1809 he was greeted at the gangway by Lieutenant Hagenmeister of the *Neva*. Asking whether the ship was English or American, and told that it was Russian, the king responded: "*Maikai* — good." Then a handsome scarlet cloak, edged and ornamented with ermine, was presented to him as a gift from the governor of the Aleutian Islands. But, adds Archibald Campbell, "After trying it on, he gave it to his attendants to be taken on shore. I never saw him use it afterwards."

Yet for several years the claws of the Russian bear reached out into the Pacific, and for a time the flag of the Czar waved over a part of Hawaii Nei.

Spearhead of the Czar's imperialistic drive, the Russian American Company was chartered in 1799 and headquarters were set up at Sitka, Alaska. To seek a good route for their supply vessels and fur cargoes, the first Russian around-the-world expedition touched Hawaii in June, 1804. The two ships were the *Nadeshda* under Adam Johann von Krusenstern and the *Neva* under Urey Lisiansky. The *Neva* spent some time off the Big Island and Kauai. More than a year later, while the *Neva* was on the way to Canton with a load of furs, it grounded on a shoal near Midway Island, and while they were getting afloat the captain explored a nearby islet which still bears his name to remind us that the Russians once cruised the archipelago. Lisiansky's account of his visit is valuable, and an appendix includes the first printed Hawaiian-Russian vocabulary, with such useful phrases as "Why do you make a noise?", "Hold your tongue," and "Have you swine?"

The *Neva* was seen again in the islands in 1809, commanded by Hagenmeister. Campbell, who after losing his feet in Alaska was brought on this ship as far as Hawaii, averred that Hagenmeister was ordered to start a settlement; but the time was not ripe, and all that the voyage accomplished was a load of salt for Alaska.

The Russians turned now to an attempt to erect a post at Fort Ross on the California coast, and did not send another ship to Hawaii for six years. This was the *Bering*, formerly the *Atahualpa*, which they had bought at a bargain from the Yankees during the War of 1812. It loaded a cargo at Oahu, but on the last night of January, 1815, it was wrecked in a storm off Waimea, Kauai.

The need to reclaim this cargo, which had been salvaged by King Kaumualii's subjects, offered an excellent chance for the governor of Alaska to try setting up a Russian settlement in the islands. Trouble came when he assigned this task to a German adventurer, Dr. George Anton Scheffer.

Scheffer had been a surgeon for the Moscow police in 1808, and in 1812 he was busy building balloons from which to observe the movements of Napoleon's invaders. He became a ship's doctor and had spent a year at Sitka when he was sent to Hawaii in the fall of 1815 as advance agent. Russian ships with colonists were to follow later.

Posing as a botanist, Scheffer won the confidence of Kamehameha, cured the king of a feverish cold, and was given land on Oahu. The same medical skill, as well as expensive gifts, charmed Kaumualii of Kauai. Scheffer spent some time on Oahu building a blockhouse on the waterfront and laying out plans for a fort alongside. These warlike preparations, coupled with the sacrilegious violation by the Russians of a nearby heiau, caused old John Young to become worried. He soon obtained orders from Kamehameha for the work to cease. Young decided that a fort was not a bad idea, however, and his men finished the job of building it. (The memory of it still survives in the name of Fort Street in downtown Honolulu.)

New details on the Scheffer story are given in a recent book on the Russian American Company by a Soviet historian, S. B. Okun, based on Russian archives. "In the six months between Scheffer's arrival and that of the Company vessels," writes Okun, "he built a few houses on the plantations assigned to him and started to raise tobacco and various other plants. He strove to expand the territory he had received as a 'gift' by buying up land from the natives. It was not long before his activities aroused the American traders against him, for, aside from everything else, it seems that he was claiming the exclusive rights to the export trade in sandalwood."

Scheffer, reinforced by three Russian ships, withdrew to Kauai, and there found a king ready to take advantage of his offers.

Kaumualii was still afraid that his overlord, Kamehameha, would come and take over the island which Kaumualii had promised to him. He therefore signed, on May 21, 1816, a treasonous document putting Kauai under the protection of Czar Alexander Pavlovich. He also promised to give the czar one half of Oahu in return for the help of Dr. Scheffer's army in capturing it.

The Russian flag now waved over Kauai, and the energetic doctor was busier than ever. He built a strong fort at Waimea and breast-works in the valley of Hanalei, which he renamed "Schefferovaya Dolina."

But the American traders were outspoken in their dread of a Russian monopoly in the North Pacific, and Kaumualii began to weary of his bargain. Under orders from Kamehameha and after some bloodshed (the story that Scheffer tried to kidnap Kaumualii and take him to St. Petersburg is probably an exaggeration), the Russian ships were sent on their way to the coast, failing even to recover the salvaged goods from the *Bering*. Scheffer escaped to Canton on an American ship and continued to urge his dreams before the czar, but the government had meanwhile disowned him. The bear withdrew his paws from the Pacific, and henceforth Russian sovereignty never prevailed over any part of the Sandwich Islands.

Lieutenant Otto von Kotzebue disclaimed Scheffer's acts when he established relations with Kamehameha in November, 1816. He was commander of the little ship *Rurik*, making an around-the-world trip seeking the fabled Northwest Passage. As a lad he had visited Hawaii with his uncle, Krusenstern, and like him was a Baltic German and a Russian subject. Now, when he first arrived off the Big Island, the pilot who came out was so terrified upon hearing that the vessel was Russian that he tried to jump overboard. Kotzebue found out later that Scheffer's baneful influence had also spread to Oahu. When men from the *Rurik* were surveying the harbor of Honolulu, they used long poles with flags on them; but these had to be replaced with brooms when the people protested, for they remembered that Scheffer had once hoisted a flag there and claimed possession for Russia. Kotzebue made a prophetic remark after a visit to Pearl Harbor: "If this place were in the hands of Europeans, they would find means to make it one of the best harbors in the world."

Kotzebue was a son of the famed playwright, who has been called "perhaps the strongest single influence on the development of European drama." Otto shared his father's graphic pen, and his volumes on the *Rurik* voyage and on the later voyage of the *Predpriyatie* (1823-1826) offer colorful pictures of the Pacific of his time. On the *Rurik* he was accompanied by two other gifted men who wrote accounts of the voyage. One was the artist Louis Choris, whose watercolors give us the best early views of the Hawaiian scene, its rulers, and its people. Choris was murdered some years later by Mexican bandits. The other was the fine naturalist Adelbert von Chamisso, who named many a Pacific plant. He is still best known, perhaps, for having published in 1814 his tale of Peter Schlemihl, who sold his shadow to the devil and wandered about the world in search of it.

Last commander of a Russian warship to interview Kamehameha was Captain V. M. Golovnin of the sloop *Kamchatka*, on his way in the fall of 1818 to investigate the declining fur company at Sitka. From his pen we get a view of the king in his sunset years: "Kamehameha is already very old; he considers himself to be seventy-nine years of age. It is probable that his exact age is unknown even to himself, but his appearance shows that there cannot be such a great disparity between the real age and his estimation. However, he is alert, strong, and active; he is temperate and sober; he never takes strong drinks and eats very moderately. In him one sees a most amazing mixture of childish deeds and of ripe judgment and actions, that would not disgrace even a European ruler."

Golovnin's book offers other revealing stories of the king's life after his retirement to Kailua on the Kona coast. The Russian also spent some pleasant times on Oahu and Kauai. His most amusing yarn, however, is his account of the first Hawaiian to visit Russia. This was a young stowaway named Lauri, who was taken back to St. Petersburg and taught to speak Russian. Lauri liked civilization for a while, but hated ice and snow and beards. Clearly, Russia was no place for Lauri, and he was sent back home on the *Kutuzov* the next year.

Golovnin acted as a prophet when he set down in his journal these words: "Were it possible to introduce the Christian faith and the art of writing among the Sandwich Islanders they would in one century reach a state of civilization unparalleled in history. . . . If a few well educated, patient people, capable of observing things carefully, like the missionaries of old, should settle in the Sandwich Islands, there is no doubt that they would soon become famous as enlighteners of this people and would have an excellent opportunity to observe . . . the gradual transition of man from a wild state into that of a civilized being." Sixteen months later the first shipload of missionaries to Hawaii hove over the horizon.

Puritans in Paradise

A DARK-FACED LAD IN ROUGH SAILOR GARB SAT WEEPING ON THE STEPS of Yale College in New England. To the students who paused by his side, he explained that he wept because he was ashamed of his ignorance. Would they help him to learn about the world and the meaning of Christianity?

A resident graduate, Edward W. Dwight, inquired further. The youth's name was Henry Opukahaia. He had been born in the Sandwich Islands about 1792. Orphaned at the age of twelve by tribal wars, he had been adopted by an uncle who was a kahuna who had taught him the pagan rites at the heiau where Cook had been worshiped as Lono. But the boy had run away to sea; he had been brought to New Haven by Captain Caleb Brintnall on the *Triumph* in 1809 and now lived with that seaman's family. Touched by the story, Dwight and other students volunteered to be Henry's tutors.

The young Hawaiian was an eager pupil. He was noted not only for his piety and industry, but also for a good-natured habit of mimicry. He would ask, "Who dis?" and then imitate someone with humorous fidelity.

Obookiah, as he was called, became celebrated in New England. He was sent to the foreign mission school which was started at Cornwall, Connecticut, for the purpose of training Sandwich Islanders, American Indians, and others who might serve as interpreters in the missionary field. Henry became an ardent Christian, started to translate the Bible into his native tongue, and yearned to go back to his islands as a missionary.

It was not to be. He died of typhus fever at the mission school on February 17, 1818. But through death he achieved a greater influence, perhaps, than if he had lived to sail back to Hawaii. The funeral sermon preached by the Reverend Lyman Beecher was widely printed. A little book, *Memoirs of Henry Obookiah*, went through several editions and spread further the wave of interest. The story of the boy who wept in heathen darkness was the beginning of the first Christian mission to the Sandwich Islands.

Odyssey of the "First Company"

JUST TWO HUNDRED YEARS AFTER THE PILGRIM FATHERS STEPPED ashore at Plymouth, a new band of truth-bringers was destined to land on the rock-bound coast of Hawaii. This group had been brought together by an association of New England churches which, inspired by the success of the London Missionary Society in the South Seas, had set up in 1810 the American Board of Commissioners for Foreign Missions. The influence of this Board was to become as impressive as its lengthy name.

Thus, on October 23, 1819, the first Sandwich Islands missionary party to be sent out by the Board gathered on the Long Wharf of Boston and sang "When shall we all meet again?" Moored in the harbor was the brig *Thaddeus*, Captain Andrew Blanchard, which was to be the new *Mayflower* that would transport these latter-day Puritans to the islands of the idolaters who had killed Captain Cook forty years before.

The roll of the "First Company" is still remembered in Hawaii. The seven families were led by the Reverend Hiram Bingham of Middlebury College and the Reverend Asa Thurston of Yale. Daniel Chamberlain, a militia captain and farmer, was expected to train the natives in the methods of New England agriculture; his wife and five children would help. Samuel Whitney was a schoolmaster and mechanic. Samuel Ruggles was likewise a schoolmaster. Elisha Loomis had been trained as a printer; his press and fonts of type were stowed aboard. Dr. Thomas Holman was what would now be called a medical missionary.

All except the Chamberlains had been recently married. To provide helpmates for the unmarried men, and perhaps to protect them from temptation on the far side of Cape Horn, the American Board had suggested that they find wives before their departure; and in at least one instance, members of the Board had nominated the chosen lady. Lucy Goodale Thurston was a bride of less than a fortnight.

Four young Sandwich Islanders were also on the *Thaddeus* passenger list. They had been gathered together and trained at the school at Cornwall, and it was hoped that they would not only be useful as interpreters but would also incline the sympathies of the Hawaiian chiefs toward the establishment of mission stations in the islands. The four converts were Thomas Hopu (who had come to New England with Opukahaia and had served on a privateer in the War of 1812), William Kanui, John Honolii, and George Kaumualii. An engraving of the boys, taken from portraits painted by Professor Samuel F. B. Morse, was sold for the benefit of their mission.

High hopes were held for George P. (for "prince") Kaumualii, or "Tamoree." He was the son, by a commoner, of the king of Kauai, who, when the boy was about seven, to save him from the malice of the queen, had paid Captain Rowan to take the lad to Massachusetts and give him an education. When funds ran out and Rowan died, George enlisted in the Navy and served in the War of 1812. He was wounded by a boarding pike when the *Enterprise* fought the *Boxer;* he went also on the cruise of the *Guerrière* against the pirates of Algiers. George finally found himself at the Cornwall school, where he cheerfully attended the lessons and re-learned his native language. He had picked up a fair amount of English, and on October 19, 1816, he wrote his royal father that he hoped to return to Kauai. "You must not expect yet a while," he wrote, "but if God spars my life I shall be there in a few yers [sic]." He was to fulfill his promise, with the help of the missionaries, who wisely guessed what would be the effect of restoring his long-lost son to the ruler of the leeward isle of Kauai.

The "First Company" and the four Hawaiian youths were rowed out to the *Thaddeus,* which immediately weighed anchor for its journey around the Horn. They were spared a rough passage of Cape Stiff, and the five-month voyage was not too unpleasant. The chief hardships were storms, cold, seasickness, the strictures of communal ownership of food and supplies, and confinement to cramped quarters. The narrow stowage space of the *Thaddeus* was overflowing with a variety of goods considered suitable for setting up a mission in the oceanic wilderness. Many of the commodities were gifts: a baptismal font, a communion plate, a rocking chair, and plentiful supplies of writing materials. About a ton of books were aboard — mainly Bibles and hymnals, and mainly in English. But there was no room for bedsteads, tables, or chairs. A Boston shipping firm had donated an entire frame house in pieces, to be erected for the comfort of the ladies, but it could not be loaded on the *Thaddeus* and the house did not arrive in the islands until the end of the year.

Early in March, 1820, the missionary ship was sailing the tropics of the world's largest ocean, in whose waters Brother Bingham and some others could cool themselves by swimming overside. One day, after a brush with a shark, Bingham expressed his pity for the Hawaiian nation which regarded this monster as a god. The missionaries were drawing near a shore where, unsuspected by them, the shark god and the rest of the heathen idols had already been smashed. The apostles of Jehovah could not have chosen a more auspicious time to arrive in the islands where Ku and Kane no longer openly reigned.

Landfall — the snow-capped summit of the volcanic "white mountain," Mauna Kea — was sighted early on March 30. Skirting the Hamakua Coast of the island of Hawaii, the missionaries, peering through spyglasses, could see ashore their future converts, moving about in field and village.

The returning "missionary boys" were keenly excited at the prospect of setting foot once more on native soil. The *Thaddeus* rounded the northern tip of Hawaii, leaving the grim cliffs of Maui to starboard. Still no canoes paddled out to the ship. James Hunnewell, supercargo, launched a boat, and Hopu and Honolii piled in. They returned three hours later without touching land. Some fishermen offshore had given them news too good to keep.

Splintered Images

THE OLD PAGAN EMPEROR, KAMEHAMEHA I, HAD BEEN DEAD FOR almost a year. Down the coast at Kailua, the ancient warrior had died on May 8, 1819, still true to the violent war god that he had served and that had served him. At the last he had wavered. Following the custom, when his end was near a new rock temple or heiau was built. A human sacrifice was demanded — so the priests told him again and again. Kamehameha refused, saying, "The men are *kapu* for the king." He meant that his son Liholiho would need all the living men he could find to uphold the throne.

Thus, although in all other ways the tribal ceremonies were performed in a way befitting the death of a great conqueror, the customary blood sacrifice was not made. Amid a saturnalia of wailing, riot, and self-mutilation, "The Lonely One" passed into a greater loneliness. His bones were concealed in a secret cave by his faithful comrade Hoapili, as was the ancient burial practice among the Hawaiian *alii*. "Only the stars of the heavens know the resting place of Kamehameha."

Liholiho, a young man of twenty-three, was proclaimed ruler under the title of Kamehameha II. Amiable but often weak, he was not too weak to take the lead in the religious revolution that was brewing. Besides, his father had appointed strong advisers to guide him. The old king's favorite wife, Kaahumanu, now forty-six years old, had been created *kuhina nui*, or chief adviser, an office that made her virtually a co-ruler with the young king. Chief Kalanimoku, whom admiring white men had nicknamed "Billy Pitt" because his statesmanship resembled that of King George's great premier, was still prime minister. Keopuolani, Liholiho's mother, was a third member of the privy council. Together they took the first dramatic step in overthrowing the ancient Hawaiian system of tabu.

Many natives had secretly begun to doubt the power of the hideous idols on the heiau. Foreign sea captains had laughed, and told of more potent gods above. News came that the Polynesians of Tahiti had abolished idolatry. Even the high priest Hewahewa had lost his conviction that the old images could kill blasphemers. Now a daring experiment would be tried. The court of Liholiho would break an old and powerful tabu.

The ancient faith had forbidden men and women to eat together, and no woman was allowed to eat pork, bananas, coconuts, or certain fish. The *kapu* lay more heavily on the feminine sex, and perhaps the dominance of women in Liholiho's counsels urged the open act of defiance that followed. This symbolic act was to be no less than *ai noa*, or "free eating."

Liholiho ordered a public banquet at Kailua during the first week of November. At this table, for the first time in history, Hawaiian women openly ate with their menfolk. The lightning did not strike, and when the meal was over, the young king commanded that all the old temples should be toppled and the idols hacked to bits.

Not without a struggle was this done. Liholiho's cousin, Kekuaokalani, had been made defender of the war god Kukailimoku, a post in which the old Kamehameha had risen to great power. Insurrection flared, and the supporters of the ancient ways rejected an embassy of peace. Battle was joined at Kuamoo in December. Kekuaokalani's wife Manono, as was the old custom, fought by his side. He was killed, and her body, pierced by a musket ball, fell beside his. Thereafter the idols were worshiped only in secret.

Here was rich news for the white kahunas in the ship from America! The story was confirmed next day, when the ship anchored in Kawaihae Bay. Gifts — canoeloads of coconuts, bananas, and hogs — came out, and later Billy Pitt himself, the "iron cable of Hawaii," came aboard to shake hands and shout "*Aloha!*" The portly prime minister was elegant in a white dimity jacket, black silk vest, nankeen pantaloons, white cotton stockings, shoes, a plaid cravat, and a top hat. He was accompanied by several lady chiefs, beautifully obese and swathed in folds of kapa. The natives were hospitable, but only the king, Billy Pitt said, could give permission for the missionaries to stay. He offered to accompany them on their ship down the coast to Kailua, where the court resided.

On Sunday, Brother Bingham was shown around the abandoned heiau at Kawaihae, the most celebrated shrine in the islands. It had been built for old Kamehameha, who himself had laid the cornerstone. Overlooking the sea rose many roomy terraces, on which in the old days hundreds of worshipers could stand while the priests offered prayers and sacrifices. Now the shrines were burned to ashes, in which were mingled the bones of many human beings and the charred remains of beasts, fish, and fruits. The newcomers rejoiced that no longer would human beings be killed to appease demons.

That afternoon Billy Pitt and his entourage came aboard, and voyaged with the missionaries to Kailua. There, on April 4, the first audience was held with Liholiho, at his residence near the shore. He was dining with his five wives, two of whom were his sisters and one the former wife of his father. He received calmly "the most important message that could be sent to any earthly potentate," accepted thankfully the gift of a spyglass sent by the American Board, but was in no haste to make promises.

While the king deliberated, the Americans made friends with the English-speaking governor of the Big Island, Kuakini, nicknamed "John Adams" after our second President, and with old John Young, still after all these years an active adviser to the court. Hewahewa the tabu-breaker offered his friendship, and on his introduction to Bingham "expressed much satisfaction in meeting with a brother priest from America."

Liholiho was still raising objections to the establishment of mission stations in his islands. This was a new idea, and should be considered deeply. English and French advisers observed that Americans might cause trouble if allowed to settle among the people and preach a new mode of living. After four days of parley, Liholiho agreed that the newcomers might land at Kailua and stay for only a year, on trial. Four days more of diplomacy were required before the king gave permission for a party to be allowed to settle at the growing commercial port of Honolulu.

Then the *Thaddeus* company said farewells and scattered to their first fields of endeavor. The Reverend Asa Thurston was chosen by ballot to stay at Kailua, along with his wife and the Holmans and two of the Cornwall boys. Brother Loomis and his wife Maria went to Honolulu, but he was later to be called back to Kawaihae to teach Billy Pitt and his family the mysteries of the new religion. The rest of the company also went to Honolulu, and there set up their homes in grass shacks on the dusty plain of Kawaiahao.

Liholiho and the Longnecks

THE FIRST WHITE WOMEN EVER SEEN IN THE SANDWICH ISLANDS (except for wives of sea captains) were objects of high curiosity when they landed at the port of Honolulu in 1820.

The town was a far cry from their own remembered villages. Along the waterfront lay ship-chandlers' shops, adobe storehouses, and one tavern after another. The rest of the settlement was "a mass of brown huts, looking precisely like so many haystacks in the country; not one white cottage, no church spire, not a garden or a tree to be seen save the grove of coconuts." Through this scene walked the women, while a growing throng of natives ran to peer beneath their poke bonnets and exclaim to each other: "Their faces are small and set far back, and they have long necks!"

Thereafter the Longnecks were a cynosure. Day and night, large-eyed Hawaiians stared through the doors and windows of the mission quarters, and audibly wondered why these foreigners had come to the kingdom. Suspicions that the new arrivals might be bent on conquest were set at rest by the query: "Would a war-party bring women and children with them?" To the child-loving Hawaiians, the Chamberlain family made such questions absurd.

The lady missionaries served their cause not only by teaching in the schools they set up, but also by their needlework. The mountainous chieftainesses demanded dresses made in the latest haole style; the ladies turned out yards of cambric Mother Hubbards, and made shirts and suits for the chiefs as well. The king put in his order for a dozen ruffled shirts and a broadcloth coat.

Life in Missionary Row demanded great exertions. Six months of laundry work had piled up, for there had been no chance to wash clothes on the *Thaddeus*. The dirt-floored houses had to be made into homes, with the aid of gifts from friendly Honolulu merchants. In such a grass house was born, on July 16, 1820, Levi Sartwell Loomis, first white child to see the light in the Sandwich Islands.

The frame house sent from Boston finally arrived on December 25 on the *Tartar* — a very welcome Christmas gift. This was not the first frame house to be erected in the islands, for several of the chiefs had purchased such dwellings from the traders; but it was the most impressive. The visitor can walk through the rooms of that house today, for it still stands on King Street in Honolulu.

The missionary band sought to teach the meaning of Christianity in their schools before engaging in wholesale conversions. The rulers said from the first: "If the *palapala* — the written word — is good, we wish to possess it first ourselves; if it is bad, we do not intend our subjects to know the evil of it." Thus the first pupils were of chief's rank. "The king forbids our teaching any but the blood royal," wrote Mrs. Holman. The strategy of starting with the more important personages appealed likewise to the missionaries, still in the islands on sufferance.

By the end of the year of trial, the various mission schools had about a hundred pupils of both sexes and all ages, but mainly adults and mainly of the chieftain class. In spite of some opposition from rum sellers and impious sea captains, the missionaries had made themselves a familiar part of island life, and Liholiho granted permission for them to stay indefinitely.

Soon after the landing in Honolulu, Brothers Whitney and Ruggles had been deputed to return to his home the wandering son of the king of Kauai. Kaumualii gave an affecting welcome to his long-lost George, and rewarded Captain Blanchard with a load of sandalwood worth a thousand dollars. Kaumualii had an interpreter — a traveled native who had once been the dinner guest of George Washington in New York — but the king himself knew enough English to express his gratitude and to ask that a mission station be set up at Waimea.

Kaumualii nowadays stood out among his subjects for his noble Roman face, his taciturnity, and his fondness for fine European dress. He soon forsook the gin bottle and acted like an exemplary Christian. So religious did he become that when he went swimming, he paddled around with one hand and with the other held the Bible before his eyes. He placed his son George second in command only to himself, and smiled when that son displayed his accomplishments — attractive manners, easy English, and the ability to accompany hymn-singing sessions by playing on a treasured bass viol. But this idyl could not last.

Liholiho had not forgotten that Kaumualii had once promised that, when he died, he would yield the sovereignty of Kauai to the heir of his old enemy, Kamehameha I. Deciding to obtain a renewal of that pledge in person, Liholiho impulsively set out with Boki on July 21, 1821, to sail to Kauai, which he had never seen in his life. All the objections of his terrified followers he put aside — a hundred miles of rough channel to be crossed in a small open boat crowded with thirty persons, the lack of food or water, the possibility that Kaumualii would prove hostile. The need for a compass he supplied merely by pointing with his finger. When the boat was twice nearly capsized, he replied: "Bail out the water and sail on; if you return with the boat, I will jump overboard and swim to Kauai!" Through a day and a night Liholiho, with a courage verging on foolhardiness, urged them on.

Liholiho survived the sea and was welcomed by Kaumualii. High pledges of trust were made on both sides; but at the end of a pleasant visit, the king of Kauai was decoyed aboard the royal vessel, *Cleopatra's Barge*, and brought to Oahu as a virtual hostage. Good behavior was assured when the unlucky monarch was married to Kaahumanu, the powerful *kuhina nui*; it made no difference that he had left a queen, Kapule, behind on Kauai. To make assurance doubly sure, Kaahumanu also married her husband's son Kealiiahonui, the young heir apparent. Kapule, the deposed queen, took the name of "Deborah" and cheerfully began operating an inn at Wailua that for many years was the most celebrated stopping place between Lihue and Hanalei.

George P. Kaumualii, prince returned from exile, now began backsliding. From playing the bass viol he went on to more

violent diversions. Merely because a certain Captain Masters denied the young man a bottle of gin, George set fire to the captain's
dwelling houses on Kauai and destroyed property worth $2500.
The fact that the old king indemnified the loss at the request of
John Coffin Jones, American agent in the islands, did not mollify
Jones, who referred to Mr. George as "one of the most finished
rascals the islands offer."

Meanwhile the missionaries had been busy. The first Christian
church in the islands was dedicated September 15, 1821, on the site of
the present Kawaiahao Church. The printing press ran off, on January 7, 1822, the first sheet of what were to be millions of pages
of reading matter. The first Christian marriage in the islands, celebrated August 11, 1822, united Thomas Hopu, Cornwall boy and
friend of Opukahaia, with his bride Delia. The first chiefs to be
married were Hoapili and his second wife, Kalakua, one of the
widows of Kamehameha; the ceremony was performed October 19,
1823.

The weekly preaching had been helped by the arrival on the
cutter *Mermaid*, in April, 1822, of a party of visitors from the
London Missionary Society which included Daniel Tyerman,
George Bennett, and William Ellis. Ellis, who knew the language of
Tahiti and soon learned that of Hawaii, was the first person to
preach a sermon in Hawaiian. He was liked so well that he agreed
to return and make his home in the islands the following year. The
missionary contingent was further reinforced on April 27, 1823,
with the arrival of the "Second Company" on the ship *Thames*. By
the end of that year, the Kailua station, abandoned when the king
moved his capital to Honolulu, was again running; and a busy station was opened at the port of Lahaina on Maui. Another station
on Hawaii was started in 1824, at Hilo.

The missionaries preached every Sunday, but baptism into the
church was not easily earned. The queen mother, Keopuolani, was
baptized only an hour before her death on September 16, 1823;
but the next baptism did not come until July 10, 1825, when a

celebrated blind convert, Puaaiki or "Bartimeus," was taken into the Lahaina congregation. On December 5, eight Hawaiians — most of them of high rank — were baptized in Honolulu. Long before that time, Liholiho had made a decision that would prove fatal.

Remembering his father's words to Captain Vancouver, Liholiho considered himself and his kingdom to be under the aegis of Great Britain. This allegiance had been strengthened in the spring of 1822 by the gift from the British government of a six-gun schooner, the *Prince Regent*, built in Australia. Hence, in the fall of 1823, he decided to visit England, fountainhead of the new civilization opening before him. He wanted to exchange ideas with his fellow monarch King George.

Liholiho and his party — including his favorite wife Kamamalu, Governor Boki of Oahu and his wife Liliha, and the king's secretary, the Frenchman John Rives — embarked on the English whaleship *L'Aigle* on November 27, 1823. The royal party arrived at Portsmouth the following May, and were settled in a luxurious London hotel. They purchased and donned clothing of the latest mode. Before the program of regal entertainment had well begun, however, the king and queen, and several others in the party, were stricken with a disease that, in spite of every care, was to prove quickly lethal. It was the measles. Kamamalu succumbed on July 8, 1824, and Liholiho, stricken with grief, lasted only until July 14.

Before his departure Liholiho, who with five wives had no child, had named his nine-year-old brother as his heir. The kingdom was really run by the dowager queen Kaahumanu as regent, and her attitude was to be of most influence upon the conversion of the islanders.

Kaahumanu (her name means "feather cloak") was indeed an imposing figure. She was six feet tall and weighed over three hundred pounds, but she was well formed and Vancouver had testified that she was attractive in the eyes of white men. Eldest daughter of Keeaumoku, she had been the favorite queen of Kamehameha I. The great king had been deeply in love with her, and so jealous that, although she was entitled by her rank to have an extra husband of her own choice, Kamehameha refused her this privilege.

As regent, Kaahumanu was the virtual head of the kingdom. She was now the wife of Kaumualii, the unlucky king of Kauai, but by no means allowed that fact to prejudice the interests of the absent Liholiho. The royal captive from Kauai survived until May 26, 1824. His will fulfilled his promise that at his death the kingdom to the northwest would be bestowed upon the heir of Kamehameha.

George P. Kaumualii felt that he had been disinherited. He confided to Bingham his belief that "the old gentleman was poisoned," and feared for his own life. Persuaded by a group of malcontent chiefs, George led an attack on Sunday, August 8, against the old Russian fort at Waimea, Kauai, manned by a handful of Liholiho's soldiers. In spite of the leadership of the young veteran of the War of 1812, the attack failed bloodily and Billy Pitt soon put down the rebellion. George, who had been hiding in the mountains with his wife Betty, daughter of Isaac Davis, was taken in honorable captivity to Honolulu. (His child, born during the brief civil war, always bore the name of Wahine Kipi — "rebel woman.") There, on May 3, 1826, a prisoner of Kaahumanu, died the prince in whom the missionaries of the *Thaddeus* had placed so many high hopes.

Although Queen Kaahumanu had taken the lead in overthrowing the idols, her attitude toward the missionaries had at first been quite offhand. She thought little of coming to call on them right after bathing in the ocean, wearing only the dress of Eden and dripping sea water on the floor of their sitting room. Her pride was so great that she had haughtily extended her little finger to them instead of a hearty handshake, but gradually her interest in the new teachings became so strong that she interrupted her card games to puzzle out the letters in a spelling book. Solving the mystery of the vowels, she exclaimed to her women: "*Ua loaa iau* — I have got it!" About 1824 she took the lead in promoting the Christianization of the realm. Often she attended the preachings, drawn by six servitors pulling a little American-built wagon.

Another amazon of high rank, Kapiolani, sensationally testified to her faith in December, 1824. She conceived the idea of helping the Hilo mission by defying the fire goddess Pele at the very lip of the bubbling crater that was the dwelling place of this most revered Hawaiian deity.

Kapiolani led a hundred-mile march from Kona, through tropical undergrowth and across knife-edged lava flows, to the smoky pit of Kilauea, on the slopes of massive Mauna Loa. About noon on December 21, the party arrived to find Joseph Goodrich of the Hilo mission waiting for them. Together they gazed down upon the spouting billows of molten rock four hundred feet below.

That night, in a grass hut built for her among the giant tree ferns on the ledge above the crater, several members of the old faith tried to dissuade her and predicted her death. She replied: "I should not die by your god. That fire was kindled by my God." Next morning, on the way to the rim, a priestess again attempted to dissuade her by waving a piece of kapa which was supposed to be a *palapala*, or scroll, from Pele. "I too have a *palapala*," responded Kapiolani. She then read from a Hawaiian book of hymns and a missionary spelling book.

At the edge of the fiery pit Kapiolani broke an old ritual. A visitor was always supposed to tear off a branch of berry-bearing ohelo, throw half of it into the crater, and proclaim: "Pele, here are your ohelos; I offer some to you, some I also eat." Kapiolani broke a branch but ate all the berries, pointedly refusing to share with the goddess. Then, above the roaring flames and the smoke of cinder cones, she uttered her famous challenge: "Jehovah is my God. I fear not Pele. Should I perish by her anger, then you may fear her powers. But if Jehovah saves me, then you must fear and serve Jehovah." A hymn was sung and a prayer uttered, and the party withdrew without being overwhelmed by fire from an enraged heaven.

Kapiolani had flouted the old *kapu*, and was to live to tell the tale for seventeen years. Alfred Lord Tennyson, who heard in England about her feat, wrote a poem in her praise. Brother Goodrich found that the act of defiance was of immediate aid to the Hilo mission, where Kapiolani spent the Christmas season. "We have reason to think that Kapiolani did as much good by her visit here of ten or twelve days as we have done in nearly a year," he wrote, "for since her departure we have upwards of ninety scholars."

Through Missionary Eyes

THE MISSIONARIES CAME AT A CRITICAL MOMENT IN HAWAIIAN history, and they did much to change the course of that history. They were voluminous writers, and in their letters, journals, and reports may be found dozens of colorful vignettes of the islands during the time of transition from a feudal culture to a sometimes pathetic mimicry of white civilization. Here are a few scenes of life in the early days of the mission.

Treatment of a pagan priest who tenaciously adhered to the idols, as told by Lucy Goodale Thurston: "In the presence of the king he was brought to the test of renouncing the system of idolatry by being required to eat some poi from the women's calabash. He *would not* do it. As a consequence, the king required him to drink a whole quart bottle of whisky. The natives then placed him perpendicularly by the body of a tree, and lashed him to it with a rope, in such a snug manner that in a short time it squeezed the very life out of him."

Only one instance is recorded in which a missionary lady was molested by a Hawaiian. It happened to Mrs. Thurston in the first year of the station at Kailua, when she was in her dwelling, teaching the young prince. "A pagan priest of the old religion, somewhat intoxicated, entered, and with insolent manners divested himself of his girdle. Before I was aware, every individual had left the house and yard. The priest and I stood face to face, *alone*. As he advanced, I receded. Thus we performed many evolutions around the room. In a retired corner stood a high post bedstead. He threw himself upon the bed and seemed to enjoy the luxury of rolling from side to side upon its white covering. On leaving it he again approached and pursued me with increased eagerness. My tactics were then changed. I went out at one front door, and he after me. I entered the other front door, and he after me. Thus out and in, out and in, we continued to make many circuits. The scene of action was next in the dooryard. There, being nearly entrapped in a corner, having a substantial stick in my hand, I gave the fellow a severe blow across the arm. As he drew back under the smart, I slipped by and escaped. Loss and pain together so enraged him that he picked up clubs and threw them at me. There we parted, without his ever touching me with a finger."

Preparation of the main course for a feast in commemoration of the death of Kamehameha I, according to Mrs. Thurston: "For two days we heard one continuous yell of dogs. I visited their prison. Between one and two hundred were thrown in groups on the ground, utterly unable to move, having their forelegs brought over their backs and bound together. Some had burst the bands that confined their mouths, and some had expired. Their piteous moans would excite the compassion of any feeling heart. Natives consider baked dog a great delicacy, too much so in the days of their idolatry ever to allow it to pass the lips of women. They never offer it to foreigners, who hold it in great abhorrence. Once they mischievously attached a pig's head to a dog's body, and thus inveigled a foreigner to partake of it to his great acceptance."

Aftermath of a visit of an American ship at Kailua, Hawaii, in 1820: "Then a whole sisterhood, embracing fifteen or twenty, assembled and took seats in a conspicuous part of the village to display themselves. Before the arrival of that ship, they were simply attired in native cloth. After her sailing, each one was arrayed in a foreign article, obtained from that very ship. Their own relatives

and friends, perhaps fathers or brothers, or husbands, had paddled off that whole company of women and girls, to spend the night
on board that ship, specially for the gratification of its inmates.
When they returned, each one flaunted her base reward of foreign
cloth."

A native of renown, encountered by Mrs. Laura Fish Judd on a
visit to Kona: "Kealakekua is an historical spot. I write this in
sight of the very rock where the celebrated Captain Cook was killed,
and I have seen the man who *ate his heart*. He stole it from a tree,
supposing it to be a swine's heart hung there to dry, and was horrified when he discovered the truth. The Sandwich Islanders never
were cannibals. This made him famous, and he is always spoken of
as the man who ate Lono's heart."

From the journal of Samuel Whitney on Kauai, January 5,
1822: "Just been refreshed with what we call an American dish,
consisting of salt beef, mutton, cabbage, potatoes, string beans,
cucumbers, horseradish, warm bread and butter and apple pie.
This may appear a strange compound; indeed it is for the Sandwich
Islands, but all of it the produce of the Island except bread and
pie."

Skin infections were prevalent, "so much so that a smooth and
unbroken skin is far more uncommon here than the reverse is at
home." The Reverend C. S. Stewart, soon after his arrival, while
shaking hands with a high chief was startled at being asked: "Do
you have anything to cure the itch?"

Young Hawaiians of the *alii* class enjoyed complete freedom. "I
have seen a young chief, apparently not three years old," Mr. Stewart noted, "walking the streets of Honolulu as naked as when born,
with the exception of a pair of green morocco shoes on his feet,
followed by ten or twelve stout men, and as many boys, carrying
umbrellas, and kahilis, and spit-boxes, and fans, and the various
trappings of chieftainship. The young noble was evidently under
no control but his own will, and enjoyed already the privileges of
his birth in choosing his own path, and doing whatever he pleased."

Privileged pets at the court of Liholiho: "Whatever pets the ladies may have, whether pigs or dogs, and most have one of either, share in the common dishes without disturbance, unless perhaps they should be so ill-bred as to put their *forefeet*, as well as their *noses*, into the food, when a gentle tap may remind them of better manners. The pets of the nobles, of whatever kind, have in many cases unlimited privileges. There is at present attached to the palace a hog of this character, weighing four or five hundred pounds, called 'Kaahumanu,' after the haughty dowager of that name, which is permitted to range at pleasure, within doors as well as without; and not unfrequently finds a bed among the satins and velvets of the royal couches."

Henry Lyman tells how a native couple brought their child to be baptized with the Biblical cognomen of "Beelzebub." When their shocking request was refused, they compromised by naming the child "Mikalakeke," or "Mr. Richards," after his baptiser.

Ladies of the mission were the first to view the sights of Kilauea Crater. While Mr. and Mrs. E. W. Clark were spending four months teaching at Hilo, "a company of sixty, including Mr. and Mrs. Goodrich and Mr. and Mrs. Clark, set off for a visit to the volcano. They spent the first night at Olaa and the next day reached the volcano. These two ladies were the first foreign ladies to see the fires at Kilauea."

The joys of travel by native schooner in 1828, according to Laura Fish Judd: "When the ladies in Clinton, N. Y., were preparing my outfit, good old Mrs. T—— suggested a blue calico and some checked aprons. She said she heard I was expecting to spend a good deal of my time in visiting the different islands, but should think that I would find it my duty to stay at home and work. Dear old soul, how I wish she could know something of the *pleasure* of these voyages! They are made in a little schooner, stowed to its utmost capacity with men, women, and children, lumber, poi, poultry, horses, horned cattle, pet pigs and dogs, and all manner of creeping things; and we are utterly prostrated and helpless, with that merciless malady, which falls on all alike, master and servant, the *mal de mer*. The native navigators often go to sleep even at the helm, though the trade wind may blow a gale. The sea is often very rough, and then again we are under a lee shore, in a dead calm, with the sails flapping and the schooner pitching in the trough of the sea, with enough violence to take the masts out of her, not to say the breath out of our bodies. If I had ever dreamed of 'yachting by moonlight among the Isles of the Pacific,' one trip has dispelled the illusion forever." On another journey she cited as an instance of Hawaiian skill in navigation "a violent altercation most of the night between the captain and the cabin boy, whether the point of land, visible through the haze and rain, was the island of Molokai, or Barber's Point on Oahu."

The school for Hawaiian women in Honolulu in 1828 met when a flag was raised by Mrs. Bingham and Mrs. Judd. The flag came from a wrecked ship, the *Superb*, and bore that name in white letters on a red ground. "Superb schoolmistresses," Mr. Bingham called them.

No substitute had been found for human toil as late as 1837, according to Mrs. Judd. "The walls of the king's chapel are commenced, and many natives are employed in cutting and dragging coral stones from the seashore. It is a Herculean task to perform this work without beasts of burden, or the aid of any labor-saving machinery. The nation is still destitute of masons, carpenters, and blacksmiths. The only implement used is a narrow spade for agricultural purposes. When timber is required from the mountain, they form a company and drag it over hill and dale with ropes, at a great waste of human strength and sinew. Horses are scarce and kept only for pleasure-riding."

Communion at Laupahoehoe in 1846, described by C. S. Lyman: "The elements of the communion service were taro and water, the one cut up in pieces and served in a tin and earthen plate, and the other distributed in two little yellow earthen mugs and a tin pint basin which we had in our calabashes." On the same trail, travelers spending the night in a native shack sometimes heard gnashing of teeth as their mules ate up the sides of the grass hut.

When Kamehameha III began attending church regularly, about 1845, the problem arose of finding a suitable seat for him, for according to Hawaiian etiquette, no one must sit above the king. In olden times, death was the penalty for climbing a tree or housetop under which a chief sat. Now, the galleries of the church allowed commoners to sit over the head of his majesty. "There was some strong feeling upon the subject among some of the old chiefs and their retainers," wrote Mrs. Judd, "but the king ended the difficulty by saying: 'Old things are passed away. I prefer a place near the pulpit and by a window, so as to have fresh air. I do not care who is in the galleries, if they do not break through.'"

"The Isles
Shall Wait for His Law"

MISSIONARY LABORS WENT FORWARD ENTHUSIASTICALLY IN THE EARLY years. The pagan faith had been overthrown, and the deeply reverent Hawaiian nature yearned for a new faith which would combine old beliefs with a novel approach.

Two qualities in the haole religion appealed in particular. One was the satisfying emotional tone of Christianity. The other was the opportunity for the letterless Hawaiians to acquire the book learning of the outer world.

The great message brought by the missionaries was eagerly accepted. Perhaps some of the finer points of doctrine were missed by the converts, but there was no doubt that they enjoyed the preaching — to which hundreds of listeners flocked from the countryside by foot, horseback, and canoe — and especially the hymn-singing, which brought out the love of music always found in the Polynesian race. They also enjoyed the prayer meetings. Even the frequent regular church services did not satisfy the new yearning for soul-searching. Shortly thousands of men and women joined lay groups — something on the order of the modern Oxford Movement — at which they discussed the state of their souls, recited their sins, and forswore future immorality. These were called "*kapu* meetings" by the natives and "moral societies" by the missionaries, who after three years suppressed the movement. "Their influence, we found, was to foster pride and self-righteousness," they concluded. "We have reason to fear that many individuals in these associations have relied upon their membership, more than upon Jesus Christ, for the salvation of their souls."

The Ten Tabus of Jehovah

THE IDEA OF TABU HAD ALWAYS BEEN A STRIKING PART OF POLYnesian worship, and the Ten Commandments were quickly received as a new sort of *kapu*. In fact, in 1825 the chiefs seriously considered incorporating them into the law of the land.

Sunday was as rigidly observed as in a New England village. William Ellis found that his first Sabbath in Hawaii was "truly gratifying. No athletic sports were seen on the beach; no noise of playful children shouting as they gamboled in the surf, nor distant sound of the cloth-beating mallet was heard throughout the day; no persons were seen carrying burdens in and out of the village, nor any canoes passing across the calm surface of the bay." Sunday horseback riding was in particular banned by the chiefs.

Although only about one person in twenty among the foreign residents attended church, visiting ship captains were often seen at the services; and the idea of Sabbath observance spread sometimes to these mariners. Hiram Bingham proudly reported in the *Missionary Herald* for 1833 that a certain Captain B. decided not to take any more whales on Sunday. "After forming this resolution he was singularly tried by seeing whales chiefly on the Sabbath for several weeks; but holding . . . to the resolution not to take a whale on the Sabbath if he got no more during the voyage, he at length had as many shown him on the six days as he wanted."

The Puritan ideal was allied with Hawaiian tabus in other ways. Clearly beneficial was the missionary battle to curb the traffic in liquors, which had badly demoralized the Hawaiians, especially those living near the busy harbors. They had been taught the art of distilling, said Stewart, by several convicts escaped from Botany Bay, and used for the purpose not only sugar cane and sweet potatoes but particularly the roasted root of the ti plant. The resulting brew, called *okolehao*, or "iron bottom," derived its name from the fact that the primitive still consisted of a musket barrel draining into an iron pot.

Unscrupulous traders had early gained favors by introducing the chiefs to the fiery waters of the white man, and there was strong opposition to the missionary temperance preachings which had resulted in periodic closing of grogshops and punishment for drunkenness. At least one chief, Boki, was in the liquor business, and in 1836 the king himself owned three distilleries and a seamen's pub. But by 1838 the Cold Water Army of the church "embraced legions of valiant champions, who mustered occasionally in holiday dress and marched with flaunting standards of 'Down with Rum' and 'Cold Water Only.' "

Adultery was likewise rife. Since the days of Cook, the ports of Paradise had long been used to the sight of Cytherean wahines swarming by boatloads to a ship newly arrived at anchor; and as one early seafarer observed, "not many of the crew proved to be Josephs." As soon as they could, the missionaries got the chiefs to promulgate edicts putting a stop to this hospitable gesture. The resentment of the seamen was often violent. A group of sailors from the U.S.S. *Dolphin* broke into the Honolulu house of "Billy Pitt" Kalanimoku on Sunday, February 26, 1826, and demanded repeal of the rule. Being driven away, they tried to kill Mr. Bingham, who was protected by his native flock. But on the demand of the *Dolphin's* captain, "Mad Jack" Percival, the port was again declared wide open.

No less than three such attacks were made on the mission at Lahaina, a popular anchorage for whalers. A mob from the British whaleship *Daniel* besieged the house of the Reverend William Richards in October, 1825, and was driven away by the natives. Other seamen invaded the station in the minister's absence in 1826 and destroyed property. In the fall of 1827, while the captain of the *John Palmer* was detained at the governor's house, his crew loaded their cannon and bombarded the mission. One cannon ball that had made a hole in its wall was preserved for years. Later in 1827 Richards was called to Honolulu because Captain Buckle had resented the publication in the United States of the missionary account of the *Daniel* outrage. Not only was Richards declared innocent of wrongdoing, but the meeting of the chiefs led to the passage of a new set of laws for the Sandwich Islands. They were short and simple. Murder was prohibited under penalty of death; theft and adultery were to be punished by confinement in irons. No longer would Honolulu be a fair haven for Commandment-breakers.

Theft had long been a Hawaiian custom approaching the status of a sport, even though death had always been the penalty for stealing from the king. In the olden time, a fire in a dwelling had been the signal for licensed pillage of the occupants. Stealing, be it recalled, had been the main cause of friction leading to the death of Captain Cook. Although most of the high chiefs soon learned to disdain the practice and often punished offenders, a few chiefs took along in their trains servants who were adept at thievery. Again and again the missionaries were bereft of property ranging in value from handkerchiefs to entire trunkloads of goods. "In two or three instances," remarked Mr. Stewart, "clothes to a very considerable amount have been taken from trunks, the locks of which are broken while the persons have been sitting upon them, and apparently deeply interested in conversation with some of the family. In these instances, however, they were dressed in large *ki-heis* [shawls], which gave concealment to their movements, and afforded a cover for the booty in their retreat." Eventually, punishment by the chiefs rendered open thievery unpopular.

Concern over modesty in raiment was early displayed by the missionaries. The busy needles of the ladies quickly devised a sort of Mother Hubbard which clothed a woman from neck to foot. A fancier variation with a long train was named the *holoku*. Men were also encouraged to forsake the loincloth malo for more civilized garb, often with odd sartorial results.

Sports and games were frowned upon, as associated with the old pagan immorality. The *hale ume*, at which partners for a night's pleasure were chosen by the touch of a feather wand, was closed. The hula and other folk rituals were condemned. Mr. Richards, although conceding that some of the ancient songs had high literary merit, felt that most were immoral and exerted the worst possible influence. Even the old ti-leaf slides above the sea were made *kapu*. Captain von Kotzebue complained as early as 1825 that joyous abandon had been replaced by an endless round of prayers. "The streets, formerly so full of life and animation, are now deserted; games of all kinds, even the most innocent, are sternly prohibited; singing is a punishable offense [Kotzebue was being a bit sarcastic here]; and the consummate profligacy of attempting to dance would certainly find no mercy."

The vice of using tobacco was also objurgated. Mrs. Richards, while her husband was away in the fall of 1832, led a campaign at Lahaina against the noxious weed, regarded as "one of the fires that kindle the thirst for spiritous liquors." No less than twenty-five hundred men were persuaded by their spouses within a few days to bring their treasured pipes to the mission for sacrifice to the new *kapu*. On the island of Hawaii in 1839, Titus Coan reported that as a result of the revival there, "pipes were brought in great numbers and burnt, and most of the plantations of tobacco in Kohala were destroyed."

Monogamy made heavy advances. The chiefs in 1829 ordered the separation of all couples not formally married, foreigners as well as natives. By 1830 the mission reported that few couples were living within convenient distance who had not been united in matrimony. Mr. Richards wedded more than six hundred couples in a few months in 1828; the grooms of Lahaina, influenced by seaport lingo, often varied the ritual by loudly responding "Aye, aye!" instead of "I do."

The Pule *and the* Palapala

THE SECOND GREAT APPEAL OF THE EVANGELISTS WAS THEIR KNOWLedge of the three R's. Hand in hand with the *pule*, or religious instruction, went the *palapala*, or religious education through reading and writing.

A program of teaching was immediately launched, at first under the direction of Mrs. Bingham. By the end of the first few months, the various mission schools were teaching about a hundred pupils, men and women, mainly of high family. The king himself started to school, but soon wearied and appointed two young men to take his place. Most of the work of the schoolroom was conducted by the missionary wives as one of their manifold duties. Little could be done until the newcomers learned Hawaiian, but thereafter instruction went swimmingly.

Von Kotzebue noted that the schools in Honolulu could "easily be recognized afar off," for the pupils recited their lessons aloud in chorus. Like most peoples without written traditions, the Hawaiians enjoyed excellent memory. "One school recited the 103rd Psalm, and another Christ's Sermon on the Mount," said Mrs. Judd; "another repeated the 15th chapter of John, and the Dukes of Esau and Edom. Their power of memory is wonderful, acquired, as I suppose, by the habit of committing and reciting traditions, and the genealogies of their kings and priests." She remarked also that "they teach each other, making use of banana leaves, smooth stones, and the wet sand on the sea beach as tablets. Some read equally well with the book upside down or sidewise, as four or five of them learn from the same book with one teacher, crowding around him as closely as possible."

The work was rapidly extended by using native teachers. The better students were quickly given schools of their own in other districts. Although in 1824 there were only about two thousand students in all the schools, two years later the number had risen to twenty-five thousand, and more than four hundred native teachers were at work. A decade after the landing of the *Thaddeus* company, no less than eleven hundred common schools were scattered about the islands.

Curiously, all this while there had been few children sitting on the school benches. They had to wait until their elders had learned the *palapala*, for parents did not want their youngsters to achieve this new knowledge until they themselves had done so. Not until 1832 was the first group of children rounded up, clothed, washed, and set to work at their slates.

Hawaii's first school system, operated by the missionaries, reached its peak of usefulness about 1832, when more than half the adult population had learned to read. By then the novelty had worn off, and it was clear that education would have to be put on an organized basis by the government.

The art of writing was unknown to the Hawaiians. Kamehameha II asked a missionary to write his name on a piece of paper. Looking at the letters spelling out "Liholiho," the king remarked: "It looks neither like myself nor any other man." There is a story that one missionary sent a present of seven melons to another, with a note mentioning the number. The native messenger delivered only six. Asked where the missing one was, he complained: "How could you know there were seven? The other melons could not tell you, for I hid from them when I ate the seventh!"

The newcomers could not spread their learning until an alphabet for transcribing Hawaiian was invented. This the missionaries did, with the help of William Ellis. To the five vowels were given the Italian pronunciations, and these, together with seven consonants — *h, k, l, m, n, p,* and *w* — enabled any Hawaiian word to be written down. The printing press could now come into play.

The Pilgrims of Hawaii brought with them on the *Thaddeus* a second-hand Ramage press and several fonts of type. Their purpose was to make the Bible and other religious works available to the islanders who had just overthrown their ancient Baals.

Elisha Loomis had more urgent duties than setting type during his first two years. The youthful printer — he was only twenty when he arrived in Hawaii, and was probably not as old as his press — finally set up shop in a grass-roofed house in Honolulu, and on January 7, 1822, proofed the first sheet ever printed in the North Pacific region. It was part of an eight-page spelling book in Hawaiian. Chief Keeaumoku had the honor of pulling this historic first impression. A few weeks later, Liholiho — for whom Loomis had issued a handbill of port regulations, the first printed edict in the islands — visited the shop and ran off a page with his royal hands.

Now that reading matter was available, school classes grew. A month after the printing work began, Bingham estimated that he had more than five hundred scholars from the nobility of Honolulu.

Loomis moved the press in 1823 to a shop made of coral blocks (the building is still standing on King Street and can be visited today). Here he embarked on jobs which were the genesis of the important printing industry of modern times. One of his first books was a 60-page hymnal, *Na Himeni Hawaii,* prepared by William Ellis and Hiram Bingham. It contained only the words of songs; not until 1837 was a volume of music printed. As a service to a committee of sea captains, the mission press printed in 1824 a handbill signed by eleven of these mariners, designed to "check among their crews the excessive use of ardent spirits." Before the end of that year the first commercial job was run by the press — some blank bills of lading.

The most popular early publication was *Ka Pi-a-pa*, an eight-page leaflet that ran through nine editions. It showed the alphabet, numerals, punctuation marks, lists of words, verses of Scripture, and a few short poems, and was the main reading matter in half the schools until at least 1832. Paper was scarce in the middle of the Pacific, and half the first edition of *Ka Pi-a-pa* was run on paper donated by Chief Boki — paper designed for making gun cartridges. At the same time Loomis experimented, unsuccessfully, in printing the hymn book on native *kapa*.

The wooden press was beginning to show the strain, and the printer likewise. "Our printing press is materially damaged and may fail utterly at any time," Bingham wrote on August 20, 1825. "The nut in which the screw plays is cracked quite in two." Somehow the work continued and better equipment arrived, although Loomis's illness became worse and finally caused him to sail back to the United States early in 1827, with the idea of continuing to print mission material in New York State.

One big problem for Loomis had been the fact that, since the Hawaiian alphabet had been standardized at twelve letters only, most of the type in his English fonts was not used, while he rapidly ran out of certain letters. To be useful, a three-hundred-pound English font required four thousand additional *a*'s and three thousand additional *k*'s. The arrival in June, 1827, of new fonts with plenty of these "sorts" made possible the setting of fifty-six pages of Hawaiian at a time.

The project of printing the entire Bible in Hawaiian had not been forgotten. But it could not issue from the press until the missionaries had learned the language and had translated the Scripture word by patient word. "We have made translations of a few pages of Scripture," Loomis had written in his journal on December 14, 1820, "among which are the Commandments. These the scholars repeat in concert each day at the close of school." Twenty years were to pass, however, before a complete translation of the Bible was in print.

Henry Opukahaia, the exile who had grieved in Connecticut that his people had no Bible, had translated the Book of Genesis as early as 1816. The great task was begun in Honolulu in 1824 when Hiram Bingham started on the text of Matthew, and the other Gospels followed. Eight missionary scholars divided up the labor and worked on first drafts, made from the original Hebrew and Greek, which were then circulated for criticism by their fellows and by educated Hawaiians. William Richards translated about a third of the entire Bible; Asa Thurston nearly a fourth; Hiram Bingham a fifth; Artemas Bishop a seventh. The remainder was the work of Jonathan S. Green, Lorrin Andrews, Ephraim Weston Clark, and Sheldon Dibble.

The translators encountered many words for which no Hawaiian equivalent could be found. "Even the common terms, 'faith,' 'holiness,' 'throne,' 'dominion,' 'angel,' 'demoniac,' which so frequently occur in the New Testament, cannot be expressed with precision by any terms in the Hawaiian language. The natives call an angel either an *akua*, a god, or a *kanaka lele*, flying man." Sometimes, when no Hawaiian word could be discovered for a term such as "covenant," the original Hebrew word, *berita*, was kept.

Over a period of twenty years the Scriptures were issued piecemeal as fast as printed, and were eagerly devoured by the new reading public that the mission schools created. No less than eighteen thousand copies of the Sermon on the Mount came from the press in 1826, and in the next year twenty-five thousand were circulated.

The Hawaiians, with the thirst of the newly literate, eagerly bartered for the pages that came from the press. Bishop's translation of II Samuel came out in 1834, and was rationed among the various islands. William P. Alexander, head of the Kauai mission, wrote on October 4: "The people are panting after Samuels, which I have encouraged them to expect soon." On December 1 he added: "My division of the books" — Samuel — "for Kauai is nearly exhausted. I could sell 200 more for *pia* [arrowroot] — the ½ who can read are not supplied. We are anxious to get the *Io-pu-a* [Book of

Joshua]." The islanders were so avid to get this reading matter that they offered in trade not only arrowroot, but also taro, potatoes, cabbages, bananas, coconuts, sugar cane, eggs, firewood, fish, and even their canoe paddles! Those who came empty-handed were given books, but selling them was thought by the missionaries to encourage thrift.

The first edition of the New Testament was completed in 1832, and soon there was scarcely a family without a copy to read. One of the first off the press was neatly bound in red morocco and presented to Queen Kaahumanu, then stricken with her fatal illness.

Other editions of the New Testament came out in 1835 and 1837. The last verse of the Old Testament was translated on March 25, 1839, and the complete Bible was first available on May 10 of that year. Some parts had been printed in Rochester, New York, from copy sent to Elisha Loomis; but most of it was the work of Hawaiian printers.

This first edition of *Ka Palapala Hemolele*, as it was called, ran to 2331 duodecimo pages, and was usually bound in three volumes, with a separate title page for each. The first title would read, in English: "The Holy Scripture of Jehovah Our God. The Old Testament translated from the Hebrew. Book I. Printed for the American Bible Society. Oahu: Printed by the Missionaries. 1838." Unusual is the fact that the poetical parts were recognized as such by the printers, and were set in lines similar to free verse.

Later editions of the Hawaiian Bible include an octavo edition printed at the mission press in 1843; this and the earlier duodecimo issue ran to a total of about twenty thousand copies. Several editions of the New Testament were printed separately. Many later editions were issued in the United States by the American Bible Society; one of these was the Hawaiian-English New Testament of 1857, aimed to facilitate the learning of English. The Bible in Hawaiian is still in print and in demand.

Nearly four hundred thousand copies of twenty-eight different books and tracts were issued by the Honolulu press by March,

1830. A second printing house was set up at the Lahainaluna School on Maui, a high school started in 1831 by the Reverend Lorrin Andrews which included a good deal of vocational training. At first, the students learning to set type there had to make their own composing sticks. The first book printed at Lahainaluna was a translation of Worcester's *Scripture Geography*. This school press was also responsible for the first periodical ever issued in the North Pacific region. It was a modest four-page weekly in the Hawaiian language. Two hundred copies, illustrated with woodcuts, were run off for circulation at the school. *Ka Lama Hawaii*, or "The Hawaiian Luminary," first appeared on February 14, 1834. In October of that year a little religious paper, *Ke Kumu Hawaii*, was put out by the mission at Honolulu. These antedated by two years the appearance of the first general newspaper printed in the North Pacific.

Several curious and useful books were issued by the Lahainaluna press, where in 1835 Edmund H. Rogers became the first professional printer. One was an 184-page English-Hawaiian dictionary designed to help the people of Hawaii to learn the stranger's tongue; it was prepared by Joseph S. Emerson and Artemas Bishop and appeared in 1845. Instruction in engraving and bookbinding was also given. The Lahainaluna press ran until 1859, when it was closed and the equipment was sold.

The quality of the mission printing, performed by willing but often inexperienced hands, may not have been high, but the quantity was tremendous, considering the primitive equipment used. During the first twenty years of their existence, up to 1842, the two missionary presses ran off a total of 113,017,173 pages. About sixty different books or pamphlets were printed, including not only the Bible and tracts, but hymnals, sermons, legal documents, dictionaries, a translation of *The Pilgrim's Progress* (*Hele Malihini Ana*), and textbooks in geography, mathematics, astronomy, natural history, and anatomy. Mrs. Judd proudly claimed that the proportion of those in Hawaii who could read and write was "greater than in any other country in the world, except Scotland and New England." The contribution of the printing press to the Christianizing of the islands was immense. Great was the power of the *palapala!*

Year of Pentecost

ALL WAS NOT SMOOTH SAILING FOR THE MISSIONARY BAND DURING their earlier years. Several strong and vexatious influences arose that acted as drawbacks to the great work.

One of these influences was the antagonism of some of the other foreign inhabitants. The dislike of certain sea captains for the killjoys who objected to rum and romance has already been remarked. Ellis and Stewart one evening at Lahaina came upon some irreligious foreigners who were entertaining Governor Adams by pretending to pray and writing on a slate "some of the basest words in our language."

The chief reason for fearing the missionaries was political. When the *Thaddeus* group first requested permission to settle in 1820, John Young and others had expressed fear that the newcomers might obtain trade preferences for the United States and thus disturb the old friendliness with Britain.

This friendship was reinforced when the 46-gun frigate *Blonde* reached Honolulu on May 6, 1825, bearing home in state the survivors of the royal party from London and the bodies of Liholiho and Kamamalu. The coffined monarchs were brought ashore on May 11 amid decorous expressions of grief, in which the commander of the *Blonde* took the lead.

He was George Anson, Captain the Right Honorable Lord Byron, R.N. Unlike his famed poet cousin, this Lord Byron was always tactful and affable. He carried with him secret instructions to cultivate amiable relations with the Hawaiians, and not to interfere with their government unless British subjects were threatened or unless some other power tried to annex the islands. At a national council of the ruling chiefs on June 6, he offered a number of useful suggestions on government — trial by jury was introduced as a result of one of these proposals — but he made it clear that the chiefs must now make their own laws and enforce them without the aid of the British Navy.

Thereafter the business of lawmaking received much attention from the chiefs, and it was only natural that they should call more and more upon the wisdom of the kahunas from America, who seemed to know a great deal about good laws.

For his first sermon in the islands, Hiram Bingham had uncovered a splendid text in Isaiah 42:4: "He shall not fail nor be discouraged, till he have set judgment in the earth: *and the isles shall wait for his law.*" The chiefs, learning the Commandments in the mission schools, wondered how they might be enacted into regulations for their people. During the rebellion on Kauai in 1824, some of the chiefs consulted William Richards about proper action. Shortly after the conversion of Kaahumanu in 1825, the chiefs asked the missionaries to draft suitable laws for the kingdom. Four years later, the king proclaimed: "The laws of my country prohibit murder, theft, adultery, fornication, retailing ardent spirits at houses for selling spirits, amusements on the Sabbath day, gambling and betting on the Sabbath day and at all times."

These laws were extended to apply to foreigners, and their strict enforcement by native police aroused the further enmity of the whaling and trading population. Police entered a foreign home while dinner was being served and ordered the host to remove liquor from the table; at another home a billiard game was interrupted; and several persons who were "rolling ninepins" found their balls and pins confiscated.

Yet the need for a code of law persisted. Richards was asked in 1838 to take an official position as adviser to the king and his councillors. He resigned from the mission and thereafter until his death took a leading part in the government. Other missionaries, particularly Dr. Gerrit P. Judd and the Reverend Richard Armstrong, became cabinet ministers of the kingdom. Despite grumblings from the populace, the American preachers succeeded well in having many of their ideas put into secular force.

Another hindrance to missionary labors was the character of the young king, Kauikeauoli ("Suspended in the Blue Sky"), who had succeeded his elder brother under the title of Kamehameha III. So long as the strong hand of Kaahumanu guided the lad's minority all was well, but at her death in 1832 she was followed by Kinau, a daughter of Kamehameha I. Kinau ruled jointly for a year with the eighteen-year-old monarch, but in 1833 he resentfully threw off all restraint. Led astray by Kaomi, a favorite of Tahitian descent, he repealed all laws except those against theft and murder, revived the ancient Hawaiian sports, and began a course of wild oats. In a reaction against imported morality, he led his people into scenes of immorality of both imported and native origin, in which gambling and drunkenness were by no means the worst acts.

After two years, however, the king became reconciled with Kinau and agreed to proclaim a code that would punish not only homicide and theft, but also adultery, fraud, and drunkenness, and would apply not only to Hawaiians but to foreign residents. Legality was thenceforth to triumph over absolute monarchy.

A third cause of disappointment was the tendency of the Hawaiians to backslide when the novelty of conversion and schooling had worn off. After the death of Kaahumanu, said Sheldon Dibble, "Congregations on the Sabbath were diminished, many schools were deserted, and some companies of men revived, for a short time, their heathen worship. At Honolulu, the grogshops were opened; and in various parts of the islands, rude distilleries were put in operation." The pious books turned out by the press lay unbought on the shelves.

But as the result of an evangelical crusade that swept the mission stations from 1838 to 1840, more than twenty thousand natives joined the church, whereas only thirteen hundred had been admitted in the previous seventeen years. This was the "Great Revival," comparable to the Great Awakening in the American colonies almost a century before.

One drawback to conversion had been the inability of the happy Hawaiians to picture the pangs of hell. They simply remained cheerful despite sermons which, in the opinion of the Reverend Lowell Smith, "would cause a congregation in New England to quake with forebodings of eternal death." But around 1838 revivalism reached a tide.

The deep-seated reason was probably a growing fear by the Hawaiians that their race was threatened with decay. Back in 1826 old John Young had written from Kawaihae, "During the forty years that I have resided here, I have . . . seen this large island, once filled with inhabitants, dwindle down to its present few in numbers through wars and disease, and I am persuaded that nothing but Christianity can preserve them from total extinction." J. S. Emerson reported in 1832 that the chief at Waialua, Oahu, found that in four months there, births had been but twenty and deaths forty-four, with no special sickness in the place. "Oh, what a dying people this is!" exclaimed E. O. Hall in 1837. "They drop down on all sides of us and it seems that the nation must speedily become extinct. . . . What we do for people must be done quickly." The missionaries furnished as much medical attention as they could, but in ministering to the sick they had to fight poverty, filth, and superstition. The yearning for salvation was all too often motivated by despair.

The revival call sounded at every station, but most successful of the evangelists were Titus Coan, formerly of the mission to Patagonia, at Hilo; Lorenzo Lyons at Waimea, Hawaii; and Richard Armstrong at Wailuku, Maui. The Polynesian version of an old-time camp meeting would reveal five or six thousand sinners shouting and praying. Cripples led the blind to mass conversions. The doorstep of Dr. Dwight Baldwin at Lahaina, moistened by the tears of penitents, was "scarcely to be dry for the whole day together."

On one Sabbath in July, 1838, the missionaries at Hilo baptized 1705 converts and gave communion to 2400 church members before sunset. Three years later, seven thousand people belonged to Coan's church, making it the largest Protestant congregation in the world.

The power of Christianity was officially proclaimed by the kingdom of Hawaii in 1840 when its first Constitution declared that "no law shall be enacted which is at variance with the word of the Lord Jehovah." In the same year, the first hanging was performed in the islands, when a chief named Kamanawa was executed at the old fort for poisoning his wife.

Crosses and Cannons

A FINAL AND HEAVY HINDRANCE TO THE COMPLETE SUCCESS OF THE Protestant missionaries was the incursion of competing Catholic missionaries, who in turn involved the French government in the simmering pot of international dissension.

The idea of setting up a Catholic colony in the Sandwich Islands originated with John Rives, the Frenchman who had gone to London with Liholiho. After the king's death Rives went to France and there proposed such a plan. Rives never returned to Hawaii, but on July 7, 1827, the ship *Comète* deposited in Honolulu the pioneer French mission. It consisted of three priests of the Order of the Sacred Hearts of Jesus and Mary — Fathers Alexis Bachelot, Abraham Armand, and Patrick Short, an Englishman. They were supported by a choir brother and two lay brothers, a few French farmers, and a young lawyer named Auguste de Morineau.

Kaahumanu ordered that the *Comète* take the group away again, but the surly Captain La Plassard refused, saying that they might take passage in another ship after a while, or that she might put them in a cask and ship them aboard a whaler. The group remained even though permission to settle had not been granted.

Their first Mass on *terra firma* was celebrated on Bastille Day, July 14. The first baptism was given on November 30, to a child of Marín the Spaniard, and up to the end of 1828 the priests baptized children only, including those of three foreign residents; but in the next year they gave this sacrament to sixty-five adults and seventeen children. Morineau obtained from the king a piece of land for the use of the lay brothers, and in January, 1828, the first Catholic chapel in the islands was opened at Honolulu.

The work of the new mission went forward for some time without strong opposition. The priests enjoyed the protection of the governor of Oahu, Boki — not so much because Boki was pious, but because his animosity toward Kaahumanu led him to join any opposition to the *kuhina nui*.

Boki, or Poki (one theory has it that he took the name of a haole dog, "Bossie"), was a younger brother of Billy Pitt who had made his way in the world. He and his wife Liliha had accompanied Liholiho to London, where their picture had been painted by John Hayter, immortalizing them in the particular ethereal pose suitable to the noble savage of the eighteenth-century artists. On his return with Lord Byron, Boki had started a tavern, the Blonde Hotel, named for the ship on which he had returned from King George's court. He also made a brave attempt to operate the first sugar plantation and cane grinding mill on Oahu. Boki combined a yearning for the old feudal order with a liking for capitalist enterprise among traders and ship captains. "His levy of sandalwood," wrote Mrs. Judd, "has kept the poor people in the mountains for months together, cutting it without food or shelter, other than that afforded by the forests." The protection of this local magnate enabled the Catholics to work along quietly for some while.

The Protestants did not at first see any danger in the rival mission, for they expected that the Hawaiians would immediately recognize the falsity of the new doctrine; but as time went on they promoted efforts to have the priests deported. They had the full support of the other chiefs, who conceived that Protestantism was now virtually the state religion and who began punishing for insubordination and idolatry the growing number of Catholic converts. Natives were forbidden in August, 1829, to attend Catholic services, but some of them continued to go to the chapel, and during the next ten years a number of them were severely punished for their religious beliefs.

The support of Boki was withdrawn toward the end of 1829. He had started to lead a revolt against Kaahumanu the previous year, but had abandoned this plan and instead had expanded into various trading enterprises which sank him deeply in debt. When an Australian ship brought a story of a South Pacific island that was covered with valuable sandalwood trees, Boki decided that he would take a last gamble to recoup his fortunes. Fitting out two vessels, the *Kamehameha* and the *Becket*, he put on board some five hundred of his followers and sailed in search of the fabulous island. The ships separated somewhere in the Fiji group. Eight months later the *Becket* limped back to Honolulu with only twenty survivors aboard. The island had been found, but a quarrel with the inhabitants had resulted in bloodshed, and on the return a disease had broken out that killed almost two hundred of the crew. The flower of Boki's following thus vanished from the scene, for the *Kamehameha* was never heard of again. "As the lower deck of the brig," hazarded Mrs. Judd, "was strewed with bags of gunpowder, upon which the men sat and smoked, it is reasonable to infer that the vessel was blown up, and that all on board perished."

Madame Boki took over the governorship, refusing to believe that her husband would not return. (Her faith passed into a proverb; "when Boki comes back" came to mean "never.") But she was soon removed from her place, and the family was no longer in a position to shelter Catholics.

The chiefs on April 2, 1831, read a decree of banishment to Fathers Bachelot and Short, but when the months passed and they showed no intention of complying, the chiefs fitted out one of their own vessels, the brig *Waverley*, and shipped the priests off to Mexican California, leaving behind only one lay brother to represent the mission. Persecution of native converts greatly died down in the next few years, partly as a result of a plea for toleration made by Commodore John Downes of the American frigate *Potomac*.

The second attempt to found a Catholic mission was made in 1835. The Church had created the Vicariate Apostolic of Eastern Oceania, and Father Bachelot had been made prefect of the area north of the equator. Bishop Jerome Rouchouze sent from Mangareva an advance agent to investigate the situation in Hawaii. He was Brother Columba Murphy, a jolly Irish catechist who was a British subject. After looking over the ground, Murphy went to California; but failing to meet with Bachelot and Short, he went on to Valparaiso in Chile. There it was decided to send the youthful Father Arsenius Walsh to Honolulu. It was thought that Walsh, also a British subject, might arouse less opposition than would a Frenchman.

Father Walsh arrived on September 30, 1836, and was immediately ordered to leave; but through the persuasion of the commander of the French corvette of war *La Bonite* he received permission to stay and minister to the foreigners but not the Hawaiians. The right of the Catholics to teach the natives was unsuccessfully urged by Lord Edward Russell, commander of the British war vessel *Acteon*, which anchored as *La Bonite* was departing. Father Walsh did nevertheless manage to baptize a few Hawaiians in the next four years.

The banished priests Bachelot and Short returned from California on April 17, 1837. They were suffered to stay on shore for a fortnight, since the king and Kinau were at Lahaina. But, despite their argument that the decree of banishment in 1831 had neglected to state that they were supposed to stay away forever, the royal edict was issued on April 30 that the two priests should go away on the same ship that brought them.

A fine international dust-up resulted. The *Clementine* was owned by a Frenchman, Jules Dudoit, but sailed under the British flag, and during the passage from California had been chartered by an American merchant. Dudoit, a fiery soul, said that he was not responsible for bringing the priests and would not accept them as return passengers unless their fare was paid and they went willingly. The British and American consuls sided with Dudoit against the chiefs. When the priests were finally compelled to go back on board the ship, Dudoit hauled down the British flag and gave it to the British consul, Richard Charlton, who publicly burned it, claiming that it had been insulted by the Hawaiian government.

The priests were kept on the *Clementine* until early July, when two warships hove into port. These were the British *Sulphur* under Captain Sir Edward Belcher and the French *La Vénus* under Captain A. du Petit-Thouars. Belcher, after an argument with Kinau, "recaptured" the *Clementine* with a company of marines, and then he and the French commander escorted the priests ashore. A few days later, however, the king arrived in town and received pledges from the two visiting captains that the priests would leave at the first opportunity.

Father Short did sail from Honolulu at the end of October, but a few days later, two more priests sent by Bishop Rouchouze arrived on the scene. These were the Reverend Columba Murphy, who now returned to Hawaii, and the Reverend L. D. Maigret, who had recently been deported from Tahiti at the request of the Protestant missionaries there. The newcomers were at once forbidden to land, but the fact that Murphy had recently been ordained was not revealed, and when the British consul stated that he was not a priest, Murphy was permitted to reside ashore. Father Maigret bought a schooner from Dudoit and together with Bachelot, who was still waiting for transportation, sailed on November 23 for the South Pacific.

Soon after their departure, Kamehameha III issued a ban against the teaching or practice of Catholicism, and persecution of native Catholics was for a while renewed. Forces for greater tolerance were, however, at work. These included the moderating advice of resident foreigners, the death of Kinau on April 4, 1839, and the threat of reprisals by the French government, which considered itself the protector of all Catholic missionaries in the Pacific. What amounted to an edict of religious toleration was issued by the king in June, 1839, stating that Catholics should no longer be punished for their beliefs.

The following month, though, another French warship arrived in Honolulu with orders from Paris to use force of arms, if necessary, to make the island chiefs realize that they should beware of incurring "the wrath of France." Captain du Petit-Thouars had obtained, the previous autumn, reparations from the Polynesian ruler of Tahiti for having expelled French priests. Now Captain C. P. T. Laplace and the 60-gun frigate *Artémise* touched at Honolulu on an around-the-world trip to promote French commerce.

Mindful of his orders, Laplace paused only to obtain a highly colored view of the situation from Dudoit, the French consul, and then sent a "manifesto" to the Hawaiian government, accusing the chiefs of having broken the treaty made with Thouars. Laplace leveled his cannon at Honolulu and demanded a new treaty. It provided that Catholicism should be allowed, that land be given for a Catholic church in the town, that the French flag be saluted with twenty-one guns, and that the Hawaiians deposit $20,000 in cash with him as a guarantee of good behavior.

Laplace trained his guns and prepared to land his forces. The foreign residents of the town were guaranteed protection, but this guarantee did not extend to the Protestant missionary families, on whom Laplace blamed the "insults" given to France. "For me they compose a part of the native population," he declared, "and must undergo the unhappy consequences of a war which they shall have brought upon this country."

War was averted, however, when the treaty was immediately signed by the *kuhina nui*, Kekauluohi, and the governor of Oahu, since the king was at Lahaina. Raising the cash was difficult, but most of the merchants lent all they had on hand. (A French admiral brought back the money in 1846, when relations had improved; the coins were still packed in the original boxes handed over to Laplace.)

The king agreed to all the demands when he returned, but in the brief interim Laplace had thought up a treaty still more favorable to the French. Two articles were especially unpalatable. One gave to Frenchmen accused of crime in the kingdom the right to be tried by a jury of foreigners named by the French consul. The other provided that French merchandise, especially wines and brandies, should be freely imported at a low duty. (Ever since that day, the Hawaiian word *palani* has meant both "Frenchman" and "brandy.") This demand nullified the prohibition law of 1838, but the Hawaiian capital was under the guns of the French. Kamehameha III signed. Laplace came ashore for the first time, and the treaty was sealed by a military Mass on Sunday, July 14 — another Bastille Day.

The Catholic missionaries were thus free to proselyte without opposition. The first publications written by them in the Hawaiian language were distributed in August. The mission was on a firm basis when on May 15, 1840, Bishop Rouchouze himself arrived in Honolulu, along with three other priests — one of them the expelled Father Maigret. At last the Protestants had energetic competition in the vineyard. "Rum and Romanism together allow me but little time to sit in my study," wrote Richard Armstrong.

A Catholic church of stone was soon begun, and schools on other islands were started to advance the mission labors. Six more workers arrived on November 9, and before the end of 1840 no less than 2049 converts were baptized on Oahu. The first Catholic printing press was set up in November, 1841, and operated for fifty years; its first publication was *He Vahi Hoike Katolika* (*An Explanation of the Catholic Religion*).

Many legal difficulties arose in connection with the Catholic mission, and Dudoit asked that all the Catholics submit their grievances to him, to be enforced by France if necéssary. It seemed to many people that pretexts were being sought for French seizure of the islands. Du Petit-Thouars, now an admiral, took possession of the Marquesas Islands in July, 1842, and from there sent a sloop of war, the *Embuscade*, to Hawaii. Captain S. Mallet, on his arrival, handed a letter to the king which claimed violation of the Laplace treaty and made further demands on the Hawaiians. Yielding to these demands would have given the Catholic priests the right to appoint certain officials of the Hawaiian government and, in general, would have given the Catholics a position much more favored than that granted to the Protestants.

This time Kamehameha III stood firm. He could not yield another inch without giving up his rights as head of the Hawaiian people. He had sent ministers to his brother monarch of France to obtain a new and more general treaty that would recognize Hawaiian independence in the eyes of all the world. Mallet sailed away on September 8 without a new treaty. Gunboat diplomacy had by no means been abandoned in Hawaiian waters; but the question was to become less religious than political in future days.

Despite irritations and drawbacks, the success of the American Protestants in their mission to the North Pacific islands was remarkable. As one ship after another deposited its missionary contingent, the field force was increased to more than fifty men and women before 1832. By 1840 missionaries coming from nearly every state in the Union could be found in every accessible part of the kingdom. In 1863 — within the lifetimes of some of the *Thaddeus* pilgrims — the job of converting Hawaii was complete, in the judgment of the American Board. Hawaii was declared a "home mission," and a base for missionary work in other islands to the south. The task was done; the mission folk could go back home if they desired. Many of them chose to stay.

A strong secular effect of the missionary enterprise was the bringing to the islands of a new population segment that was to become a dynamic force in its history. In thirty-five years, no less than fifteen "companies" of missionaries arrived; even today genealogies are traced back, say, to an ancestor who came with the Third Company on the ship *Parthian* on March 29, 1828. They were prolific; Mrs. Thurston counted no less than forty-seven children at the General Meeting of 1834. As missionary parents addressed each other as brother and sister, their children decided that they should call each other "cousin." From this custom grew the Cousins' Society, which still holds an annual reunion of the old families.

The roll of the "companies" echoes the names of the most influential group of American families in Hawaiian history: Bishop, Richards, Bingham, Andrews, Gulick, Judd, Baldwin, Bond, Dibble, Alexander, Emerson, Hitchcock, Lyons, Lyman, Spalding, Parker, Armstrong, Castle, Cooke, Wilcox, Rice, Dwight, Dole. These names crop up again and again; for many of the missionaries did not go back to the United States when the American Board ended the official mission in 1863. They had spent their best years in Hawaii and wanted to remain. Their children had grown up as islanders, at home in Hawaii. The property of the mission was divided among the individual workers (until 1838, the missionaries had lived under the "common stock system," sharing supplies as needed and receiving no salaries). After 1863, although some of the older missionaries continued to receive salaries, many of their children could stay in the islands only if they went into education, or political life, or business. The founding of several of the great mercantile enterprises dates from this time when mission families were forced to earn their livings in other ways.

Gunboats and
Whaling Ships

THE REIGN OF KAMEHAMEHA III SAW A LIVELY GROWTH IN COM-
merce. The sandalwood trade declined after 1830, but thereafter the
rise of whaling more than made up for the loss. Honolulu soon
became the business capital of the Pacific, and its harbor held merchant ships from China, Peru, Mexico, California, Great Britain,
and the Atlantic coast of the United States.

As early as 1817, to sell off a cargo, James Hunnewell set up
a store in Honolulu. A few years later, five mercantile houses were
doing a thriving business. The needs of the island shoppers and
the visiting whalemen resulted in a wide choice of imported goods
in the town. Among the ladings sent to Hunnewell between 1826
and 1830 were such varied articles as would stock a first-class store
in any civilized country.

John Coffin Jones, an early merchant, wrote in 1821 that the dumping of cheap trade goods on the chiefs was already impossible, and that only superfine materials would sell. "The natives are now too much enlightened; they know well the value of every article; if they do not there are plenty of canting, hypocritical missionaries to inform them, even though unasked." Two years later he wrote to Boston: "The king, too, is very anxious to have a billiard table; one that you might get for two hundred dollars would command at least $1500. If a steamboat could be brought here, it would command any price."

The goods were tempting. The Hudson's Bay Company store started in Honolulu in 1834 by George Pelly was nicknamed Aienui, "the big debt," by the Hawaiian people who ran up large bills there.

Honolulu was also a warehouse center for the ocean area. In 1840 it was estimated that half the goods of American or European origin which were landed at this port were transshipped to California, the Russian settlements, or the islands of the South Pacific. Some Honolulu shipowners picked up a little extra money by smuggling skins, silks, tea, and specie into California. According to R. H. Dana, Jr., a vessel with a moderate cargo would enter Monterey, pay the heavy Mexican customs duties, and do a little local trading. She would then rendezvous off Catalina with a sister ship from Oahu, transfer a heavy cargo, and sell it, duty-free, at other California ports.

The Treaty Hunters

TRADE WAS HAMPERED IN THE EARLY YEARS BY THE BARTER SYSTEM and the use of specie from many other countries. A businessman in Hawaii in the nineteenth century had to be familiar with more than a hundred and fifty gold and silver coins from all the trading nations of the world, including the United States, Great Britain, France, Mexico, and some of the South American republics. The lack of small currency was especially troublesome; when the United States Exploring Expedition under Lieutenant Charles Wilkes visited the islands in 1840, the commander had Spanish dollars chopped into quarters and eighths to use for change. But the growing predominance of American trade favored the dollars-and-cents standard, and when in 1846 the kingdom set up its first monetary system, it was based on a penny that was called *hapa-haneri*, the "hundredth part" of a dollar, or *kala*. Coins were minted also in half dollars, quarters, eighths, and sixteenths. The copper penny bore the head of "Kamehameha III — Ka Moi" and on the reverse the words "Aupuni [government] Hawaii." No provision was made for accepting dimes and nickels, and these small American coins were virtually worthless until 1859, when a law made them legal tender in the kingdom.

Trade was enlivened by the rise of commercial publications. The first secular newspaper in the islands, and the first printed in English west of the Rocky Mountains, appeared in July, 1836. It was the *Sandwich Island Gazette*, printed by two Americans named Nelson Hall and S. D. MacIntosh, and it appeared weekly for three years. It was followed by the *Sandwich Island Mirror*, issued monthly for a year.

A more pretentious newspaper, the *Polynesian*, began in June, 1840; it was re-established in May, 1844, after having suspended publication for two and a half years, as the official journal of the government. Its editor, James J. Jarves, was given the title of Director of Government Printing. Jarves, son of the founder of the famous glass factory at Sandwich, Massachusetts, was the stormy petrel of Hawaiian journalism; his editorial duties allowed him time to write a volume of sketches on island life, an early history of Hawaii, and even a romantic novel about sixteenth-century Spanish castaways on the Big Island.

The Friend was established in 1843 by the seamen's chaplain, the Reverend S. C. Damon, and is still being published in Honolulu after more than a century. This monthly had occasionally been

critical of the government, but in September, 1846, the opposition
set up its own organ, the *Sandwich Island News*, which ran for
about two years. In the next few years two other opposition papers
were founded: the Honolulu *Times* and the *Weekly Argus*.

A literary journal was one of the earliest periodicals in the Pacific;
the *Hawaiian Spectator*, a 100-page quarterly, began publication at
the American mission in January, 1838, "conducted by an association of gentlemen."

The *Oahu Fountain*, a temperance monthly, was founded in
1846 but ceased publication after ten months.

Kamehameha III, "Ka Moi," sobered by responsibilities, held the
throne for almost thirty years, and lived to see his realm take its
place among the family of Christian nations as a thriving constitutional monarchy.

Law enforcement in the islands was a problem mainly because the
rights of foreigners and foreign residents had never been clearly
stated. Should people from other countries be allowed to live in the
kingdom? Could they own land or engage in business? If they
obtained land, could they build on it or sell their rights to others?
During the early years, many of the haoles who settled in Hawaii
did not understand the old landholding system or scorned to abide
by it, and felt that they should have the same rights in Hawaii as
in their homelands. Some of these settlers denied the right of the
king of Hawaii to restrict their enterprises, and began to appeal to
their own governments for protection. The appearance of a warship in Hawaiian waters, they believed, might help the chiefs to
listen to reason. Slowly it was realized that special rights could be
established only if Hawaii signed treaties with various maritime
nations of the world.

First, however, the Hawaiians had to put their own legal house in
order. The council of chiefs, still under the guidance of William
Richards, began working toward a written constitution for the
people. The first result was the "Hawaiian Magna Charta," the
declaration of rights and laws of June 7, 1839, in which

Kamehameha III voluntarily gave up many of his regal powers. Its preamble, reminiscent of the American Declaration of Independence, stated that "God has bestowed certain rights alike on all men, and all chiefs, and all people of all lands: . . . life, limb, liberty, the labor of his hands, and productions of his mind."

The rights and civil statutes proclaimed in 1839 were embodied in the Constitution of 1840, signed by the king and the *kuhina nui*, Kekauluohi, on October 8. The document conferred some new and broad rights never previously enjoyed. First of these was the creation of a "representative body" of lawmakers elected by the people; thus, for the first time, the common man had a share in politics. Another was the formation of a supreme court made up of the king, the *kuhina nui*, and four judges appointed by the House of Representatives. Executive power remained with Kamehameha and the *kuhina nui*, aided by four island governors appointed by the king. The king and the *kuhina nui*, who had to sign all laws, were also members of the council of chiefs, which met annually along with the lower house to legislate by majority vote. An even more liberal form of government was incorporated a dozen years later into the Constitution of 1852.

Annexation of the Hawaiian Islands by a foreign power seemed frighteningly close in 1840. Great Britain had just taken over the Polynesian islands of New Zealand, and Richard Charlton, who had been British consul since 1825, seemed determined to get his government to intervene in Hawaiian affairs. He put in a claim in 1840 for a parcel of land that he said had been given to him by Billy Pitt some years before. The claim was vague if not actually a fraud, but Charlton used it to stir up trouble through these critical years, and in 1847 he finally got possession of the land.

Relations with France in 1840 were still touchy, and it seemed more than likely that Hawaii would wind up as a French colony like the Marquesas and the Society Islands.

American businessmen were interested in developing Hawaiian trade and agriculture, but were held back because the independence of the Hawaiian Kingdom had never been recognized by any nation of the world. The first efforts toward obtaining this recognition were, as a matter of fact, undertaken in 1840 by a visiting American lawyer, Thomas J. Farnham, but they came to nothing. Another American, Peter A. Brinsmade, was more closely concerned. He was promoting the development of a land grant to be given to Ladd & Company on the contingency that Hawaiian independence be recognized. Brinsmade went to Washington and urged Daniel Webster, then Secretary of State, to give the idea full consideration.

Great help was given by Sir George Simpson, an official of the Hudson's Bay Company who visited Hawaii on a tour of the world. He suggested that two commissioners be sent from Hawaii with the power to negotiate treaties with Great Britain, France, and the United States. Simpson was asked to serve on the commission when he returned to London, where he was to meet the two emissaries. These men were William Richards and Timothy Haalilio, a young Hawaiian who had been the king's private secretary.

The two set out on July 18, 1842, on their search for recognition of Hawaii's place in the circle of nations. They first went to Washington, and before the end of the year obtained from the American government a formal statement that the United States was more interested in the Hawaiian Islands than any other nation could be. The document also proclaimed that no power ought to conquer these islands or colonize them, nor should any power seek undue control over their government or obtain any exclusive commercial privileges.

Fortified by this declaration, Richards and Haalilio arrived in London early in 1843 and began negotiations with the head of the British Foreign Office. Their efforts were hampered by the arrival of Consul Charlton, who had hastened from Honolulu to London to complain against the Hawaiian government. They had better luck on the Continent, and in Paris the foreign minister gave a verbal promise of French recognition. Just as this promise was to be received in written form, however, word arrived in Paris that the

Hawaiian Islands had been taken over — lock, stock, and barrel — by a British naval officer. At once it became clear that Hawaiian independence was a grave issue that would have to be settled on a high level among the three nations most concerned.

Britannic Interlude

THE OLD BRITISH PRESTIGE IN THE ISLANDS HAD DECLINED DURING the past twenty years. Charlton left behind as acting consul a man of devious mind, a lover of intrigue who believed that his aim should be to find a pretext for adding the Sandwich Islands to the British Empire. This man was Alexander Simpson — a cousin of Sir George, but opposed to Sir George's ideas.

On his way to London, Charlton had complained to British authorities in Mexico concerning the situation in Honolulu. Unaware of the current policy of his government in London, Rear Admiral Richard Thomas, commander of the Pacific squadron, sent a frigate to Hawaii to protect British interests there.

The *Carysfort* arrived on February 10, 1843, commanded by Lord George Paulet, and Simpson went on board at once and poured out his complaints. Among these was the fact that the Hawaiian government, irked by his behavior, had refused to acknowledge his official position. The king, hastily summoned from Lahaina, was ordered at once to recognize Simpson or suffer the consequences: a broadside against the town from the guns of the *Carysfort*.

Before the eight-hour term expired, the king agreed to acknowledge Her Britannic Majesty's consul in Honolulu. This was only the beginning of a series of demands upon the harassed monarch, including an indemnity of more than $100,000 from the island treasury. Lord George refused to accept as the king's spokesman Dr. Gerrit P. Judd, a medical missionary who had taken the place of Richards as "translator and recorder." Clearly, it was Paulet's intention to annex the country. After anxious deliberation under the guns of the frigate, the king decided to yield under protest, trusting that the commissioners in London would persuade the British government to redress the wrong.

The Hawaiian flag was lowered on February 25, a salute of twenty-one guns was fired, and British soldiers marched into the fort to the strains of "God Save the Queen." The ship's band also played "Isle of Beauty, Fare Thee Well" — a refinement of cruelty inspired, it was said, by some lady friends of Lord George.

Paulet commandeered three of Kamehameha's schooners and changed their names to *Albert*, *Victoria*, and *Adelaide*. The *Albert* sailed on March 11 for Mexico with Alexander Simpson aboard, carrying Paulet's report on the annexation. On the same vessel was a young American merchant, James F. B. Marshall, ostensibly acting as agent for Ladd & Company. Unknown to Simpson, Marshall had secretly been commissioned as envoy extraordinary and minister plenipotentiary to present the Hawaiian side of the story. He carried with him documents that had been drafted by Dr. Judd in the privacy of the royal tombs, using the coffin of the great Kaahumanu as a writing desk. The reports that each of these rival messengers carried were finally to arrive on the same desk in the British Foreign Office.

The Union Jack flew over the Hawaiian Islands for five months. The cession provided that the government should lie in the hands of the king (or his deputy), Captain Paulet, and two other British officers. Dr. Judd, appointed to serve as the king's deputy, strove to maintain good feeling, but soon the naval officers began, contrary to the cession deed, to meddle with internal affairs. Laws on liquor control were relaxed and a new police force was set up. A body of native troops called the "Queen's Regiment" was formed, to be paid from the king's treasury. Dr. Judd, after protests, resigned on May 11, and the remaining officials became even more autocratic. To prevent their seizure of the public archives, Dr. Judd took away these documents and hid them in the royal tomb.

The growing resistance to the annexation was strengthened by the arrival of Commodore Lawrence Kearney in his flagship, U.S.S. *Constellation*, with the rumor that the United States had recognized the independence of the islands. Kearney protested against the cession, and an open break was averted only by the arrival of the large British man-of-war *Dublin*, flying the flag of Rear Admiral Thomas himself. He had come to repair the damage done by the forced cession, and after arranging terms with the king to safeguard British interests, he took the lead in an impressive restoration ceremony.

Paulet had destroyed every Hawaiian flag he could find, flattering himself that none would ever again be needed. The admiral had a new one made on board the *Dublin*, and on the morning of July 31, the banner once more flew over the islands. Before a great crowd, Kamehameha III, on horseback, was given a salute of twenty-one guns from the warships, in recognition of his restored sovereignty. The king and chiefs then went to Kawaiahao Church for a thanksgiving service at which the king proclaimed that his hope that the land would be restored had come true. At this time, it is said, he used the words that are still the motto of the Hawaiian Islands: "*Ua mau ke ea o ka aina i ka pono* (The life of the land is preserved in righteousness)."

The site of the restoration ceremony was named Thomas Square in honor of the merry admiral, who went ashore to live in Honolulu for the next six months and soon won the hearts of the people. He took the lead in giving a round of dinner parties for the diplomatic corps, which now included no less than fourteen foreign representatives.

A horrified observer of the way in which the common people celebrated the restoration of sovereignty was an errant seaman named Herman Melville, whose ramblings in the South Seas were to result in such famed novels as *Typee*, *Omoo*, and *Moby Dick*. Melville had been discharged from the Nantucket whaler *Charles and Henry* at Lahaina on May 2 and then had come to Honolulu, where for a while he seems to have earned his living setting up pins in a bowling alley. On June 1 he was indentured as a clerk to Isaac Montgomery, merchant, at a salary of $150 a year plus board, room, and laundry. His decision not to linger in the islands may have cost American literature many a bright page on Hawaii; but Ishmael was anxious to return to New York, and on August 17 signed on as ordinary seaman on the frigate *United States*. Concerning the restoration ceremonies, Melville was later to write in *Typee:*

"Who that happened to be at Honolulu during those ten memorable days will ever forget them! The spectacle of universal broadday debauchery, which was then exhibited, beggars description. The natives of the surrounding islands flocked to Honolulu by hundreds, and the crews of two frigates, opportunely let loose like so many demons to swell the heathenish uproar, gave the crowning flourish to the scene. It was a sort of Polynesian Saturnalia. Deeds too atrocious to be mentioned were done at noonday in the open street."

The Ten Demands of Tromelin

THE DEPUTATION OF RICHARDS, HAALILIO, AND SIR GEORGE SIMPSON won a victory when a declaration was signed in London on November 28, 1843, in which the independence of the Sandwich Islands was formally recognized by the Queen of Great Britain and the King of the French. The United States declined to sign this declaration, acting on its policy of avoiding entangling alliances; but to Richards and Haalilio, in the summer of 1844, Secretary of State John C. Calhoun reaffirmed American recognition of Hawaiian independence.

When William Miller, the new British consul general, arrived in Honolulu in February, 1844, he brought with him a treaty identical with the objectionable one forced upon Kamehameha III by the French in 1839. The government had no choice but to accept it in full or go without any treaty at all; and it was signed on February

12. Unfortunately, the envoys had not been able to get a new treaty with France. They left the United States and embarked for Hawaii in November, 1844; but Haalilio died at sea, his health ruined by his foreign travels. Richards arrived in Honolulu in March, 1845, having been abroad for almost three years.

During his absence, the king, aided by other skilled advisers, had been pushing further constitutional reforms. A treasury board was appointed to control government funds, and within a few years the national debt was paid off. A young American lawyer, John Ricord, was named attorney general in March, 1844, and he ably handled many of the lawsuits that were being brought into the courts by foreign plaintiffs. In his leisure hours Ricord worked out a series of reforms which were approved by the legislature and codified in a series of Organic Acts.

The first of these acts went into effect in March, 1846. It divided the executive branch into five departments with a minister at the head of each. These ministers, the four governors of islands, and other members appointed by the king were to form the privy council, a body which was to become a highly important influence in the kingdom. The third Organic Act, which went into operation early in 1848, improved the entire judiciary system, setting up a supreme court, four circuit courts, and twenty-four district courts. The first chief justice was William L. Lee, another young American lawyer, who had completed the plans worked out by Ricord before he left the islands. Associate justices were Lorrin Andrews and John Ii, a Hawaiian who had been educated in the mission schools.

The second Organic Act, which went into effect in 1846, supplied further details for the operation of the executive departments. Its most startling result, however, was the sweeping away of the outworn system of feudal landholding. A "land commission" set up under the act was part of a broad scheme for giving clear titles to all landholders in the kingdom. This division of lands was called the Great Mahele. First, all the land in the kingdom was divided between the king and his chiefs. Then the king divided his land into two parts: "crown lands" which he kept for his own use, and "government lands" which he turned over to the government. Many chiefs surrendered part of their lands to the government and thus obtained fee-simple title to the remainder. Then the government lands could be sold to commoners and also to foreigners. The revolution was complete when the *kuleanas* — lands lived on and cultivated by the common people — were taken from the holdings of king, chief, or government and given outright to the occupants. All these changes were recorded in the Mahele Book, and the claims approved by the Land Commission are still the basis of all titles to holdings covered by these awards. Now a person could own land without fear of sudden eviction, and plan ahead for its fruitful use.

The recognition of Hawaiian independence in 1843 was followed, during the next decade, by the attempt of the able and patient Robert C. Wyllie to obtain equitable treaties with the various powers. A treaty with the kingdom of Denmark was signed in 1846. In the same year Kamehameha III was offered treaties by England and France which were not completely satisfactory, but which he signed in the hope of getting better terms later.

A new French consul, Guillaume Patrice Dillon, who replaced Dudoit in 1848, proved to be so chauvinistic that in April, 1849, his recall was requested. Dillon asked for help from his government, and in the middle of August, Rear Admiral Legoarant de Tromelin arrived in Honolulu with two war vessels, *La Poursuivante* and the steam-corvette *Gassendi* (not the first steamship in the islands, for the British sidewheeler *Cormorant* arrived in 1846). The admiral sent the king ten demands, which included equality of worship, reduction of duty on French brandy, and the punishment of certain native schoolboys who had impiously put their hands in holy water. To enforce his demands, Tromelin landed a French force that took over the customs house and other government buildings. At the fort all the guns were spiked, the powder was poured into the sea, and everything in the building was smashed, including an old clock in the governor's house. The king's yacht and some foreign vessels were seized. Ten days after this French victory, the admiral departed, taking the consul with him. This display of power was in odd contrast with the magnitude of French interests in the islands, for aside from the priests, only twelve French subjects were living there. Some reparation was made ten years later when Napoleon III presented a six-hundred-piece silver dinner service to the Hawaiian royal family.

To obtain redress and to ask for a new treaty, a mission was sent to France, headed by Dr. Judd. It arrived in Paris early in 1850 and spent several months in futile attempts to obtain satisfaction. Dr. Judd took with him the two younger princes, Alexander Liholiho and Lot Kamehameha, both of whom were later to rule Hawaii. On the journey, during which both England and the United States were visited, the future monarchs obtained a view of the world abroad that was to influence their ideas greatly.

The final attempt of France to overawe the islands by cannon balls came shortly after Dr. Judd's return. The warship *Sérieuse* arrived bearing a French commissioner named Emile Perrin, who on February 1, 1851, repeated the famous ten demands of Tromelin. The king protected himself by signing a secret proclamation which placed his kingdom under the protection of the United States should the French try to seize the islands. Luther Severance, the new United States commissioner, consulted with Captain W. H. Gardner of the U.S.S. *Vandalia* and they agreed that the American flag, if raised over Hawaii, would be defended by firing on the *Sérieuse* if necessary. When this news came to Perrin, he modified his demands, signed a temporary agreement, and returned to France. Thereafter the old shadow of French annexation was lifted. In the same year, an equitable treaty was signed between Great Britain and the Hawaiian Kingdom.

Relations with the United States were hampered at first by the lack of skilled men in the Honolulu post. George Brown, the first commissioner, was appointed in 1843, but was soon recalled, and his successor, Anthony Ten Eyck, was no better.

The need for good relations with the Americans was hastened by the news brought on June 17, 1848, by the schooner *Louise* that gold had been discovered in California. J. F. B. Marshall, who returned to Honolulu in March, 1849, wrote that "the wild rush to California had almost depopulated the place. The *dolce far niente* character of the group was gone forever, and a feverish, bustling, hurry-scurry sort of life had taken its place. More than half the white population, and many of the natives, had gone to the coast, in whatever craft they could secure a passage. Condemned hulks, which the old salts declared were but floating coffins, had been hurriedly patched up and speedily filled with freight and passengers for the new land of promise. Everything was changed. Prices of both native and foreign articles were enormously high. Wages had doubled and trebled."

When the Reverend S. C. Damon visited the mines of the Sierra in 1849, he found a group of Christian Hawaiians on the American River who gathered about him and loaded him with bags of gold dust for relatives back in the Sandwich Islands. Both William Kanui and Thomas Hopu, the Cornwall boys who had come in the *Thaddeus*, had caught the gold fever, and Damon encountered them both in Sacramento, where Kanui was running a small restaurant. Today only a few names on the old maps, like Kanaka Bar and Kanaka Glade, remind the student of the part played by gold-hungry Hawaiians in the California story.

The march of the United States to the Pacific Coast made it seem to many people the part of "manifest destiny" that Hawaii would be annexed after the gold rush. The king in 1849 sent a special ambassador, James J. Jarves, to Washington, and a treaty was signed that went into effect in 1850. But in the fall of 1851, the king was fearful that filibusters might descend on the islands from the Pacific Coast and take over the government.

Actually, Sam Brannan and two dozen soldiers of fortune arrived from San Francisco in November on the clipper *Game Cock*, hoping the kingdom would fall into their hands; but they were soon warned off by Marshal William C. Parke. Many Americans from California had settled in Hawaii, and some of them clamored for annexation. As a measure of protection, Kamehameha went so far as to have Wyllie draw up a treaty of annexation in consultation with David L. Gregg, the new American commissioner. The king insisted, among other points, that Hawaii should be admitted to the Union as a state and not as a territory. Final signing of the treaty was delayed, the filibusters never arrived in force, and the death of Kamehameha III ended this first rehearsal for the annexation of the islands by the United States, which did not come until almost half a century later.

"Beware the Right Whale's Flukes!"

THE MAINSTAY OF HAWAIIAN PROSPERITY FOR A GOOD MANY YEARS was the whaling trade, that great American enterprise of the nineteenth century which sent hundreds of Yankee ships to scour the globe in pursuit of the wily leviathan. In those days, America was lighted by whale-oil lamps or spermaceti candles. Sperm oil was used to make soap and paints, and to lubricate machinery. Ambergris was treasured by the perfumer.

The sperm whale and the right whale were the most fiercely sought. The sperm was found in the more temperate waters of the world. He averaged forty to fifty feet in length, but sometimes ran to eighty-five. From his gigantic head-case might be ladled as much as thirty barrels of liquid spermaceti, and the blubber of his monstrous body, when rendered out, would average 125 barrels of oil, and sometimes yield twice as much. The right whale was found more often among the icebergs of the Arctic or Antarctic, and in size approached the bulk of the sperm whale. He was sought for his oil, and also for his "whalebone." This flexible material, hundreds of thin blades of which hung in his huge throat, was used for corset stays and umbrella ribs, and was at one time worth up to $5 a pound.

Killing any type of whale on the open sea was a dangerous feat. The toothed jaws of the sperm whale were quite capable of splintering a boat's hull. The right whale defended itself with thrashing tail, and one maxim of the whalers ran: "Beware of a sperm's jaw and a right whale's flukes!" But sailors from Hawaii were especially bold in hunting the roving Moby Dick wherever he might be found, from equator to icecaps.

The Pacific, for more than half a century, was the main hunting ground of the whalers; in the 1840's and 1850's, six-sevenths of the world's whaling fleet was in this ocean. Hawaii had the only good ports within a radius of two thousand miles, and lay at the center of the main grounds. Here the ships made rendezvous, to outfit and repair, to buy supplies, to store oil and bone for shipment home, and to let the crews relax among the grogshops and dance halls of the waterfronts.

The first American whalers to reach Honolulu were the *Equator* of Nantucket under Captain Elisha Folger and the *Balaena* of New Bedford under Captain Edmund Gardner. They arrived in the fall of 1819, and soon afterwards killed a whale off Kealakekua Bay. About the same time, Captain Jonathan Winship, returning from Japan, reported great schools of sperm whales in that region. Following this hint, the *Maro* of Nantucket, first American whaler to cross the middle of the Pacific, became co-discoverer, with the *Syren* of London, of the famous "on Japan" grounds. Since Japan was closed to foreign vessels, Honolulu was the nearest port to this new domain. Before the end of the reign of Kamehameha III, the rest of the chief Pacific grounds had been discovered. They extended within a rough triangle from Cape Horn west to New Zealand and north — including the Japan ground — to the Arctic. Especially rich areas lay off the northwest coast of America, in the Seas of Okhotsk, Anadir, and Bering, and among the freezing waters north of Bering Strait.

A few figures show the rise of the whaling trade. By 1822 some sixty ships had touched at the islands. Thereafter about a hundred a year used island ports until 1840. In the following twenty years, whaling in the Pacific was at its flood, and an average of four hundred ships touched at these ports. In the banner year of 1846, no less than 596 arrivals were recorded; of these 429 touched at Lahaina and the rest at Honolulu. For a long time, Lahaina and a few other ports rivaled the capital, but although supplies and port fees were cheaper at Lahaina, the ships there had to anchor in an open roadstead. The great majority of ships coming to the islands were American; most of the remainder were British.

Honolulu remained the favorite center of the whaling business. A shipyard was started there in 1823 by James Robinson and Robert Lawrence, survivors of the wreck of an English whaler on Pearl and Hermes Reef. Other yards were soon set up for rigging and repairing hulls. The *Polynesian* boasted in 1840 that Honolulu offered opportunities for the repair of ships "not to be surpassed in any other portion of the Pacific."

The number of ships in port at any one time has been overstated; but often, it is true, a man might clamber from one end of the harbor to the other over the decks of moored vessels. The record date was November 20, 1852, when the masts of 131 whalers and 18 merchant ships forested the harbor of Honolulu. Since the average crew numbered thirty, no less than four thousand sailors might be on the beach during a busy liberty day.

Many whaleships began to prolong their voyages from one to two or even four years. They would spend the summers on the northern grounds and the winter months in cruising the equator. In spring and fall they would pass a few weeks in the Hawaiian ports. Often they would store their catch of bone and oil in Honolulu, where warehouses had been erected or unseaworthy hulks moored to provide storage space. Or the catch could be shipped home by merchant vessels; early in 1853, the clipper *Sovereign of the Seas* loaded eight thousand barrels of whale oil at Honolulu.

Spring and fall, the arrival of the whaling fleets stirred the sleepy islanders to great activity. Waterfront saloons were overflowing with thirsty seamen who had "hung their consciences on Cape Horn." Ship chandlers offered for sale the hundreds of items needed to equip a floating oil-factory. Cattle were driven to the ports or shipped by sea from the ranches of Hawaii and Maui. Forests were denuded for galley firewood. Whaling captains spent thousands of dollars a year for fresh vegetables, sugar, molasses, coffee, bananas, coconuts, breadfruit, melons, pineapples, turkeys, hogs, and goats.

The government treasury was fattened by fees and import duties, and the growing of food for whalemen brought cash to the native tillers of the soil. But this easy prosperity probably retarded the development of large-scale plantations. And the periodic arrival of hordes of riotous whalemen of many nationalities inevitably wrought violent changes in the Hawaiian social scene.

Shipmasters were ordered by their Boston owners to discharge in the islands any troublesome crew members. As early as 1822, not less than a hundred deserters from the whaleships were on the beach at Oahu. Beachcombers loafed in the streets, men who had deserted or who, sick or disabled, had been put ashore in charge of their consul. They did nothing to occupy their time except hang about in low haunts until their money was gone. Many men were paid their wages in Honolulu, but their first idea was to get rid of the money. "On one occasion," wrote Edward T. Perkins, "the Sheriff of Oahu removed from the pockets of a drunken petty officer, who was staggering through the streets, one thousand dollars in Californian ingots, which were afterwards returned to him when sober." Native constables, armed with canes, were unable to cope with the thousands of fun-hunting sailors who roamed the town for several months each year and who inevitably collided with the "blue laws" of the kingdom. A schedule of "Fines for Malconduct of Seamen" still exists. Penalties range all the way from hanging (for maliciously violating the laws controlling contagious diseases) down through $30 for adultery, $6 for desecrating the Sabbath, $5 for headlong horseback riding, and $1 for hallooing in the streets at night.

The worst outbreak came in the fall of 1852, when about a hundred and fifty ships were in Honolulu Harbor. One Henry Burns, seaman off the *Emerald*, was arrested on November 8 for disorderly conduct and imprisoned in the old fort, since there was no more room in the police lock-up. Burns, in a cell with several others, began tearing up the brick floor, and a jailer, George Sherman, was attacked when he went to quiet him. In the dark, the jailer's club struck Burns in the temple, and next morning he was found dead.

Sherman was immediately held on a charge of manslaughter. Burns's funeral on the tenth was attended by several thousand whalemen, and afterward a mob began looting the grogshops and threatening the lives of citizens. They demanded that Sherman be turned over to their vengeance, and when they were refused, finding the fort too well defended, they set fire to the police station near the foot of Nuuanu Street. One of the whaleships was licked by the flames, and only a shift in the wind saved the fleet from burning.

The next day a meeting of citizens resulted in the restoration of order. The streets were cleared by unarmed Hawaiians, and the sobered rioters were returned to their ships or held for trial. The fort had been defended by a volunteer corps of some two hundred foreign residents, and from their number was later formed the Hawaiian Guard, a militia devoted to seeing that such outbreaks did not again lead to terror and bloodshed in the port of Honolulu.

Concern for the welfare of seamen led to the founding of the Seamen's Bethel in 1833, in charge of the Reverend John Diell and his wife, who were sent out by the American Seamen's Friend Society. The hall could hold five hundred people, and the Diells distributed Bibles, tracts, and even spelling books to help sailors to read. The chaplain's concern for providing spiritual guidance to residents of the town led to the establishment, in May, 1837, of the Oahu Bethel Church, first church in Honolulu for foreigners. The work of Diell was carried on after his death by the Reverend Samuel C. Damon, who took up the chaplaincy in 1842 and carried it on for more than forty years. A Sailor's Home was erected at Bethel and Merchant Streets in 1855.

Hawaiians had always been prime seafarers, and the attractions of voyaging the world's oceans led many young men to leave home on a whaleship, to rub shoulders on its decks with runaway Yankee farm boys, Portuguese harpooners, Negroes, broken gold-rush men, natives of other Pacific islands, and the flotsam of Europe. During the three years 1845-1847, nearly two thousand Hawaiians signed articles on foreign windjammers, and in the 1850's some five hundred enlisted annually. Captains did not always live up to the laws requiring that recruits be returned home after two years, and no insignificant cause of the decline in Hawaiian population was the fact that one-fifth of the young men were sailing abroad during most of the whaling era.

Undismayed by the hazards of stalking whales from boats on the deep, or by life in a cramped and stinking forecastle, living on "salt horse" and hardtack, the Hawaiian sailor voyaged for a wage of a few dollars a month; but even so, opportunities were often greater for him at sea than ashore. The fearlessness and endurance of Hawaiian seamen were well known around the world, and the whaleships made use of these traits. An example of their prowess is given by O. N. Emerson: "Once in the icy waters of the Okhotsk Sea, a right whale was captured just at nightfall. A storm was brewing and the captain was anxious to have the body lashed to the ship before dark, but in the hurry an attempt to bend a hawser around the flukes of the whale repeatedly failed. A Hawaiian sailor seized the end of a line and, leaping into the icy waters, dove with it under the great monster, brought it up the other side and back to the ship. The hawser was quickly attached, and before it was too late the whale was made fast." Diving under whales in northern seas was all part of the day's work.

The Last of the Kamehamehas

THE ROYAL BROTHERS, ALEXANDER AND LOT, WERE EACH TO RULE FOR nine years; their successor spent only one year on the throne. The two decades 1854-1874 marked a middle period in which many changes came to the Kingdom of Hawaii, and under the leadership of able and devoted rulers it took many a step toward a position of high respect in the eyes of the world.

Visitors to the islands were often surprised by the charm and grace of the court of Kamehameha IV and Queen Emma. The behavior of the royal couple struck Dr. H. W. Baxley, an American, as more civilized than that of some of the diplomatic representatives sent to them by his own government. "The king and queen are well educated, intelligent, and courteous," he wrote, "of dignified manners, becoming their positions; and possessing a proper appreciation of the influence of their example over their people.

The king has excellent judgment, good taste, kindness of manner, and affability in social life; and on occasions of state, a calm, thoughtful, self-possessed, gentlemanly, and impressive deportment, commanding respect and admiration, and which far surpasses in appropriateness the ostentatious awkwardness and rude arrogance of some who are, unfortunately for their more pretentious nationalities, appointed to represent these at his court."

Honolulu Panorama, 1854

WHEN ALEXANDER LIHOLIHO ASCENDED THE THRONE AT THE END of 1854, under the title of Kamehameha IV, the population of the islands was at a low ebb. The census of 1853 showed a total of 73,138 — a decline of more than 35,000 from the previous census of 1835. About ten thousand people lived in Honolulu. Of these 1180 were foreign residents of many nationalities, but about 500 were Americans and 350 British.

Honolulu was, however, expanding. It had been officially declared a city in 1850 and was doing its best to deserve the title. When Sereno E. Bishop, son of a missionary family, returned there in 1853 he found it a great improvement over the "hard-looking old camp" he had left in 1840, with its scattering of grass-roofed huts, adobe courtyards, and dusty, treeless expanses of land spreading from the lanes running to the waterfront. Now, although most houses were still thatched, and shade trees rare, many residences and business edifices were built of stone, or of lumber brought from the Pacific Coast.

The downtown area spread from River Street to Alapai, and from School Street to the busy waterfront. Along the harbor rose the Honolulu Flour Mill, which first began operation in 1854; part of the first floor was occupied by the machine shop of D. M. Weston, founder of the Honolulu Iron Works. Next stood the coral-block walls of the old three-story Custom House, the premises of the firm of Ladd & Company, and the warehouse of Swan & Clifford (which offered for sale to thirsty residents a cargo of five hundred tons of ice brought from Sitka, Alaska, in October, 1854). Then came the ship-yard of Robinson & Company, and finally, spreading below the battery of cannons on Punchbowl Hill, the walled compound of the old fort, used mainly as a prison. (In 1857, the fort was to be leveled and its walls used to fill in new harborside land purchased by the government from Queen Kalama.)

The royal family resided at the palace on King Street, built of coral blocks and surrounded by a broad piazza. Its rustic simplicity led G. W. Bates to remark that "It is just such a palace as European sovereigns, when the cares of empire oppress them, may sigh after, and never obtain." In a nearby enclosure stood the royal tombs.

For years all government business had been transacted at Hono-lulu Hale, on Merchant Street near Bethel. But in 1851 was built, of coral blocks cut from the reef by jail inmates, the Courthouse, which for the next twenty years was to serve as court of justice, legislative chamber, church, meeting hall, concert hall, and ball-room. (It was sold in 1874 to H. Hackfeld & Company, and is occupied even today by that firm's successors, American Factors, Ltd.) Still other government offices were opened in March, 1854, on Hotel Street near Alakea.

A large barnlike building, put up in 1850 to replace the thatched stalls scattered about the town, was the Market that rose near the tower of Bethel Church. This was the gathering place for people of all classes, good-humoredly jostling each other and haggling for meat, poultry, and fresh vegetables. Carriers lugged through the streets their burdens on the old Hawaiian *mamake*, a pole with loads dangling at either end. Occasionally a neat carriage might roll by, but most of the traffic was made up of saddle horses, hand-drawn carts, and a few creaking ox wains.

Paul Emmert, a Swiss artist, drew in 1853 or early in 1854 a series of lithographs of Honolulu. One of these is a view of the city from the harbor reef, and the rest are panoramas from the bell tower of the Catholic Church on Fort Street near Beretania. These pictures show that the town spread in various directions and contained many edifices of two and three stories.

Residences — lovely Nuuanu Valley was a favorite site — included those of royalty and chiefs, foreign consuls and commissioners, government officials, merchants, sea captains, and missionaries. Most imposing of these homes was Washington Place, built by Captain John Dominis, a sailor from the Balearic Isles who had prospered in the trade in furs and casks of salmon from the Northwest. After his death at sea in 1846 it was rented to Anthony Ten Eyck for use as the United States Legation; it was to Ten Eyck that the house owned its name. Washington Place was to be inherited by Queen Liliuokalani, last of the Hawaiian monarchs; since 1919 it has been the official residence of the Governor of Hawaii.

The Emmert drawings show not only residences but also schools, churches, hospitals, and several hotels. The H. Hackfeld department store, founded in 1849 by a Hamburg merchant on the site now occupied by its successor, The Liberty House, offered for sale parasols, silk waistcoats, bird cages, window glass, and iron bedsteads. Other business premises included those of importers, shipping agents, medical men and dentists, jewelers, carpenters, bakers, tailors, and barbers; and there was a generous sprinkling of livery stables, pharmacies, coffee shops, billiard saloons, and bowling alleys. Taverns abounded, but since the tax of five dollars a gallon was still levied on imported liquors, a popular drink at private parties was Cologne water. "After imbibing the essence of ideality, in the shape of peppermint and wintergreen," a friend told Perkins, "we soar away to Olympus amid an atmosphere of bergamot and rosemary."

The streets were dark at night, for gas lighting was not introduced until 1859. Fire was a great and frequent danger. The first firefighting machine came to the islands in 1847, a hand engine that had to be filled from buckets. A volunteer fire company was formally organized on November 6, 1850, and on the same date went into action when eleven downtown homes were burned. The fire department was confirmed by act of the privy council on December 27. Every citizen was ordered to keep at least two buckets handy, for use only in case of fire. They were needed, even though the Honolulu Fire Department's shiny engine, named "Honolulu," was equipped with a 150-foot hose that could send a stream of water sixty feet into the heart of the blaze.

Travel by Land and by Sea

LAND TRAVEL WAS STILL SLOW AND UNSURE, AND WHENEVER POSsible, the people went from one place to another by canoe or trading vessel. Much traveling was done on foot even on Oahu, along the trails that bygone natives had trodden out. Saddle horses were still scarce and might cost $150, but within a decade after 1854 the craze for riding had spread so that the price fell to $15 or $10, and nearly everyone owned an animal on which he — or she — might career astride through the rutted lanes, in disregard of the public safety. On Saturday afternoons everybody seemed to be in the saddle, or at least riding bareback, and races and feats of horsemanship stirred up so much dust that, as one writer observed, "The mariner nearing the southern coast of Oahu during such a revel might well suppose that the crater of Punchbowl Hill had awakened from its long sleep, and was again belching forth its clouds of ashes over the devoted city."

Good roads outside of the towns were few and far between. A horse trail led through taro patches to the seaside at Waikiki, but as late as 1865 Baxley, the visiting medico, remarked that the bathers there were accommodated in cottages in the absence of any hotel — "a lucky necessity," he noted, "for those who need dietetic restrictions and renovation, rather than the poisonous pandering to the palate of these modern caravansaries."

The need to improve the footpath up Nuuanu Valley and down

the precipitous Pali to the Koolau district was often urged, and by 1845 a road suitable for riders of horses and mules was finished. The feat of driving down the Pali road with a one-horse wagon was performed in 1861 by Dr. G. P. Judd and the Reverend Eli S. Corwin, but it was many years before a safe passage over this route could be assured. A prophetic writer in the *Polynesian* in 1852 remarked that residents of Oahu would "never be satisfied till a tunnel is dug through the *pali*, suitable for the passage of carts and wagons." (More than a century was to pass before vehicles could in actuality avoid the hazards of the winding road by using a tunnel through the Koolau Range.) The first complete "round-the-island" carriage trip was not made until 1863, when W. A. Aldrich left Honolulu on a Friday and returned to town via the Pali four days later.

There were no hotels or inns outside of Honolulu and Hilo as late as 1873, but the hospitality of country home or native shack was so graciously offered that often the traveler felt that he was conferring a favor by staying there. And the roads were slow but safe. "In no part of the world is life and property more safe than in these islands," boasted the annual report of Chief Justice William L. Lee for 1852. "Murders, robberies, and the higher class of felonies are quite unknown here, and in city and country we retire to our sleep conscious of the most entire security. The stranger may travel from one end of the group to the other, over mountains and through woods, sleeping in grass huts, unarmed, alone, and unprotected, with any amount of treasure on his person, and with a tithe of the vigilance required in older and more civilized countries, go unrobbed of a penny and unharmed in a hair."

Travel by sea has always been of first importance to the people of Hawaii. In the early days the king and chiefs owned vessels, and the government remained in the shipping business until around 1846. From about 1820 on, many small ships were owned by local people and operated among the islands. None of these ran on fixed schedules, and the hazards of the sea and ignorance of navigation often made it appear that the accomplishment of a trip to another island was a minor miracle.

Journeys in these "poi clippers," as they were called, were frequently long, rough, and crowded. Cabin passengers were usually driven to seek air on the narrow decks, which were jammed with "steerage" passengers and a mixed cargo. "The schooner *Pau*," according to a Honolulu newspaper of 1853, "arrived on Thursday evening from Hawaii, having the largest load of native produce we have heard of lately. On her trip up she took to Hawaii 270 passengers, and brought back 190, 20 turkeys, 30 pigs, 75 chickens, 30 dogs (!), 1 pair oxen, 1 mule, 14 cords wood, 11 canoes, etc., altogether making decidedly a jam for a schooner of 100 tons burden." Despite the drawbacks, there was an astonishing amount of interisland junketing, especially by the footloose natives.

Freighting carried on by the small vessels sailing among the isles became an expanding business. Cargoes of sugar, molasses, wheat, and firewood were transported to Honolulu and imported goods were shipped back. In 1851, about sixty-five coasting ships, averaging about sixty tons, were registered under the Hawaiian flag.

American shipyards were asked, from the early fifties, to build vessels suitable for the Hawaiian trade. One of the first of these was the schooner *Ka Moi* (or *Sovereign*), launched at New London, Connecticut, in 1853. Two smaller companions, *Moi Wahine* and *Moi Keike*, also served for a while. Best known of these United States-built sailing ships was the clipper *Emma Rooke* and the pilotboat *Nettie Merrill*, both of which began interisland runs in 1860.

The branching out of America into the Pacific brought the first steamships to ply among the islands. Captain William A. Howard of San Francisco in 1851 obtained a franchise for interisland service, but the 600-ton propeller steamer *Constitution*, after making one round trip between Honolulu and Lahaina, was found to be too large for the needs of traffic and was sent back to the Pacific Coast.

The privy council then offered the lapsed franchise to a competing group headed by Richard H. Bowlin, a Honolulu lawyer representing a San Francisco syndicate. In the fall of 1853, this firm, the Hawaiian Steam Navigation Company, put into operation a small side-wheel vessel which began regular service under the name of the *Akamai*. They soon put two other steamers on this run, but all three were either wrecked or withdrawn within a few years, and in 1856 the franchise was declared void. Interisland steamer service did not settle to a steady basis until 1860, when the *Kilauea* began its long and checkered career as a familiar figure on the interisland lanes.

Oceanic transport of Hawaiian passengers and cargoes slowly expanded when clipper lines spread into the Pacific. During the heyday of the windships, in the fifties and sixties, many famous clipper ships of the world touched at Hawaii; and even until the end of the century, much cargo was carried to and from the islands in square-riggers and schooners. The rise of large business firms in the islands made it profitable to establish frequent sailings between Hawaiian ports and those of the United States, Great Britain and her colonies, and Germany. Certain ships of the fifties were so regular in operation between San Francisco and Honolulu that they served as packets; and in 1855 the Regular Dispatch Line began running clipper barks on fixed schedules.

Steamship lines to link Hawaii with the rest of the world were slow to start, although a trial voyage was made by the *Polynesian* as early as 1854. The potent Pacific Mail Steamship Company inaugurated a line in 1875 between San Francisco and Australasia, stopping at Honolulu on the way. In 1882, with the founding by the Oceanic Steamship Company of a semimonthly service between San Francisco and Honolulu, the people of Hawaii became more closely tied to the outer world by blue-water shipping routes.

The need for safe moorings for Pacific shipping accounted for the rise of such ports as Honolulu, Lahaina, and Hilo. Honolulu Harbor was not easily entered under sail, and ships were towed in by several small boats or by human arms; Sereno E. Bishop returned in 1853 on the clipper *Sovereign of the Seas*, which was towed by "a long line of native people who grasped the hawser and walked along the reef." Oxen were also used, and in 1854 the little steamer *Akamai* was often enlisted as a tugboat in the harbor. About this time, the need for many harbor improvements was realized by the government, and a series of dredging and filling operations began that led to much more convenience in waterfront work. The lighthouse at the entrance to the harbor was not permanently lighted, however, until 1869.

Mail service between Hawaii and the rest of the world was improving at mid-century, but the months of waiting between the writing of a letter and receipt of its reply still hampered business. A Honolulu editor wrote in 1837 that mail was frequently received "by a dilatory route, through other ports, at the age of two and even three years." Letters might reach the islands carried in ships around the Horn and forwarded from Valparaiso, Tahiti, or Sydney; and the latest European news could even come by way of China. J. F. B. Marshall wrote many years later that the annual delivery of mail, arriving some months after it had left New England, was "as eagerly welcomed as are now the latest telegraphic despatches seven days from Boston to Honolulu. My senior partner [Charles Brewer], also a Boston boy, in order to have the satisfaction of reading 'the respectable daily' every morning, was accustomed, with rare self-control, to place the year's file of the *Daily Advertiser* beside his easy chair, with the oldest date at the top, and religiously to read one paper daily, just a year old."

An overland route across Mexico was opened in the 1830's, but the postage in that country alone cost about fifty cents a letter; and, of course, the service was interrupted by the Mexican War in 1846. Until that year, the Hawaiian government did not offer any mail service whatever. Merchant ships carried the mails free, and on arrival the bags were emptied on the floor of a counting room and "those expecting letters gathered around the pile to assist in 'overhauling' or 'sorting,' picking out their own, and passing over their shoulders the letters of those standing in the outer circles."

The second Organic Act set up a postal system in 1846, but its provisions were not put into effect until four years later. In that interim, the development of the Pacific Coast caused an improvement of service there. Steamship lines ran between the Atlantic ports and Panama and between Panama and California; and from there, ships to Hawaii brought mail to the islands quicker than had been thought possible before. The *Polynesian* in 1855 remarked on the arrival of mail from New York in the record time of thirty-five days.

A treaty between Hawaii and the United States at the end of 1849 facilitated exchange of mail, and a year later a post office was set up in Honolulu, with fixed rates on letters, newspapers, and other printed matter from or to San Francisco. Henry M. Whitney, named as postmaster, began operations at once, and by 1853 about 2800 letters a month passed through the Honolulu Post Office. The rate on letters had been reduced in 1851 from ten to five cents, and the postmaster authorized to issue stamps. Whitney accordingly put out stamps with values of two, five, and thirteen cents; these are the "Missionary" stamps prized highly by collectors today. The law also provided for selling stamps for domestic use, but until 1859 this service was free, for it was feared that charging for interisland mail would "inevitably exclude from the mails a large share of the native correspondence." In that year a scale of rates went into effect, and the new scheme did not, as feared, diminish letter-writing among the people. The interisland stamps in one-cent and two-cent denominations — the "plain-border numerals" of the philatelist — became quite popular, and their sale helped to support the cost of a postal system more in keeping with the needs of nineteenth-century communication.

"*Aleck and Emma*"

THE THIRD KAMEHAMEHA DIED NEAR THE END OF 1854, AFTER almost thirty years on the throne. Childless, he was succeeded by his nephew, Alexander Liholiho, a son of Governor Mataio Kekuanaoa and Kinau, and hence a grandson of Kamehameha the Great.

Kamehameha IV, at the time of his accession on January 11, 1855, was within a month of attaining the age of twenty-one. He was tall, slim, and handsome, with high forehead and romantic beard. He was a victim of asthma, attacks of which sometimes upset his working routine. To improve his health, he once took boxing lessons from a professional named Yankee Sullivan. He had served the nation for three years as an able member of the privy council, and was in many ways well trained to become a serious ruler and leader of the Hawaiian people.

The new king was intelligent and well educated, and spoke fluent English as well as Hawaiian. At the opening of the legislature, he urged that unless his subjects learned English, their hopes of intellectual progress on a par with the foreigners would be vain. His visit to England with his elder brother Lot had aroused a strong admiration for British forms of government and religion, and his court hoped to reflect the aristocratic grandeur of St. James's.

Educated at the Chiefs' Children's School, run by missionaries, the prince had become bored with interminable sermons and prayer meetings. "Having been compelled to be good when a boy," remarked his mentor Dr. Judd, "he is determined not to be good when a man." His bias against Americans had been deepened by unpleasant experiences while traveling in the United States, such as the time when a railway conductor in New York City had mistaken the prince for a servant and ordered him out of the car. "I am disappointed at the Americans," he wrote in his diary that night. "They have no manners, no politeness, not even common civility to a stranger." His anger at racial discrimination was deepened by fear that his country might be annexed to the United States as a part of its "manifest destiny." Although some of his closest advisers were Americans, he swung gradually away from their influence, and at the end of his reign not a single American was to be found in his cabinet. His nine years on the throne were marked by a revival of British influence in the kingdom.

Aware of his duty to carry on the dynasty, Kamehameha IV in the summer of 1855 notified his council of his intention to marry. His bride-to-be was Emma, a granddaughter of old John Young and a great-granddaughter of Keliimaikai, a younger brother of Kamehameha I. She had been adopted as a child by Dr. T. C. B. Rooke, an English medical man who had married Emma's aunt. The girl had been well educated at the Chiefs' Children's School and by private tutor, and her natural gifts of amiability and warmness of heart had been strengthened by a refined upbringing. She possessed regular features, a graceful figure, and a natural nobility of manner.

The wedding on June 19, 1856, in Kawaiahao Church was an occasion of national rejoicing. The ruling couple began at once to exercise the high position in society to which their rank entitled them.

The marriage was undoubtedly a love match, and on May 20, 1858, the family was blessed by the birth of a son, who was given the official title of "His Royal Highness the Prince of Hawaii" (*Ka Haku o Hawaii*). The domestic joy of the earliest years was admired by their subjects, and such a close observer as R. C. Wyllie remarked: "We were all quite charmed with the private life of the royal pair, always addressing each other familiarly as 'Aleck' and 'Emma' and uniting in a just pride of and affection for their interesting and precocious son."

A memorable achievement of the royal pair grew out of their awareness of the need for trying to preserve the dwindling native population by setting up better medical services. Thousands of Hawaiians had died in such epidemics as those of measles in 1848 and smallpox in 1853. The legislature in 1859 passed a law permitting the establishment of hospitals on four of the main islands. The king himself went about soliciting funds for the Honolulu hospital, seeking subscriptions among businessmen, whaling captains, and even ladies attending tea parties. He obtained pledges amounting to $14,000; this fund was the beginning of the Queen's Hospital. A two-story building was erected by the end of 1860 on the site of the institution which, many times larger, stands today as a memorial to the rulers who sought to bring modern medicine to the aid of their poor and ailing countrymen.

The happiness of king and queen was not fated to last long; and the tragedy that befell them was the occasion for the rise of the Episcopal Church in Hawaii under the aegis of the monarchy. The upbringing of Queen Emma reinforced the British leanings of the king, and both were reflected in the fact that they had chosen to be married by the ritual of the Church of England. Events in the lives of both the king and his adviser Wyllie inclined them toward the comforts of religion.

The shocking affair in which the king was the principal actor happened on September 11, 1859, in the town of Lahaina, where the royal party was winding up a tour of the islands. A young American of good family, Henry A. Neilson, was in the king's suite as private secretary. Through malicious gossip, Kamehameha IV had been led to suspect an affair between Neilson and the queen. The king brooded for days, and finally decided to take action. He spent a day and part of two nights on a small vessel offshore, drinking heavily. Then he came to the town, found Neilson, and at close range shot him with a pistol.

The wound was serious but not immediately fatal, for Neilson lived more than two years longer. No legal action against the king was suggested, but he soon discovered by careful inquiry that his fears were quite unfounded, and thereafter he suffered bitter remorse. For months he spent most of his time and money in trying to make amends to the wounded man, and had to be strongly dissuaded from abdicating the throne. His self-condemnation led him toward religion and revived his old interest in establishing an Episcopal church in his kingdom.

The idea had the support of Wyllie, the Scottish-born minister of foreign relations, recently recovered from a serious illness. Wyllie had endeavored to interest both the American and English branches of the Episcopal Church. Bishop William I. Kip of California could not spare any of his clergymen to work in Hawaii, but English support of the plan was obtained as a result of negotiations through Manley Hopkins — Hawaiian consul general in London and father of the poet Gerard Manley Hopkins — which were reinforced by a letter from Kamehameha IV to Queen Victoria. The Reverend Thomas N. Staley on December 15, 1861, was consecrated as bishop of the new missionary diocese of Hawaii, and in the following August sailed with his family for his new field of endeavor.

The arrival of Bishop Staley and his party was eagerly awaited in Honolulu by the king and queen. They intended that the first ceremony would be the christening of the little prince, in whose veins ran the blood of English John Young. Queen Victoria had promised to act as godmother and had sent a magnificent silver christening cup as a baptismal gift. But long before Bishop Staley reached Honolulu on October 11, 1862, the godchild of Victoria was dead.

In his last days, the Prince of Hawaii had been baptized by the pastor of Kawaiahao Church, using the ritual of the Church of England. William W. F. Synge, new British commissioner, acted as proxy for the Prince of Wales, after whom *Ka Haku o Hawaii* was christened with the name of Albert Edward Kauikeaouli Leiopapa a Kamehameha. When he died of brain fever on August 27, the grief of his parents was shared by the entire populace; as one newspaper said, "The death of no other person could have been so severe a blow to the king and his people."

Kamehameha IV, who felt a sense of personal guilt in the death of his only child, continued his patronage of the new "English Church," as it was called. The king and queen were the first communicants, confirmed on November 28; and the king further revealed his piety by translating into Hawaiian the Episcopal Book of Common Prayer. But he did not live to see the laying of the cornerstone of the Anglican Pro-Cathedral in Honolulu in 1866. Weakened by asthma and by grief at the death of his heir, his health failed; and after a short illness, Kamehameha IV died on November 30, 1863, at the age of twenty-nine.

The Bachelor King

THE LATE KING'S ELDER BROTHER, PRINCE LOT, WAS PROMPTLY proclaimed the new ruler of Hawaii by the cabinet, the privy council and the *kuhina nui*.

Kamehameha V was not as brilliant as his brother, but he had a better control of practical affairs. He had served as minister of the interior and head of the Department of Finance. He was personally the leader of the government, and believed that as inheritor of the golden mantle of his grandfather, Kamehameha the Great, he should rule with kindly despotism over his people. His policies often aroused violent opposition, but he sincerely felt that his acts were always aimed at the highest good of the nation.

Lot Kamehameha in general pursued the policies set by his dead brother — in particular the efforts to obtain world recognition of Hawaiian independence and a treaty with the United States that would forestall demands for annexation. His main achievement, however, was the writing of a constitution that would restore strong power to the monarchy.

His attitude was revealed when, on his accession, he declined to take the customary oath to support the Constitution of 1852. He felt that some of its features limited too greatly the authority of the king and allowed too much freedom to his subjects in their current state of progress toward real democracy. He thought that voting rights should be allowed only to those who were educated and who owned property; ignorant and landless men could be too easily swayed by demagogues. Universal suffrage would, he feared, end in a Hawaiian republic that would sooner or later be annexed by the United States. "Hawaii has scarcely emerged from a feudal state," he said, "and already the American influence pushes us toward a republic."

Amid political clamor, Kamehameha V called for the election of a constitutional convention which met on July 7, 1864, to draft a new document. Opposition centered upon his insistence that the voters of the kingdom should satisfy property qualifications and a literacy test. After five weeks of debate, the king dissolved the convention on August 13 with the words: "On the part of the Sovereignty of the Hawaiian Islands, I make known today that the Constitution of 1852 is abrogated. I will give you a Constitution."

The new Constitution of 1864 promised by the king was signed by him just a week later. It strengthened the monarchy by freeing it from the control of the privy council; the office of *kuhina nui* was abolished. It also required that all voters should be property owners who, if born since 1840, could read and write. Opponents pointed out furiously that if the king could give a new constitution to serve as the law of the land, he could also take it away again when he wished. The constitutional issue bobbed up in politics for many years afterward. Despite the heavy-handed way in which it was put through, however, the Constitution of 1864 lasted longer than any other in the Hawaiian kingdom, and was not to be overthrown until twenty-three years later, and then at the point of a bayonet. During the lifetime of Lot Kamehameha, only one minor amendment to its provisions was made.

Kamehameha V came to the throne in 1863, midway in the American Civil War period. His brother, under the wise advice of Wyllie, had proclaimed a policy of Hawaiian neutrality in the event that conflict between the Blue and the Gray should break out in the Pacific. The irritations of the war years in America might well have made the Washington government fearful that anti-American sentiment lay behind the British leanings of the royal brothers of Hawaii. In spite of some coolness on each side, the governments of the United States and Hawaii strove for good relations; in 1863, for instance, as a friendly act, President Lincoln raised the status of the American representative in Honolulu to that of "minister resident." Moreover, it was during this same year that the idea was revived of a reciprocity treaty that would aid the expanding sugar industry of the islands by permitting American and Hawaiian exports to be exchanged duty-free.

The fifth Kamehameha, like his brother, reigned nine years. "There was no trivial royal nonsense about him," wrote Mark Twain, who knew the king; "he dressed plainly, poked about Honolulu, night or day, on his old horse, unattended; he was popular, greatly respected, and even beloved." His service in the Department of Finance was reflected in his personal life. All purchases for the royal household were entered in his memo book, and each morning he would hand out money to his servants with orders to pay the bills due that day. Thus he set an example of thrift and integrity for his people. The merchants of Honolulu had never before seen a king so prompt in settling his accounts.

Like his brother, Lot had been accustomed to taking a drink in his youth; but as soon as he ascended the throne he became a strong advocate of temperance. For years a law had been on the books which made it a penal offense to supply any native with intoxicating drink. When this law was about to be repealed by the legislature, the king fought to keep it, saying: "I will never sign the death warrant of my people."

One of his strongest animosities was that against hula dances. His objection lay in the fact that he found the workers on his estates would travel for thirty miles in a day to watch some dancers, or loaf about at parties and neglect to cultivate their crops. He tried to restrict the hula by laws that would prevent public performances without official licenses. Although Lot resembled in many ways the old Hawaiian chiefs, his ancestors, he felt that some customs should be forgotten; when his father died in 1868, the usual dances performed at the death of royalty were replaced by hymn singing. And the days of idleness for most of the population following such a death were filled instead by useful labors in which the king took the lead.

The last of the Kamehamehas was large and heavy of body, and sometimes had trouble getting about. He liked to visit his friend John Cummins at his plantation at Waimanalo, on the eastern side of Oahu, but he disliked the harsh and hazardous ride over the Pali trail. Therefore he purchased a small steamboat in which he could ride in style around the shore. He also arranged to have a short railway line laid down for his own use, so that he could ride in complete comfort from the boat landing to Cummins's house.

Lot was known as "the bachelor king." His sister, Victoria Kamamalu, was named as his successor. After she died in 1866, it was often suggested that the king should marry and continue the dynasty; but he never took a wife. His failure to marry may not have been a result of choice but of romantic fate.

In his youth, the story goes, he was engaged to marry Bernice Pauahi, daughter of Chief Paki and Konia. She was his foster sister and herself a descendant of Kamehameha I. One of the foremost heiresses of the kingdom, she was a most eligible lady. But instead of the future king, she chose to marry Charles Reed Bishop, an enterprising New York Stater who in the previous year had become a Hawaiian subject in order to begin a career in finance and government service. His success — he was one of the founders of the Bishop Bank in 1858 — was to enable him to establish the Bernice Pauahi Bishop Museum in Honolulu in memory of his wife, and to set up the Bishop Estate to manage her fortune under a notably sound trusteeship that has been perpetuated throughout the years.

During all the king's life he remained friendly with the Bishops. An hour before his death on December 11, 1872, he called Bernice to his bedside and told her that he wished to appoint her as his successor. She modestly declined the honor.

Bernice Pauahi supplied the funds for the erection of the Royal Mausoleum in Nuuanu Valley to house the remains of early chiefs and rulers. The bones of the Conqueror himself could, of course, not be found; but on October 30, 1865, were borne to the imposing new mausoleum the bodies of the later monarchs and their queens, as well as that of John Young and other chiefs. And to this place in his time was taken, to rest beside that of his brother, the coffin of Kamehameha V, "the last great chief of the olden type."

The Middle Years of Change

KAMEHAMEHA V DIED UNEXPECTEDLY IN 1872, AT THE VERY TIME when the nation was celebrating his forty-third birthday. He had never formally named his successor. Bernice Pauahi did not wish to accept the title, feeling that Queen Emma or Princess Ruth Keeliko-lani, the king's half sister, might better deserve it. The throne was thus vacant, and it was now the task of the legislature to elect a king from among those eligible. Never before had the subjects of the Hawaiian Kingdom been given the privilege of voting to decide who should reign over them.

The Year of Lunalilo

CAMPAIGNING AT ONCE BEGAN BY THE CHAMPIONS OF THE TWO most prominent candidates: William Charles Lunalilo and David

Kalakaua. Both came of noble families, but Prince William, as he was called, was more popular among all ranks of society, because of his personal charm, his liberal opinions, and his high birth. He was the son of Chief Charles Kanaina and Kekauluohi, who had been *kuhina nui* under Kamehameha III; through her he inherited the blood of a half brother of Kamehameha the Great. The story went that, at his christening, his mother told the Reverend Hiram Bingham that the baby should be called "Lunalilo," meaning "most high in rank."

While the body of Kamehameha V was still lying in state, because a great storm postponed the burial ceremonies, the cabinet ordered the legislature to meet on January 8; 1873, to elect a new king. Lunalilo promptly published a message to the people, submitting his qualifications and asking that a plebiscite be held to determine the popular choice. He pledged himself to restore the Constitution of 1852 and to rule as a liberal constitutional monarch. This plebiscite was arranged at a mass meeting on December 26, which ended with a resolution that the people of Honolulu instruct their legislative representatives to vote for Lunalilo and no one else.

The Kalakaua side had not been silent. They circulated a paper signed by "The Skillful Genealogist" which tried to show that Lunalilo did not belong to the Kamehameha line. This attack boomeranged, however, and people flocked to Honolulu from all the islands, intent on casting a vote for "Prince Bill."

Four days before the plebiscite, Kalakaua issued a formal appeal which was posted everywhere and which, worded in the ancient metaphorical style, uttered a clarion call: "My countrymen of old! Ho, all ye tribes! Arise! This is the voice!" Kalakaua continued with an attack on Lunalilo, charging that he was misled by foreigners, and urged the people not to vote on New Year's Day. He promised to repeal all personal taxes and to put native Hawaiians into government jobs.

But the posters and campaign talk of the Lunalilo party had a more potent effect. The votes on January 1 were almost unani-

mously in favor of Prince William. A week later, as the legislature
met with throngs of anxious citizens surrounding the building,
formal votes were cast for the new king. Every vote to the end
was for William C. Lunalilo, the people's choice.

King Lunalilo, who was inaugurated the next day at Kawaiahao
Church, moved at once to make many amendments to the Constitution, in particular to abolish the property qualification for voting. Like his three predecessors, he tried to obtain a reciprocity
treaty with the United States to bring economic health to the
kingdom. More income was badly needed, for the depression of
1872 was deeply felt. As an inducement to make such a treaty
attractive to the people of America, the idea arose of offering a
lease on the lagoon of the Pearl River on Oahu as an American naval
station. The king, on the advice of his cabinet — which consisted
heavily of men of American origin — agreed in June that the offer
of Pearl Harbor should be made. But when a storm of protest arose
against ceding territory to a foreign country, the legislature and
the king took back the proposal, and the United States did not
obtain these naval rights until fifteen years later.

The "people's king," elected by them to rule, had been born on
January 31, 1835. His mother died when he was ten, and he was
brought up as a darling of the nobility. He, like the other princes,
was given a solid education at the Chiefs' Children's School. He was
friendly and witty, and his democratic views and liking for foreigners had kept him from being offered any government positions
under Kamehameha V.

Mrs. Isabella Bird Bishop, an English traveler who saw Lunalilo at
Hilo shortly after he became king, wrote home: "The king is a
very fine-looking man of thirty-eight, tall, well formed, broad-
chested, with his head well set on his shoulders, and his feet and
hands small. His appearance is decidedly commanding and aristocratic: he is certainly handsome even according to our notions. He
has a fine open brow, significant at once of brains and straightfor-
wardness, a straight, proportionate nose, and a good mouth. The

slight tendency to Polynesian overfulness about his lips is concealed by a well-shaped mustache. He wears whiskers cut in the English fashion. His eyes are large, dark-brown of course, and equally of course, he has a superb set of teeth. Owing to a slight fulness of the lower eyelid, which Queen Emma also has, his eyes have a singularly melancholy expression, very alien, I believe, to his character. He is remarkably gentlemanly looking, and has the grace of movement which seems usual with Hawaiians."

Lunalilo could feel at home both with people of his own race and with foreign visitors. Daniel E. Bandman, an English Shakespearean actor who visited the islands on tour in 1871 and became a close friend of Lunalilo, told how a party of Europeans drove out to Waikiki to pay a call on the prince. As they approached his estate, they saw him perched high in a coconut tree, chopping fronds, clad only in "the garb of Adam before he met Eve." Fearing embarrassment all round, they drove past the gate and stopped back half an hour later. Lunalilo had caught a glimpse of them and hastily descended; when they returned, he greeted them in a conventional white suit in a parlor where on the table were scattered copies of the leading newspapers and society journals of New York and London.

Lunalilo had poor health, aggravated by an addiction to firewater, and during his reign he developed a serious case of pulmonary tuberculosis. He felt optimistic about his recovery, but his advisers were not so sanguine and began wondering who might rule the kingdom should the disease take a fatal turn.

The king's chief defect was a lack of decisiveness which, had he lived longer, might have resulted in harm to his kingdom. This weakness was revealed, for example, on the occasion of a military mutiny.

The Hawaiian army consisted at this time of a body of sixty men known as the Household Troops, whose duties were guarding some buildings and providing an escort for royalty. Their headquarters were in the barracks on Palace Walk, and their drillmaster was a

Hungarian martinet named Captain Joseph Jajczay. On Sunday, September 7, the captain attempted to enforce discipline, and was promptly knocked down. The adjutant general, Charles H. Judd, was summoned, and was likewise attacked; the orders of Governor John O. Dominis were ignored. The mutineers united in their demands to have their haole officers removed; but no action was taken until Tuesday, when a message from the king, ordering the men to return to duty, was disregarded by thirty-four of the troops.

Two companies of volunteer townsmen were called out, but were given nothing definite to do. The mutineers slammed the door of the barracks in the face of the marshal who read a warrant for their arrest. On Wednesday the king, their commander-in-chief, who was recuperating at his Waikiki cottage, interviewed three spokesmen whom he had asked to see. He ordered the troops to submit and trust to his clemency. On their return, the men and their companions stacked arms, but refused to leave the barracks, and spent the next day gathering ammunition, meanwhile asking that their king put his request in writing. Accordingly, on Friday the royal message was read to the mutineers, who were addressed therein as "my loving people" and were ordered to relinquish all government property and go home.

Reluctantly, the soldiers obeyed, and Lunalilo then decreed that the Household Troops be disbanded, leaving the country without any formal military protection. "The soldiers' mutiny had one good result," wrote Judd in a private letter, "the disbanding of a useless and expensive army."

The humiliation of the government by its own troops was shameful; but perhaps, when no firm action was taken at the outbreak of the mutiny, Lunalilo did well to move in a gingerly fashion, for a single fiery act on either side might have led to a bloody race war. It was suspected that Colonel Kalakaua, for his own political ends, might have been stirring up native resentment against all members of the haole group.

The friendliness of King Lunalilo to foreigners and foreign ideas was attacked by political foes who sought to draw to their side those of Hawaiian blood. The election of representatives to the legislative assembly was set for February 2, 1874. Meanwhile, Lunalilo was sinking further into invalidism. In mid-January he returned to Honolulu from a trip to the Big Island, with his health unimproved. He still refused to name a successor to his throne, insisting that the people should elect a person of their choice, as they had elected him.

The vote for legislators showed the rising political wind. Nearly all the men elected were natives and members of the Kalakaua faction. The next evening about nine o'clock, a bugle call sounded from the barracks. In his residence near the palace, Lunalilo had died.

Messengers flitted in the moonlight, and silently the crowd gathered. At one in the morning, a solemn procession marched to the palace with the casket containing the king's body. There he was laid out in state, wrapped in his mantle of golden feathers. So passed "the kind chief," after a reign of one year and twenty-five days.

The body of Lunalilo lay in state for three weeks and then was placed in the Royal Mausoleum until a tomb could be built for him in the churchyard of Kawaiahao. His mother, through some oversight, had not been taken to the Mausoleum with others of the Kamehameha line, and the king preferred that he should not lie there either. Accordingly, the body was transferred to a separate tomb which still stands in the Kawaiahao cemetery. The tale runs that, just as the coffin was brought through the gate, a loud roll of thunder came from the skies — a sign of heavenly recognition of the high rank of King Lunalilo.

Lunalilo is best remembered, perhaps, because he left most of his estate to found a benevolent institution. In his will he specified that a home be built to shelter the aged, poor, destitute, and infirm people of Hawaiian extraction. The Lunalilo Home in a valley near Honolulu is still a useful memorial to the generosity and kindheartedness of the first elected king of Hawaii.

The Last of the Whalers

CHANGE AND GROWTH MARKED THE YEARS 1854-1874 THAT LIE between the reigns of Kamehameha III and Kalakaua. The Polynesian kingdom was moving steadily toward an economic pattern closer to that of the American continent. Farms and cattle ranches dotted the countryside, and green fields of rippling sugar cane spread in the sunshine.

Fortunately, the rise of a plantation economy offset the slow but heavy loss of income resulting from the decline in the whaling trade. The annual average of whaleship arrivals during the first three years of Kamehameha IV was four hundred; in 1870-1872 it was less than fifty. In the best year, 1852, whalers brought almost 375,000 barrels of oil into Hawaiian ports. In 1860 the catch was down to 63,000, and in 1872 it dropped to 20,000. This period saw the rise of locally owned whaleships and the practice of "bay whaling" off the coasts of the islands.

The first whaler under the Hawaiian flag was the *Denmark Hill*, fitted out in 1832 by Henry A. Peirce and Captain G. W. Cole, who commanded the vessel. He returned with a thousand barrels of sperm oil, but only a few other local ventures were made before 1851, when the business began in earnest. In that year the *Chariot* sailed to the Northwest under Captain Thomas Spencer, a Rhode Islander. The crew was hampered by bad weather — they saw only one clear day in five months — but after her first voyage the luck of the *Chariot* improved; and by the time she was laid up in 1855, a number of other vessels — *Juno, Magdalene, Hansa, Wilhelmina, Pfeil, Liholiho,* and *Black Warrior* — were whaling for the benefit of Honolulu owners. In 1862-1863, the brig *Kohala* and the bark *Zoe* wintered in the Arctic and brought back good catches, as well

as furs and ivory traded from the Eskimos, although Captain Bru-
merhopp of the *Kohala* was killed by a treacherous native of the
north.

The busiest year was 1858, when nineteen ships formed the
Honolulu whaling fleet. The average dropped to about a dozen
during the next decade, and the business was dead by 1880. Not all
the island-owned ships sailed under Hawaiian registry. There was a
high mortality rate in ships as a result of wrecks, decay, and high
repair costs.

Offshore whaling never amounted to much. The Ministry of the
Interior on November 1, 1847, issued an exclusive charter to James
Hough, a Hawaiian subject, to hunt whales off the island of Maui
from Lahaina to Honuaula, provided he paid the government one-
thirtieth of the oil taken. No further requests for such rights
were made until Christmas, 1854, when a one-year charter was
issued to C. J. Clark and H. Sherman to take whales in Maalaea Bay.
In 1858, "bay whaling" became a regular practice, with gangs at
several points from Lahaina to Kalepolepo Bay. E. M. Mayor was
granted permission in that year to start a whaling station on the
islet of Kahoolawe. By 1862, bay whaling off Maui had become so
successful that O. J. Harris erected a tryworks at his Kalepolepo
station. In 1870 Captain Roys of the *Anne* shot two hundred
whales in Kalepolepo Bay with a newly invented whale gun. But
thereafter the whales seemed to shy away from the bays of Maui,
and shore-based hunting died out.

The Hawaiian Islands were the favorite rendezvous of the
whale fleets during the palmy days, in spite of the competition of
San Francisco. Mark Twain wrote in 1866: "In facilities for shipping
crews, in economy of time and distance of travel of a voyage, in
facilities for insuring, in cheapness of money, in facilities for
transshipping cargoes, ditto ditto for chartering and equipping
vessels, and ditto ditto for communicating with owners, Honolulu
cannot begin to compete with San Francisco." He explained the
popularity of the islands by their comparative freedom from "land-

sharks" who preyed on the ship and her crew. The whaling captain in Honolulu was "the biggest frog in the pond," and the agents took care of all his shore business so well that his stay in port was bound to be a complete holiday.

A number of reasons for the decline in the whaling trade can be found. Foremost was the growing scarcity of whales, as the ocean was steadily fished out. Between 1835 and 1872, almost three hundred thousand whales were killed around the globe. Slaughtering these giant mammals was a wasteful business. The *Hope* in 1844 reported that only one whale out of every three killed was saved; the rest sank or were lost. Another ship lost twenty out of thirty-one killed. It was said that not more than half of all the whales killed were saved and not more than one-fifth of those struck were secured.

Other causes of decline were the necessity of longer voyages, which involved heavier expenses for refitting at points far from home; the rising cost of operating ships and the difficulty of getting insurance; and the competition of illuminating gas, kerosene, and oils refined from petroleum after the first successful oil well was drilled in Pennsylvania in 1859. A graver cause was the lack of skilled seamen to operate the whaleships and handle the harpoons. The life was so hard that, particularly in the Pacific, desertions were frequent. Sometimes a whaling captain would not dock in the islands, but would sail "off and on," to prevent his men from disappearing ashore. Toward the end of the whaling era, desertions in Hawaii were so frequent that head money was paid for the capture of a runaway. Sometimes a man was encouraged to hide in a home outside of town, so that later he could be turned over to the police and bring a reward to his faithless host. The decline in wages resulted, by the last quarter of the century, in having the whaleships manned by the least able sort of crewman.

The Civil War brought a heavy mortality in whaleships. Forty of them were sunk to form a barrier in the harbor of Charleston, South Carolina, during the blockade in 1862. The heaviest blow came in 1865, when the Confederate privateers *Shenandoah* and

Alabama sank fifty more. The celebrated *Shenandoah* — which was said to number a dozen native Hawaiians in its crew — was viciously active in the Pacific. Almost the entire New England fleet was hunting whales among the ice floes of the Bering Sea grounds, and thither sailed the *Shenandoah*. The Hawaiian bark *Victoria* hurried north from Honolulu with the news that Lee had surrendered, and notified Captain James I. Waddell that any further destruction of ships would be piracy. Some of the whalers, warned by the *Victoria*, retreated to the shallows; but others, loaded with oil and bone at the end of the season, were easy prey. On one day eleven ships were captured, and most of them were burned, while the helpless crews watched with rage as their hard-earned treasure went up in oily flames. Waddell was notified three times that the war was over, but in all he destroyed twenty-five ships of the Arctic fleet, at least three of them being Hawaiian-owned vessels.

After the war, the main hunting ground was the cold and foggy region north of Bering Strait, where the whale hunters killed walruses and traded with the Eskimos. The dangers of staying too long near the permanent Arctic barrier ice were shown in 1869. In that year the brig *Kohola* under Captain Tripp left the grounds on September 20, but nevertheless four men froze on that day. Destruction of ships in subzero weather reached its height in the terrible year 1871. More than thirty vessels (seven of them Hawaiian) were caught in the ice north of the Strait late in August and were either crushed or else held so fast that they had to be abandoned. The crews — including some women and children — struggled south down the coast and made their way in open whaleboats through choppy seas to board a few ships that had not been caught in the ice.

Five of these ships escaped to the islands, including the *Kohola*, the lone surviving Hawaiian vessel. Amazingly, although twelve hundred seamen were wrecked in the disaster, not one life was lost. But the loss of the ships and the income they would have brought to Hawaii was keenly felt. In a similar Arctic calamity in 1876, however, fifty lives were lost and thirteen ships (two of them Hawaiian) were caught in the floes and abandoned. After that, whaling ceased to be of any great importance to the Hawaiian Islands.

The Sweet Story of Sugar

THE DECLINE IN THE WHALING TRADE WAS FORTUNATELY TO BE more than compensated by the rise of a thriving plantation economy. The foremost crop, then as now, was sugar.

Captain Cook had seen cane fields planted by the natives, and the idea of cultivating sugar had long been dreamed about in Hawaii. Thomas Manby, one of Vancouver's men, wrote: "The sugar cane grows to a prodigious size and is spontaneous in many places; they fatten all their hogs on it, which gives the pork a very superior richness to any I ever tasted in Europe. The lower class of people are constantly sucking this valuable stalk, which gives them both health and strength by its salutary effects. The leaves of this valuable plant are not without their utility, as it is in common used to thatch their habitations. Should Great Britain ever attempt to colonize any part of the Northwest Coast of America, these islands will give them a very ample store of provisions and provided industry is closely pursued, a sufficiency of rum and sugar might with ease be produced, not only to supply our own settlements, but to carry a large quantity annually to the Chinese market." In 1793 Peter Puget thought that "the large and luxurious growth" of cane on Hawaii "would abundantly repay in quantity any labor bestowed on it in sugar and rum." Dr. G. H. von Langsdorff, naturalist with Krusenstern, said of the native cane: "If this were cultivated to any degree of perfection, in time Kamchatka and indeed all Siberia might be supplied with sugar from hence."

A Chinese named Wong Tze Chun on the island of Lanai, it is said, produced a little sugar as early as 1802, on a crude stone mill brought from his homeland; and Marín the Spaniard manufactured some in 1819. An Italian named Lavinia, according to Theodore Morgan, produced sugar in 1823, having natives crush the cane on poi-boards with stone beaters, and boiling the juice in a copper kettle. In the early days, interest in making rum was strong. John Wilkinson, a Britisher whom Chief Boki had brought to the islands on the *Blonde* to carry out European agricultural methods, laid out a sugar plantation in Manoa Valley in the fall of 1825. In spite of the high cost of labor with native tools, Wilkinson put under cultivation during the first year about a hundred acres of cane, as well as a number of coffee trees; but then he died, and although some cane was manufactured into sugar, molasses, and rum, the Manoa plantation was abandoned about 1829. Thereafter, rum was not commonly distilled in the islands.

The first extensive sugar planting was not begun until about 1835, when the energetic American firm of Ladd & Company got a fifty-year lease on a tract at Koloa, Kauai. After heartbreaking efforts to get started, they produced about two tons of sugar in 1837, along with 2700 gallons of molasses. The sugar was of poor quality and even by 1842 was only of fair grade. The first mill at Koloa, set up in 1836, was a crude press whose wooden rollers wore out very soon; but the next year one with iron rollers was used, and in 1841 an improved model run by water power came into operation. S. E. Bishop recalled that "The boiling train was composed of rather flat pans. The syrup was crystallized in large jars like conical flowerpots, with a hole at the apex, corked with cane-bagasse, which when opened allowed the molasses to drain out." The plantation struggled on for years without marked success until Dr. R. W. Wood obtained full possession in 1848 and thereafter gave it a strong management. Koloa Plantation is still in operation today.

Mills were set up after 1838 in various parts of the kingdom, by missionaries and others, to grind cane for native growers on shares. C. S. Lyman, staying with Titus Coan at Hilo in 1846, visited a mill operated by five Chinese. "Their mill is like a cider mill with three cylinders, the middle one turning the other two. They use horse power. In the boiling house there were three large boilers in operation. I understood them to say that an acre of cane would yield three thousand pounds of sugar."

Sugar was exported in 1836, only four tons of it; by 1850, the figure had risen to 375 tons, and at the end of the reign of Kamehameha V, the output averaged 9586 tons a year. These figures are trifling in comparison with the latter-day average of more than a million tons. But the effect of the expanding sugar trade, despite its many ups and downs, was a rising income that — in the face of overexpansion, lack of a ready labor supply, bankruptcy, manipulation by speculators, and periodic depressions — brought a golden prosperity to the kingdom and led to recurring demands for a reciprocity treaty that would admit Hawaiian-grown sugar and other articles into the United States without duty. After long negotiations, such a treaty was put into effect in 1875. It brought the islands firmly into the sphere of American business influence, and started a boom in production that led to an amazing increase in Hawaiian agriculture. Fifteen years after the treaty was signed, the tonnage had increased ten times, and thereafter the amount of sugar shipped doubled every ten years!

Part of the success of the sugar industry was due to ingenuity in improving the methods of work, such as the invention of a deep plow by Samuel Burbank of Koloa Plantation and the devising in 1851 by David M. Weston of a centrifugal machine for separating sugar from molasses. This "whirl-dry" method did well in a few minutes what had formerly taken weeks to do poorly. The vacuum pan, which enabled the mill to boil sugar at a lower temperature and without scorching, was introduced early in the 1860's. Steam power was applied extensively in the mills, using as fuel the pressed cane stalks, or bagasse. The sugar that was shipped came to be of such a high grade that it could be sold to groceries for table use without being refined. In addition to export, sugar was also sold to local dealers and to visiting ships.

Selection of better cane stocks led to great increases in output.

The first planters used native cuttings, and boasted of obtaining as much as four tons of cane an acre. In 1854 a better variety was imported from Tahiti which was called Lahaina cane, because it arrived first at that port. One of its descendants, "H 109," in recent years has produced up to a hundred tons of cane an acre, or enough to make fourteen tons of sugar. Around the end of the century the Lahaina cane developed a baffling root rot. Scientists carrying on research for the Hawaiian Sugar Planters' Association, founded in 1895, began breeding new varieties from the microscopically small seeds of the sugar plant. Painstakingly, pollen was gathered and crossed with West Indian varieties, and 5252 small seedlings sprouted. Out of all these, the strain labeled "H 109" was found to be resistant to the deadly Lahaina disease, and was a favorite until about 1930, when still better varieties developed by the scientists were able to make Hawaiian cane yield the highest sugar output per acre in the world.

The ancient Hawaiian custom of irrigating the fields was revived by the sugar planters in 1856, and thereafter few plantations could survive without irrigation, since four thousand tons of water are needed to grow enough cane for one ton of sugar! In that year a ten-mile ditch was dug to supply the Lihue Plantation on Kauai. The greatest early venture was the Hamakua Ditch on Maui, designed to bring water from the wet northern slopes of Haleakala around its flanks to the sun-baked central plain at Paia. Two partners, S. T. Alexander and H. P. Baldwin, both sons of missionaries, borrowed money and began the work in 1876. The cost was about $80,000 — a gigantic project for that time.

To get the water across the ravines on the slopes, large and heavy pipes had to be laid down each side and across the deep gashes in the earth, to make an inverted siphon. The final obstacle was the gorge of Maliko, and here the construction hands would have to lower themselves on ropes down the cliff. They refused, and the work stopped. Then Manager Baldwin had to show the way. He had lost one of his arms in a mill accident, but he slid down the rope using his legs and then, with his good arm, he successively gripped and released the rope and grabbed a new hold lower down. Shamed by this exhibition of courage, the men followed Baldwin; but to keep them heartened and to inspect progress, he went through this daring performance day after day.

The Hamakua Ditch, finished in 1878, ran for seventeen miles and had a daily capacity of forty million gallons. Soon Claus Spreckels, a sugar promoter from California, ran a second ditch below it, which was twice as long and had a capacity of fifty million gallons. Several other long ditches later paralleled the line, and on the plains of central Maui, once fit only for "the razorback hog, prickly pear, and wild indigo," tall cane flourished. Under Baldwin's supervision in 1891, a large ditch was dug on Kauai to deliver thirty-five million gallons daily to the Makaweli Plantation. Big as they seemed then, these earlier projects were to be overshadowed by those of today. One modern ditch carries sixty million gallons of water daily, through a tunnel six miles long.

The first artesian well was bored in July, 1879, at Ewa Plantation on Oahu, and thereafter the underground water supply was made available; nowadays Ewa's sixty wells furnish more than a hundred million gallons a day, almost enough to supply the needs of the city of San Francisco. Great reservoirs have been built for storage; the Wahiawa Reservoir on Oahu, largest in the islands, has a capacity of two and a half billion gallons.

The rise of larger plantations inevitably caused closer relationships between the growers and the businessmen of Honolulu. Here was the beginning of the agency system, strange to American economy, which led to later accusations that the life of the islands was dominated by a few big, paternalistic companies. The system had existed before the rise of sugar prosperity, but it expanded heavily during the middle period. The large business houses were obvious sources of risk capital and also drifted into acting as agents to handle marketing, accounting, purchasing, shipping, insurance, research, industrial relations, and many other central services.

The earliest agency was Ladd & Company, which started the Koloa Plantation in 1835. The boom in sugar exports during the Civil War, when Louisiana shipping was cut off, made the business houses of Honolulu take notice of the new industry. The oldest surviving agency, first of the group later called the "Big Five," is C. Brewer & Company; it took this name in 1843, but went back to Captain James Hunnewell's firm started in 1826. In 1863 the Brewer firm took over the agency for three plantations, and finding it "more profitable than whaleships," turned to sugar instead of sperm oil. Another agency, started by R. C. Jannion in 1845 with a stock of trade goods owned by a Liverpool firm, became Theo. H. Davies & Company in 1868 when the business changed hands. Captain Henry Hackfeld's firm kept his name until World War I, when it was reorganized as American Factors, Ltd. Samuel N. Castle and Amos Starr Cooke began a partnership in 1851. Thus four of Hawaii's future "Big Five," or their predecessors, became agents for sugar plantations during the middle period. The fifth, Alexander & Baldwin, began as an informal partnership in the 1870's but did not formally organize until 1895.

A large amount of capital to develop the sugar industry was brought into the islands from the United States. The most prominent promoter was Claus Spreckels, who had already made a fortune as a sugar refiner in California. He and his son, J. D. Spreckels, who founded the Oceanic Steamship Company, became prominent in business and politics in Hawaii. Aside from sons of missionaries, other sugar magnates were often men from other parts of the world. James Campbell was an Irish sailor and carpenter who settled in the islands and founded the Pioneer Mill Company in 1861. Valdemar Knudsen, the son of a premier of Norway, lost the gold he acquired in the California rush but made a new fortune in Hawaiian sugar. Captain James Makee, a Massachusetts whaling captain put ashore near death after being attacked by a ship's cook, lived to become King Kalakaua's partner in sugar planting. Paul Isenberg, son of a German pastor, rose from overseer on a Kauai estate to become a large estate owner. An ex-seaman named Benjamin F. Dillingham discovered that one could drill to the subsoil pools on Oahu and irrigate the fields with this life-giving water.

Other crops than sugar were raised in the middle period. Coffee as an export product also had its beginnings on Wilkinson's plantation in Manoa, using nursery trees brought by Lord Byron from Rio de Janeiro. Other plants were brought from Manila and set out in Kalihi and Niu Valleys near Honolulu. Missionaries around 1828 began growing coffee at Kona on the Big Island, a district now famous for this crop. The first large coffee plantations, however, were on Kauai, mainly around Hanalei Valley. Other early developments were on Oahu and at Hilo. The first coffee was exported in 1845, only 248 pounds of it. Disasters struck the industry, such as labor troubles, drought, flood, and an insect blight which caused the Hanalei estates to be converted to sugar; finally, the culture was localized around Kona, where a suitable climate made it profitable for individual growers to cultivate small acreages. Production varied greatly from year to year. Today, coffee is Hawaii's third most important export crop, with a total of about eight million pounds; most of it is shipped to the mainland for blending use. Gathering the ripe beans is so much of a task that the public schools of Kona run until August and open in November, so that children as well as adults can harvest coffee.

Wheat-growing for the milling of flour caused a flurry of activity from 1855 to 1865, but did not become a permanent industry. The Irish potato was a money crop from 1840 to 1850, especially on Maui, where hundreds of bushels were sold to whaleships. A boom came during the California gold rush, when raising potatoes at Kula might yield a fortune quicker than panning placer gold in the creeks of the Sierra Nevadas. But as soon as the Americans of the western states began growing their own potatoes, the boom collapsed.

Rice-planting, to supply the needs of the growing Chinese population of the islands, produced another staple crop. In 1860, trial plantings of seed from South Carolina gave such large yields that a craze for rice raising swept the islands, and in some places, growing taro was pulled up to be replaced with rice plants. In a few years, rice was the second most important crop, next after sugar. Toward the end of the 1870's, well over a million pounds of rice were exported, and probably another million were consumed at home. Most rice-raising was done by Chinese, using centuries-old hand methods; they brought in water buffalos with which to till the swampy ground. But by the end of the century, when skilled workers could no longer be brought in from China, it became cheaper to ship rice into Hawaii from Texas and California.

Silk production was another experiment in developing new industry. Koloa and Hanalei, Kauai, were the sites of this effort from 1836 to 1845. Charles Titcomb of Hanalei read about silk culture, planted mulberry trees for feed, and imported eggs from China and America. Natives were taught to tend the cocoonery, but although small shipments of raw silk were exported about 1844, droughts, heavy winds, and insect pests caused heavy losses. Lack of skilled labor was aggravated by the hostility of neighboring chiefs, who put a tabu on the paper script paid as wages; but G. W. Bates blamed the destruction of the industry upon the religious zeal of the natives, who refused to feed the silkworms on Sunday.

Tobacco was tried at Hanalei, but frequent rains led to failure. A more suitable climate was found on the south side of Kauai. "Here," said Bates, "the plant attains a large size, and is of superior quality. One leaf was three feet long and twenty inches broad." Tobacco never became an important export.

Indigo was brought into the islands in 1832 by Dr. A. P. Servier from Batavia and planted at Waikiki and Pearl Harbor. It was not commercially successful, but it grew luxuriantly and ran wild, covering acres with tough weeds.

Cotton growing began early; in 1825 it was reported that the

natives were raising a cotton plant of fine quality. Under sponsorship of the American missionary board, Miss Lydia Brown in 1835
began teaching the art of spinning and weaving at Wailuku, Maui.
After a year and a half, a class of young Hawaiian women was grad-
uated "clothed in garments of their own manufacture." The governor of the Big Island ordered the building of a cotton factory
at Kailua, Hawaii, in 1837. By the spring of 1839 about six hundred
yards of cotton cloth had been woven at Wailuku and four hundred
yards at Kailua. Fields were planted in various places, and the Civil
War gave an impetus to the idea of exporting cotton to the northern
states. A six-hundred-pound bale was shipped to Boston in April,
1863, and export continued for some years, but the largest amount
in any year was only about 22,000 pounds in 1866. Ten years later,
export ceased. Foreign competition, supplying cotton goods of superior quality and low price, led to importation of yardage in later
times.

Small quantities of fruits and vegetables were exported in the
middle period, especially bananas, oranges, and peanuts. A few
pineapples were also shipped, but the fruit was not of select quality. The government introduced cinnamon, allspice, and pepper
plants, but spice-raising did not prosper. Thousands of pounds of
a fungus that grows on decaying trunks of kukui trees were shipped
to China as a food.

A strange export of this period was pulu, a fuzzy fiber stripped
from the base of tree-fern fronds. It was found to be excellent as a
stuffing for pillows and mattresses. San Francisco was a good market
for pulu, which was exported for more than thirty years. The gathering of this material in the damp forests of the Big Island worked
hardships on the poor laborers and reminded people of the old days
of forced sandalwood collection. Exporters offered four dollars a
hundredweight for pulu. To work in the forests, Hawaiian families
neglected their taro patches, and then spent the dollars to buy the
white man's flour, which they boiled in water and vinegar to make a
horrible substitute for their nourishing native poi.

Home on the Hawaiian Range

CATTLE RANCHES AND TROPICAL ISLANDS DO NOT USUALLY MIX. YET Hawaiian cowboys were lassoing wild bulls and branding mavericks some decades before the cattle industry became important in the American West.

The longhorns brought in by Vancouver in 1793 from Santa Barbara, California, protected by the king's *kapu*, ran wild on the hills and multiplied to the point where they laid waste the forests and in some places drove out the natives by trampling the unfenced taro patches and truck gardens. John Palmer Parker, born in 1790 in Newton, Massachusetts, settled at Waimea, Hawaii, in 1815; his job for the king was to shoot the cattle, prepare their hides, and salt the beef for sale to visiting ships. This old Nimrod in 1853 showed G. W. Bates a rifle with which he had shot twelve hundred head of wild cattle. Through years of skillful management, the business was built into the great Parker Ranch of today, second largest ranch under the American flag.

Before 1830, a high chief visiting California persuaded some Spanish *vaqueros* from the ranches there to come to the islands and teach the Hawaiians how to ride and rope. They brought with them their high-horned saddles and sheathed stirrups, their long spurs and braided lariats. The Hawaiians found this dashing outdoor life to be highly congenial, and soon mastered the ranch hand's trade; but the word for cowboy in their language today is still *paniolo* (from *español* or Spaniard), after their galloping tutors of early days.

The king owned all the wild herds, and the right to slaughter them was let out on contract. "Bullock hunters" roamed the Waimea region in the 1840's. F. A. Olmstead saw some that were Spaniards from California; and all wore ponchos and slit trouser legs, and used long spurs and Spanish saddles for roping work. Wild bulls were also trapped in pits dug near the trails. David Douglas, Scottish naturalist, was supposed to have been gored and trampled to death when he tumbled into such a pit in 1834, although an American cattleman named Hall suspected that Douglas had been murdered for his gold, since some wounds on his head could not have been made by horns or hoofs.

Gradually the wild animals were thinned out and, after the Great Mahele divided up the lands, selected herds were settled on spreading ranches. A report in 1851 to the Royal Hawaiian Agricultural Society, founded the previous year, gives the first record of the importation of breeding cattle, Aberdeen Angus and Hereford. A Durham bull was imported in 1854 and Devon cattle in 1855 — "a bull calf, a cow named Edith, and a bull named Herod." Dexter and Shorthorn cattle were brought to the islands in the early 1860's. It was estimated in 1852 that there were about forty thousand head of cattle in the kingdom, including at least twelve thousand wild ones. About two thousand hides a year were exported, and the carcasses were boiled down to tallow in huge vats. As late as 1875, hides and tallow were of more value than the beef, but today the twelve thousand cattle in Hawaii do not begin to supply the local demand for meat. About a fourth of all land in the islands is still pasture today, whereas all the sugar is grown on less than six per cent of the total area — or 345 square miles, about the size of New York City.

The Hawaiian cowboy's working outfit was fully as colorful as that of his American counterpart. He wore a huge sombrero of woven pandanus, decked with a *lei* of fresh flowers. He flaunted at his neck a red silk bandanna and his sash was made of the same material. The shirt was a blue cotton plaid called *palaka*, woven especially for island sale. Over his shoes, which did not have high heels, he wore leggings of decorated leather. The leggings not only protected the rider from thorny brush but also served as a sheath for his long knife. One edge of this fine steel instrument was a sharp saw. When an animal was first roped, the cowboy leaped off his horse and sawed off the pointed horns, to protect himself, his horse, and other cattle when the wild beast was driven to fenced pasture.

The *paniolo* was an expert with his seven-fathom lasso, with which he could noose a running bull and hold him by hauling the rope taut around the high Spanish saddle horn. Special spurs made by a local blacksmith included a small piece of iron hung on a chain so that it struck the spur and made a loud jingling sound as the cowboy rode along. His trousers were tailor-made of white cloth, and at the roundup, which was often a social event witnessed by nobility and even royalty, the proud *paniolo* rode and roped all day attired in this garb. When evening came, every cowpuncher whose otherwise spotless pants showed only rope marks was rewarded by a *lei* from the queen of the roundup.

Many mainland rodeo events have been won by a *paniolo* from Hawaii. The world's best roper, Angus McPhee, was twice beaten by Maikai Keliilike, who roped his animal the second time in one minute flat. Ikua Purdy made a record at the Cheyenne Frontier Days celebration in 1908 by roping, busting, and hog-tying his animal in 56 seconds. Eben P. K. Low, grandson of the founder of the Parker Ranch, who was born in 1864 and lived to be eighty-nine, often challenged any man to "outshine him either in clothes or in roping ability." Before "Rawhide Ben," as he was called, lost one hand in a roping accident, he was a star performer, and even later, in 1908, he was crowned at Cheyenne as the one-handed champion roper of the world.

The cowboys of Hawaii had to know how to ride the waves as well as the mountains. Armine von Tempski described the shipping of cattle raised on the windy slopes of Haleakala, where in the lee of that massive crater the pastures are so waterless that in the past century most cows on the ranches there grew up without ever getting a drink of water, existing on the heavy dews. A steamer anchored half a mile off Makena, Maui, and the mounted cattlemen, dodging sharks, herded the animals into the shallow bay. "A whaleboat was lowered and began to come in. Dad went into the corrals and maneuvered among the steers. The boat anchored about fifty feet from the beach and the sailors called out greetings. Holomalia and Eole guarded the open gate of the corral. When everything was ready Dad roped a steer about the horns and dashed out, Hauki galloping beside the captive. They rushed across the beach at full speed and hit the sea. A great splash went up into the air, then they began swimming for the boat. Flinging the manila rope, which was about the steer's horns, to one of the men in the boat, Daddy wheeled. . . . The boat had to anchor far enough out so the struggling cattle couldn't get their feet on the bottom and tear free. Eight animals on each side constituted a boatload. When it had its quota it was drawn back to the ship by a long rope, as oars could not be used with the animals floating on each side. When it reached the ship the cattle would have a sling put around them and be hoisted aboard." Similar loading scenes were enacted also at Kawaihae Bay, even after World War II.

The Life of the Land

HIGH SOCIETY IN HONOLULU, UNDER THE LEADERSHIP OF THE COURT, had a cosmopolitan flavor in the middle period. "As to society," wrote Perkins in 1849, "Honolulu is not a whit behind the age, and the associations of refinement pertaining to more extensive communities may here be enjoyed, though in a minor degree, and fetes, balls, and excursions are frequently the order of the day." When Lady Jane Franklin, widow of the lost explorer Sir John, visited the islands in 1861, she was entertained at a state dinner, going in on the arm of Kamehameha IV. "The dinner was as well appointed as it would have been in London — the table covered with candelabra, epergnes, vases of flowers, fruit." The butler had recently come from a post at the Crystal Palace in England.

Tragedians and Travelers

ASIDE FROM DINING AND DANCING, SOCIAL DIVERSIONS INCLUDED visits aboard ships in the harbor, parties to welcome travelers, Sunday-school strawberry festivals, moonlight rides on horseback, charitable work, sewing bees, agricultural fairs, cribbage, and the enacting of tableaux. Nearly every foreign house in town had a pianoforte and a sewing machine. It was the latest fashion to go to the Daguerrean Gallery and have one's photograph taken, to be framed in gilt or else enshrined in a gold locket on a gold chain.

A number of clubs and fraternal and social organizations had been started, as well as literary and musical societies for the cultural improvement of members. From time to time, city folk might choose to attend a circus on the Esplanade, a minstrel show, fireworks display, concert, lecture, debate, or amateur play. Visitors were likely then, as now, to be invited to a native *luau* and a performance of the hula, which, although frowned upon by Kamehameha V in his later days, was still offered even before such distinguished tourists as H. R. H. the Duke of Edinburgh.

Honolulu's first theater, the Thespian, sponsored by a group of business people, opened in 1847 in an adobe structure at King and Maunakea Streets. The house held seventy-five people in the boxes (at one dollar a head) and two hundred in the pit (at fifty cents). Community interest in the drama at once became so strong that stock was sold to erect a building to be used primarily as a theater. This was the Royal Hawaiian, seating five hundred, not counting an occasional centipede occupying a box seat. This playhouse at the corner of Hotel and Alakea Streets had its *première* on June 17, 1848. The first season was cut short by the departure of many actors and audience members for the gold fields of California; but thereafter the Royal Hawaiian was the scene of much theatrical activity.

Under the vigorous management of Charles Derby, who slept in the greenroom and cooked his meals under the stage, eking out his income by giving lessons in music, dancing, and fencing, this theater was sometimes used for repertory performances by traveling British and American companies. Charles Mathews, who played there in 1873-1874 by command of Kamehameha V, wrote: "A really elegant-looking audience; tickets ten shillings each, evening dresses, uniforms of every cut and country; chiefesses and ladies of every tinge in dresses of every color; flowers and jewels in profusion, satin playbills. . . . The whole thing was like nothing but a midsummer night's dream." Not only dramas and skits, but singers, minstrels, cyclorama and diorama displays, trained poodles, dissolving views, and even grand opera appeared on the stage of the Royal Hawaiian. Derby left the management when the authorities confined him as a leper in 1875; he escaped to New England, where he died in a Salem almshouse in 1883.

Not the least diverting production at this theater was one managed by the celebrated Edwin Booth, then aged twenty-one, who was returning in 1855 from a tour of Australia. The play was the Colley Cibber version of Shakespeare's *Richard III*, and during rehearsals Laura Keene, the leading lady, quit the company and left for home. In desperation Booth drafted, to play the part of Lady Anne, an American stage hand with a Dutch accent. He was under five feet tall, was bowlegged and cross-eyed, and had two teeth missing in front. In feminine dress he looked even worse, and when Booth began what seemed to himself an interminable dialogue with the words: "Divine perfection of a woman," the tragedian's despair was not lightened by the smothered shrieks of laughter from fellow actors in the wings. Kamehameha IV, who was still in mourning but who did not want to miss the show, watched from an armchair offstage. At the end he patted Booth's shoulder and told him that as a boy he had seen Booth's father, Junius Brutus, play the same role in New York.

The Varieties Theater opened in 1853 in competition with the Royal Hawaiian, and later Buffum's Hall and several other buildings were used for plays and readings. In short, Honolulu became more of a "show town" than many an American provincial city of its size. It even included a Chinese playhouse built in 1879 for the satisfaction of the growing Oriental community. In this theater, single acts often ran from 4 P.M. to midnight, and often several weeks were required to present an entire play. "These ancient histories of China are interspersed with tumbling, singing, fighting, dancing, wrestling, joking, laughing, screeching, howling, and various *ing's* too numerous to mention," a reporter noted. The din bothered neighbors, and in 1884 the group moved to a new building on Beretania Street.

Singers of international note sometimes gave concerts at the Courthouse. Miss Catherine Hayes appeared there in 1854, and Madame Anna Bishop gave two concerts in 1866 to full audiences. Lady Franklin attended a concert in 1861 by the Amateur Musical Society, and the performers, both vocal and instrumental, reached such a high standard that she was not surprised to hear that the Choral Society of Honolulu had recently rendered *Il Trovatore*. Opera was, in fact, favored by music-hungry Honolulu audiences, who greeted with delight in 1871 the visiting troupe of the famed Madame Agatha States. The season included *Lucia*, *Il Trovatore*, *Faust*, and *The Barber of Seville*.

Theater lovers in 1880 incorporated as the Musical Hall Association of Honolulu and built a brick structure across from the palace, on the present site of the Federal Building. The New Theater or the Music Hall, as it was called, cost $40,000, and the interior was modeled on that of the Bush Street Theater in San Francisco. King Kalakaua was in the royal box when the house opened in January, 1881, with a melodrama, *The Marble Heart*. Forced to depend on casual touring companies for professional shows, and closed for many months by the smallpox epidemic of 1881, the playhouse went through bankruptcy in 1883 but was renovated and rechristened the Royal Opera House. Here visiting troupes performed such favorites as *Rip Van Winkle*, *East Lynne*, *Hazel Kirk*, *The Two Or-*

phans, The Lady of Lyons, The Ticket-of-Leave Man, Uncle Tom's Cabin, Mazeppa, and *Little Lord Fauntleroy.* Henry Berger, brought from Germany in 1872 to head the Royal Hawaiian Band, often led the orchestra. But there was no regular season, audiences were often too noisy or too apathetic, and theatrical fare depended on the repertories of companies stopping between ships, or on barnstormers from California who, too often, would go broke and leave the actors "coral-stranded." Yet despite a serious fire in 1895, the Opera House was rebuilt and served as a theatrical center until World War I.

The Prussian Captain Berger, in his forty-three years as conductor of the Royal Hawaiian Band, composed seventy-five Hawaiian songs, including the national anthem, "Hawaii Ponoi." He is said to have so popularized European music that natives whistled grand-opera airs while they pounded poi.

To be sure, some visitors found the life even of the capital to be drowsy and indolent, and the lack of international news to be dulling to the mind. "At the principal bookstore," wrote a visitor named William R. Bliss in 1872, "a bulletin is posted every morning on which is recorded the news of the city — arrivals and clearances of sugar schooners, auction sales, ships expected, some of which are phantom cruisers; also the latest opinions, rumors, suppositions, expectations, probabilities, afloat in the town; showing how much enterprise there might be in Honolulu society, if the city were connected by telegraph with the rest of the world. But then it would be no longer Honolulu."

The canker of the foreign society on the islands, according to a British visitor, Isabella Bird Bishop, was gossip. "By gossip," she wrote home, "I don't mean scandal or malignant misrepresentations, or reports of petty strifes, intrigues, and jealousies, such as are common in all cliques and communities, but *nuhou,* mere tattle, the perpetual talking about people, and the picking to tatters of every item of personal detail, whether gathered from fact or imagination." C. W. Stoddard agreed. "It has been frequently observed that a tendency to gossip is peculiar to the climate; this and the pestiferous south wind are its only objectionable features."

An amusing — and amused — visitor arrived in Honolulu on March 18, 1866, and stayed for four months. His name was Sam Clemens, but he had recently taken to signing his newspaper articles and sketches with the pen name of "Mark Twain." An insatiable sightseer, he rode a spavined horse around the islands; he was garbed in a starched brown linen duster reaching to his ankles, and talked and gesticulated so much that people who didn't know him thought he was always drunk. After a tour of Maui, where he climbed Haleakala and viewed Iao Valley, he took a schooner to the Kona Coast, voyaged around the southern end of the Big Island (where at Waiohinu he is reputed to have planted a monkeypod tree now grown to an immense size), and then climbed around the volcano district at Kilauea. After visiting the Hamakua district he rode along Waipio Valley, crossed the Waimea tableland, and caught the little steamer *Kilauea* at Kawaihae on his return to Honolulu. Mark Twain's Sandwich Island experiences furnished him with material for twenty-five picturesque letters to the Sacramento, California, *Union*, which were drawn upon for several chapters in *Roughing It*. For the rest of his life he remembered his tour as a most refreshing interlude in a tropical paradise, and as late as 1884 he began to write a novel with a Hawaiian setting. Best of all, his visit gave him a new and lucrative profession — that of lecturer. His famous speech on the Hawaiian Islands was virtually his sole dependence on the platform for a year and a half, and for more than seven years it was his main stand-by as an international lecture artist. He lovingly referred to Hawaii, in a letter in 1908, as "the loveliest fleet of islands that lies anchored in any ocean."

A number of other notable visitors came to the islands in the latter half of the century, and more than a hundred of them wrote books that called Hawaii's scenes and scenery to the attention of the world. Among the most readable travel writers, aside from Mark Twain, were Charles Warren Stoddard; Constance F. Gordon-

Cumming, author of *Fire-Fountains;* Charles Nordhoff, grandfather of the American novelist of that name; and Isabella Bird Bishop. Mrs. Bishop, first woman fellow of the Royal Geographical Society, spent half a year in the islands in 1873, visiting most regions by sea or on horseback, galloping astride like a *paniolo* and spending many a night in a wayside hut. Both Nordhoff and Mrs. Bishop met many persons of social refinement not only in Honolulu but in the smaller towns and on the plantations. Both gave graphic descriptions of native customs and sports, particularly riding the waves on surfboards (Nordhoff noted that Hilo was one of the few places where surfriding could be seen).

Visitors and Volcanoes

THE BEGINNINGS OF THE TOURIST INDUSTRY IN THE HAWAIIAN Islands date from the 1870's, when curious travelers, vacationists, and health-seekers began to arrive on every steamer. The sightseeing route started to assume almost a standard pattern — Honolulu, Nuuanu and the Pali, the beach at Waikiki, excursions around Oahu, a circuit of Kauai from Haena to Barking Sands, and trips by sea to Maui and to the Big Island, where Kona, Hilo, and the Hamakua Coast were favorite spots.

The high point of every sojourn, though, was a visit to the volcano regions. Here the traveler could well be convinced that every one of the Hawaiian Islands is in reality the top of a volcano rising from the floor of the Pacific, part of the greatest mountain range on our earth, built up from a rift in the ocean floor by thousands upon thousands of eruptions. The colossal crater of Haleakala, dormant since around 1750, was less accessible to visitors, who more commonly journeyed to see the five volcanoes that form the island of Hawaii. Here looms Mauna Loa, world's largest single mountain mass, whose deceptively sloping sides make one forget that its volume is 125 times that of the cone of Mount Shasta in California.

The first foreigner to ascend it was the Reverend Joseph Goodrich in 1824. Archibald Menzies, naturalist on the *Blonde*, measured the summit altitude a year later, hitting close to the official height of 13,680 feet. Notable eruptions from its flanks and from Mokuaweoweo, the *caldera* on its top, have occurred thirty-seven times since 1832 — an average of one every three and a half years. In that time it has added to the bulk of the island almost four billion cubic yards of lava, not counting the molten rivers that flowed into the boiling sea. The United States Exploring Expedition in the winter of 1840-1841 ascended Mauna Loa to make scientific observations on the vibration of the pendulum. Commander Charles Wilkes and his men pitched tents on the summit, nearly fourteen thousand feet in the air, and despite snowstorms and gales, remained for three weeks. Slightly more accessible today, the summit of Mauna Loa is still not a tourist resort.

More widely popular was the volcano of Kilauea (elevation, four thousand feet), to the east of Mauna Loa and overshadowed by its bulk. Sacred to the goddess Pele, Kilauea and its fire-pit of Halemaumau had long been visited, with awe and trembling, by generations of natives. The region was first studied scientifically by Lord Byron and his men of the *Blonde* in 1825. Titus Coan, missionary at Hilo, was the foremost volcanologist of his time and made many trips to observe the outbursts of pagan Pele. Dr. G. P. Judd, guide to Commander Wilkes, while collecting lava in Kilauea in 1841, almost lost his life when a river of fire burst out and trapped him under a ledge.

The first foreign ladies to visit Kilauea were two missionary wives in 1828, and thereafter many sightseers took the trip. In April, 1861, Lady Jane Franklin, guided by a king-to-be named David Kalakaua, ascended from Hilo with a lady friend. The two rode in style in litters slung on poles between two bearers, reclining on seats stuffed with pulu. They spent two nights sleeping in grass shacks on the lip of the crater, having brought an iron bedstead with them for comfort. On one day, wearing bloomers, they

THE LIFE OF THE LAND

clambered down and peered over the edge of the cauldron and heard a priest of Pele reel off an invocation to her which ended — "cunning man as he was" — just as a flaming fountain spouted up from the boiling lake.

Later in 1865 an inn was erected on the edge of Kilauea to shelter the weary sightseers toiling up from Hilo. This was the first Volcano House, on a site not far from the present world-famed hostelry reached by automobile from Hilo in less than an hour. "The inn is a unique and interesting place," wrote Mrs. Bishop in 1873. "Its existence is strikingly precarious, for the whole region is in a state of perpetual throb from earthquakes, and the sights and sounds are gruesome and awful both by day and night. The surrounding country steams and smokes from cracks and pits, and a smell of sulphur fills the air. They cook their *kalo* in a steam apparatus of nature's own work just behind the house, and every drop of water is from a distillery similarly provided. The inn is a grass and bamboo house, very beautifully constructed without nails. . . . It is altogether a most magical building in the heart of a formidable volcanic wilderness."

Although both Mauna Loa and Kilauea have erupted many times since 1790, when a third of Keoua's army was killed, Pele has always given enough warning so that since then, not one human life has been lost. In fact, Hawaii is probably the only place in the world where spectators rush to the scene of a volcanic eruption instead of away from it. Symptoms are eagerly watched at the Hawaiian Volcano Observatory, and when an outbreak might be imminent, people from all the islands hurry to the region, hoping for fireworks.

Travel writers for more than a century have vied with each other in trying to paint word-pictures of the beauties and terrors of Kilauea. A passage from Mark Twain's *Roughing It* will serve as a sample. The volcano was not in violent eruption at the time he saw it; but the sight was enough to awe even that inveterate humorist into a serious vein. "Shortly the crater came into view. I have seen Vesuvius since, but it was a mere toy, a child's volcano, a soup kettle, compared to this. . . . Here was a vast, perpendicular, walled cellar, nine hundred feet deep in some places, thirteen hundred in others, level-floored, and *ten miles in circumference!* . . . The illumination was two miles wide and a mile high, perhaps. . . . A colossal column of cloud towered to a great height in the air immediately above the crater, and the outer swell of every one of its vast folds was dyed with a rich crimson luster, which was subdued to a pale rose tint in the depressions between. It glowed like a muffled torch and stretched upward to a dizzy height toward the zenith. . . . In the strong light every countenance glowed like red-hot iron, every shoulder was suffused with crimson and shaded rearward into dingy, shapeless obscurity! The place below looked like the infernal regions and these men like half-cooled devils just come up on a furlough. . . . The greater part of the vast floor of the desert under us was as black as ink, and apparently smooth and level; but over a mile square of it was ringed and streaked and striped with a thousand branching streams of liquid and gorgeously brilliant fire!"

Superstitions concerning the volcano goddess Pele (who even in recent years has been seen at dusk on the narrow roads of the Big Island) have not died. When the great lava flow that burst out from Mauna Loa in November, 1880, approached dangerously near a stone wall on the outskirts of Hilo, the people of that town appealed to Princess Ruth, then sixty-three, to save them. This granddaughter of Kamehameha I, armed with a bottle of brandy and all the red silk handkerchiefs she could find, advanced to the edge of the river of lava. After a prayer to Pele, she tossed the kerchiefs one by one into the flow. Last she poured out the foreign firewater as a substitute for the sacred awa. No one was surprised when, next morning, the torrent stopped at the stone wall on the edge of town. And when, fifty-five years later, another lava flow menaced Hilo and soldiers and scientists united in an attempt to divert the flow by dropping bombs from the air, there were many dire predictions that Pele's wrath would fall upon the pilots of the five Keystone planes whose rain of bombs at last stopped the fiery torrent.

Hawaiians at Home

THE INFLUX OF TOURISTS MADE PRESSING THE NEED FOR A SUITABLE hotel, and private enterprise was unable to finance one that would appeal to the carriage trade. The government accordingly took the responsibility, and with a ball on February 29, 1872, the Hawaiian Hotel (later called the Royal Hawaiian) was opened for occupancy at the corner of Richards and Hotel Streets. "All the chambers are large and airy," ran the advertisement, "and fitted with luxurious baths and other modern conveniences." The cost was more than $110,000 — a staggering sum that nearly doubled the national debt and caused the temporary fall of the two cabinet ministers who were the chief promoters of the idea.

Other public projects were carried on during the middle years at an investment of about a million dollars. Most important was the large government building called Aliiolani Hale, costing about the same as the hotel and, like it, constructed of concrete blocks. It was designed by a firm of architects in Sydney, Australia, and master mechanics were brought from that city to supervise the building. The cornerstone was laid February 19, 1872, with an elaborate Masonic ceremony, and the Hale was completed about two years later. The rest of the expenditure went for other show places — the Royal Mausoleum, Iolani Barracks, a new prison, the post office, customhouses, schools, warehouses and harbor improvements, a quarantine building, and an insane asylum. To pay the costs of progress, taxes were increased to the point where the government income averaged around $400,000 a year, but expenses were even higher, and money had to be borrowed locally, at interest rates from twelve to eighteen per cent.

Although the towns were becoming modernized, many natives still lived on their *kuleanas* as they had done for centuries. The impact of haole ways was growing stronger, however, particularly in the matter of dress. "Another absurd imitation of English or American fashions now creeping in among the native women," C. S. Lyman observed, "is the tight dress. The simple loose dress, which has been worn all over the islands, is easy, cool, and very becoming. But put these free buxom savages accustomed to the unrestrained use of the limbs into corsets and they appear like a monkey in smallclothes, in agony and ill at ease till the offensive encasement is laid aside." He also noted that "at Honolulu, before pants came into general use among the natives, those who took in clothes of foreigners to wash made quite an income by hiring them out to unpantalooned and unclothed natives to be married in, the owners of the clothes being ignorant of the whole matter." One country bridegroom, according to Jarves, borrowed of a friend a huge green blanket overcoat (the temperature was at ninety degrees), a dickey, and a pair of fisherman's boots. After the ceremony he returned the wedding clothes and passed his honeymoon, as he had his previous life, shirtless. At another wedding, described by the Reverend Henry Cheever, a squadron of couples were being married in quick succession; when one man showed up in line without his bride, he explained, "Oh, she's just outside the church door, putting on her dress!"

The Hawaiians seldom wore shoes on the road, but carried them until they arrived and then put them on. When they did wear shoes, they wore only the best — which meant the ones with the loudest squeak. The first shoes introduced were not well built, and the people got the idea that a resounding creaking noise was an important part of the total effect. Cheever tells how Father Bond at the Kohala mission was asked by a parishioner to order a pair of shoes to be made by the local cobbler. Amused, he asked the native whether he would pay one *hapaha* extra for a good squeak, or even run to a quarter's worth. "The man concluded to have the largest squeak that Crispin could build in, even if it cost as high as a dollar."

Litigation was enjoyed by the Hawaiians because it brought some excitement and notoriety. O. P. Emerson reported that two heirs of a man who died at Waialua went to district court to dispute which of them should receive a spokeshave, worth perhaps fifty cents.

The Hawaiian at home in 1873, as sketched by Nordhoff, did not present an unhappy picture. "Finally," he wrote, "the daily life of the Hawaiian, if he lives near the seacoast and is master of his own life, is divided between fishing, taro planting, poi making, and mat weaving. All these but the last are laborious occupations; but they do not make hard work of them. Two days' labor every week will provide abundant food for a man and his family. He has from five to ten dollars a year of taxes to pay, and this money he can easily earn. The sea always supplies him with fish, sea-moss, and other food. He is fond of fussing at different things; but he also lies down on the grass a good deal — why shouldn't he? — he reads his paper, he plays at cards, he rides about a good deal, he sleeps more or less, and about midnight he gets up and eats a hearty supper. Altogether he is a very happy creature, and by no means a bad one. You need not lock your door against him; and an election and a *luau* occasionally give him all the excitement he craves, and that not of an unwholesome kind. . . . It would hardly do to compare the Hawaiian people with those of New England; but they will compare favorably in comfort, in intelligence, in wealth, in morals, and in happiness with the common peoples of most European nations."

Disease was a recurrent threat to native life and happiness, and foreign germs continued to decimate the population. In 1848 and 1849 an epidemic of measles, introduced from Mexico, raged through all parts of the islands, followed by whooping cough and influenza; ten thousand people died within a year. Smallpox, called *mai puupuuliilii*, struck in 1853, and in spite of the energetic precautions of a special public health commission, 2485 people died within eight months. A fifth of the natives in Honolulu were carried off. This same scourge recurred in 1881.

Leprosy (the name has been changed by legal action in recent years to "Hansen's disease") was a grim menace. It had been brought into the kingdom during the reign of Kamehameha III, probably from China, since the native name for it was *mai pake* — the Chinese disease. It had spread unchecked over all the islands, and isolation of sufferers was thought to be the only treatment possible. A law was passed to set up a receiving station at Kalihi, near Honolulu, and for cases adjudged incurable, a settlement was founded on the barren, wave-dashed peninsula jutting from the north side of the island of Molokai. The site was accessible from shoreward only by a precipitous trail down the two-thousand-foot cliffs of the guardian mountains. By 1873, about eight hundred patients, most of them Hawaiians, had been settled at this leper station.

The need for segregation was not well understood, for family feeling has always been strong among the Hawaiians, and painful scenes were enacted when victims of the disease were taken away and sent to Molokai. "When the search for lepers was made," wrote Isabella Bird, "the natives hid their friends away under mats, and in forests and caves, till the peril of separation was over, and if they sought medical advice, they rejected foreign educated aid in favor of the highly paid services of Chinese and native quacks, who professed to work a cure by means of loathsome ointments and decoctions, and abominable broths worthy of the witches' cauldron." Often a healthy husband or wife would elect to be condemned to a lifetime exile at the colony rather than to suffer separation.

A view of the Kalawao settlement and the devoted Catholic missionaries who labored there is given by Stoddard, who made a visit in 1884: "By the roadside, in the edge of the village, between it and the sea, stood a little chapel; the cross upon its low belfry, and the larger cross in the cemetery beyond, assured us that the poor villagers were not neglected in the hour of their extremity. . . . The chapel door stood ajar; in a moment it was thrown open, and a young priest paused upon the threshold to give us welcome. His cassock was worn and faded, his hair tumbled like a schoolboy's, his hands stained and hardened by toil; but the glow of health was in his face, the buoyancy of youth in his manner; while his ringing laugh, his ready sympathy, and his inspiring magnetism told of one who in any sphere might do a noble work, and who in that which he has chosen is doing the noblest of all works. This was Father Damien, the self-exiled priest, the one clean man in the midst of his flock of lepers." Only a year later, Joseph Damien de Veuster himself showed symptoms of the fatal disease, of which he died in 1889.

The isolation village, scene of the ministrations of the "martyr of Molokai," continued in operation until the middle of the twentieth century, when it was virtually closed because modern methods of treatment made it unnecessary for patients to be banished to the barren shores of Molokai.

Saints and Scholars

THE "ENGLISH CHURCH" SET UP UNDER ROYAL AUSPICES WAS NOT the only new denomination established in the islands during the middle period. A Methodist Episcopal Church was organized in 1855, with the Reverend W. S. Turner of the California Conference as its first pastor. A church building and parsonage were built, but the congregation seems to have suffered dissension and was dissolved in 1861; the premises were taken over by the Episcopalians in 1862, before their own church was built.

The two Congregational churches already operating in Honolulu were thriving. The first of these was the Oahu Bethel Church organized in 1837, the first church for foreigners in the islands; it had grown out of the Seamen's Bethel started in 1833 by the Reverend John Diell, and was reorganized in 1850 by Samuel C. Damon. In 1852 was opened the Second Foreign Church, later called the Fort Street Church. These two rival congregations were ultimately combined to form the present Central Union Church of Honolulu.

The pioneer Protestant mission took a decisive step in 1863. For some years the American Board of Commissioners for Foreign Missions, which had controlled and in part financed the work, had felt that Hawaii was now a Christian nation and that future religious activities should be placed in the hands of the island church congregations. In that year Hawaii was declared a "home mission" and the Board withdrew from this field, leaving it under the jurisdiction of the Hawaiian Evangelical Association, which was enlarged to include native pastors and also lay delegates elected from the different islands. Hawaii, no longer a foreign field, itself became a center for missionary endeavor in the Pacific, especially Micronesia. Regular stations had been set up in the 1850's in the Gilbert, Marshall, and Caroline groups. Communication, as well as delivery of supplies, was maintained by a specially built interisland bark named the *Morning Star*. When she was worn out in serving the far-flung Micronesian stations, a series of other ships were substituted, each successive one bearing the name of *Morning Star*.

The mission to Hawaii had ended, but many of the missionaries remained. They had become identified with the life of the land, and their children had grown up in the islands. Their abilities were still needed. J. J. Jarves, no fanatical defender of the missionaries, pointed out that, to help the Hawaiian people, "no better class can be found than those who have been so instrumental in nurturing and sustaining them in their progress towards civilization. . . . Supported by the people as pastors, teachers, or physicians, and by the government as agents in various important departments, they will lead lives of greater usefulness to those they are among, and enable the Board to extend its operations elsewhere. In pursuing this policy, they and their children will become identified with the nation." Missionaries and their families, free to purchase land, start business, and engage in professional careers, did continue to serve the kingdom in many walks of life. The fiftieth anniversary of the landing of the "First Company" sent out by the American Board was celebrated in June, 1870, with a jubilee. The joys and struggles of those days of Liholiho now seemed very far away.

Another American sect was active at this time in Hawaiian missionary work. They were the Latter-Day Saints, or Mormons. A shipload of converts from the eastern states, headed by Sam Brannan, had stopped at the islands in the *Brooklyn* in 1846, on their way to California. The first Mormon missionaries arrived in Honolulu on December 12, 1850; they were ten young men from the California gold camps. They soon decided that they should learn the Hawaiian language and work among the native population if they wished to gain any great number of converts. These and other workers sent out from Utah made rapid progress. Almost from the beginning they appointed natives to various offices under the Mormon Church, and in spite of opposition from Protestants and Catholics alike, Mormonism had spread by 1854 to all parts of the kingdom.

One of the most persuasive preachers was George Q. Cannon, a member of the first group, who made the island of Maui a strong center. With the assistance of two educated Hawaiians, Cannon began early in 1852 to translate the Book of Mormon; and in exactly two years the final Hawaiian version was printed in San Francisco and ready for use in the islands.

The heads of the Mormon Church decided in 1853 to promote the "gathering" of all members of their sect back in Utah. The island of Lanai was selected as a temporary gathering place for the Hawaiian congregation. A town site was chosen, houses were built and farms started, and the "City of Joseph" rose as a Mormon stronghold. All the haole missionaries were recalled to Utah in 1858, however, because of the outbreak of the "Mormon War," and the Hawaiian church members were left to fend for themselves.

The villain of the Mormon drama arrived on July 4, 1861, in Honolulu, where he was to play an energetic role for twenty-six years. He was Walter Murray Gibson, an American adventurer whose record included an escape from jail in the Dutch East Indies, where he had been imprisoned as a filibuster. He had persuaded Brigham Young of his ability to revivify the Hawaiian mission, and to the native Saints he introduced himself under the title of "Chief President of the Islands of the Sea." Converts multiplied under his leadership, for he soon became fluent in the Hawaiian language, and donations came pouring in. Gibson augmented this income by selling church offices at prices ranging from $150 down to fifty cents. With the money collected, he built up the Lanai lands and made them his headquarters. He was excommunicated by the Mormons in 1864, but by that time all the church property was under his control, and became the basis of his large political operations that were later to aggrandize his selfish soul.

Ejected from Lanai, the Mormons under new leaders from Utah erected another gathering place in 1865 at Laie, on the northern shore of Oahu. Here the members could settle and cultivate a home garden, fish in the ocean, and raise cattle, while taking part in the communal growing of sugar cane. In spite of hardships, after some years the revenues from sugar helped to support the work of the Mormon Church in other parts of the islands and elsewhere in the Pacific. In 1879 the membership included about one tenth of the entire native population of Hawaii. The Mormon Temple at Laie, dedicated in 1919, is the center of spiritual ceremonies performed not only for Hawaiians but for members from New Zealand, Tahiti, and Samoa. The impressive stone temple, rising above the fields of cane, is a notable monument to the pioneer missionaries of the Latter-Day Saints in Hawaii.

A flare-up of nativistic religion came in 1867, when an educated Hawaiian, Joseph Kaona, returned to his birthplace at Kona and with a band of followers moved into a new church building. Ejected after some weeks, they camped on neighboring lands and refused to depart. A few months later, in 1868, Hawaii was shaken by violent earthquakes, and Kaona began preaching that the Second Coming was imminent and that only his band would be saved. When Sheriff Neville went again to eject the squatters, he and his constables clashed with a force armed with clubs, stones, lassos, and copies of the Hawaiian Bible. In the fray, Neville had his skull fractured by a stone that knocked him from his horse, and after lying for some hours he was finished off by a club. One of his constables was lassoed, dragged to the ground, and killed. Several Kaonaites also died in the encounter. A sheriff's posse arrested the religionists at the same time that a company of soldiers from Honolulu arrived off the coast. In the trial that followed, Kaona the prophet and a few of his followers were convicted of manslaughter in the second degree.

Educational methods underwent marked changes in the middle years. Government-supported institutions had long since replaced the volunteer schools of the missionaries who had shown the way. A law passed in 1840 required that common schools should be maintained in every community. One inspector for each of the five main islands was appointed, and these were to be supervised by a school superintendent. First to hold this office was David Malo, a Hawaiian minister and historian.

The Organic Acts in 1845 and 1846 set up a department of public instruction under a cabinet minister, William Richards. When he died in 1847 he was succeeded by Richard Armstrong, pastor of Kawaiahao Church. For the next dozen years, under his leadership, the trend away from denominational schools toward public schools in all communities was gradually accelerated. After 1853, official reports no longer classified government common schools under sectarian headings.

By mid-century, most Hawaiians could read and write in their own language. But English had long ago become the main language of trade and government, and many parents wished their children to become proficient in that tongue. Jarves proposed in 1845 that English should gradually be made the official language of the islands. The missionary view, however, was that in order to preserve the Hawaiian nation, its speech must also be preserved. All instruction in the common schools had been carried on in the vernacular; the study of English was not introduced at the Protestant seminary at Lahainaluna, Maui, until 1846. The acquisition of Oregon and California by the United States, however, made the missionaries recognize that English was the coming language even for the natives of Hawaii.

A law was passed in 1854 "for the encouragement and support of English schools for Hawaiian youth," and by the end of the year ten such schools were in operation. They were the start of a movement that ended some years later with the adoption of English as the chief medium of instruction in the public schools of the islands.

A number of "select" schools had grown up which were ultimately to be taken over by the government; but meanwhile, those parents who could afford to pay fees were eager to send their offspring to these private schools where English was taught and teaching standards were high. Most celebrated was the family boarding school opened in 1839, the Chiefs' Children's School. Started by Mr. and Mrs. Amos Starr Cooke, this was designated by the act of 1846 as the "Royal School" and placed under the Ministry of Public Instruction. The Cookes retired in 1850 after having educated many children of the nobility. No less than five of their pupils afterwards sat on the throne of Hawaii. English had always been the language of instruction in the Royal School, and when in 1849 the children of haole residents began attending as day students, it became a select English academy.

The Oahu Charity School, set up by Mr. and Mrs. Andrew Johnstone in 1833 near the Honolulu Mission to educate the children of foreign residents marrying Hawaiian wives, offered instruction in "all the branches of British charity education." It was finally taken over by the government in 1851 and named the Honolulu Free School, supported by a special tax on foreigners.

The leading school of the kingdom under Kamehameha III was the high school at Lahainaluna, Maui, founded by the missionaries in 1831, primarily to train native teachers and preachers. When in 1849 the American Board found it difficult to continue financial support, it was transferred to the government. Another boarding school for boys was opened at Hilo in 1836, under the Reverend

David B. Lyman. The combination of classroom instruction and manual labor was so successful that the Hilo School was used as a model some years later when General S. C. Armstrong, a distinguished Civil War soldier whose parents were missionaries in Hawaii, founded Hampton Institute in Virginia in 1868.

The Central Female Boarding Seminary was started at Wailuku, Maui, in 1837. The girls were taught history and singing, as well as domestic science. "The chief object of the school," wrote Jarves, "is to train a class of females who shall make suitable wives for the graduates of the High School [Lahainaluna], who too often, by marrying their ignorant and vicious countrywomen, have relapsed into their former barbarous habits." The plan did not work out too well, for ten years later C. S. Lyman said that at one time the men vowed that they would not go to Wailuku for wives. "Furthermore, the girls are ambitious of marrying foreigners, and the young men find it difficult to obtain them."

An academy for the education of the children of Protestant missionaries was founded on the outskirts of Honolulu in 1841 by the Reverend and Mrs. Daniel Dole. This school grew steadily and in 1853 was granted a government charter under the title of "Punahou School and Oahu College." Some California parents in the early days sent their children to Hawaii to study at this private school, and today Punahou is still thriving, celebrated as "the oldest high school west of the Rockies."

A seminary was opened in 1846 in the Koolau district of Oahu to train teachers for Catholic schools.

Public education suffered more than one slump during the middle period, but there was a steady progress toward a central system patterned on the best American methods. A three-man Board of Education replaced the ministry in 1855. It was headed by Prince Lot, and when he became king in 1863 he appointed his father to replace him; but, although Kekuanaoa had served on the board for eight years and was an able man, he was handicapped by knowing only a little English. The Reorganization Act of 1865 set up a

Bureau of Public Instruction designed to restore professional leadership in education. The first inspector general of schools was Abraham Fornander, a journalist and antiquarian who was hampered in his reforms by a lack of sympathy with the methods of the missionary schools. But the system established in 1865 eventually led, under the leadership of such men as H. R. Hitchcock, who became inspector general in 1870, and Charles R. Bishop, the banker who began serving on the board in 1869, to a highly effective school program under American ideals of democratic education. Isabella Bird Bishop, globetrotter, wrote of Hawaii in 1873: "I suppose there is not a better educated country in the world. Education is compulsory; and besides the primary schools, there are a number of academies, all under government supervision, and there are 324 teachers, or one for every twenty-seven children." Since that time, many observers have agreed that the most American institution in Hawaii is its public-school system.

Decline and Fall of the Monarchy

A STORMY ELECTION USHERED IN THE STORMY REIGN OF THE LAST male monarch of the Hawaiian Kingdom.

Kalakaua, "The Day of War," undeterred by his defeat by Lunalilo the previous year, announced his new candidacy the day following Lunalilo's death. He advertised his availability by placards that were posted even at the entrance to Kawaiahao Church. His opponent was Queen Dowager Emma, widow of Kamehameha IV. She had been living quietly since returning in 1866 from a trip abroad, where she had enjoyed the friendship of Queen Victoria. Mass meetings were held, and the contest became bitter. Native support was divided between Kalakaua and Emma, but it was felt that she would try to restore the predominance of the British community, and hence most Americans were strong for Kalakaua.

The cabinet set February 12, 1874, for the meeting of the legislative assembly that would elect the new monarch. The Courthouse was surrounded by crowds of Hawaiians, most of them supporters of the queen. When the announcement was made that Kalakaua had received thirty-nine votes against six for Emma, a roar of execration arose.

Three committeemen left the hall on their way to announce to David Kalakaua that he was king of Hawaii. As they stepped into their carriage, the crowd attacked. The plug hats of the legislators were knocked in the gutter, their tail coats were torn from their backs, and they were glad to get back into the building alive. The carriage was smashed; the mob armed themselves with spokes from the broken wheels and rushed up the Courthouse stairs. Inside, the doors were blocked by C. C. Harris and Sanford B. Dole, who by sheer will power held off the rioters for twenty minutes. But others climbed the outside stairs, dug through the door with a whaling spade, and entered the legislative hall. The building was soon a shambles. Books, furniture, and public documents were tossed out the windows. Members who had voted for Kalakaua were beaten as they tried to escape. Several were injured severely and one died as a result of his wounds.

The police were helpless; some of them stripped off their badges and joined the mob. To prevent further damage and possible killing, Kalakaua, along with Charles R. Bishop and the governor of Oahu, sent a request to the American minister and the British commissioner to land forces from three warships then in the harbor. At once armed marines from the American vessels *Portsmouth* and *Tuscarora*, and the British ship *Tenedos*, came ashore. By nightfall they had restored order, but they remained on guard for a week, by which time Kalakaua was firmly on the throne.

The Merry Monarch of Iolani

AT A SECLUDED CEREMONY AT KINAU HALE ON FEBRUARY 13, SUR-rounded by limping and bandaged legislators, Kalakaua took the usual oath to support the constitution. On the same day, Queen Emma acknowledged him as her sovereign. To settle the old question of succession, Kalakaua at once proclaimed his younger brother, the popular Prince William Pitt Leleiohoku, as his heir.

Kalakaua had been born November 16, 1836, in Honolulu, at the foot of Punchbowl Crater, the old "Hill of Sacrifice," where his grandfather, the high chief Aikanaka, had been in charge of the gun battery. David established a new dynasty, for he was not a member of the dying Kamehameha line. His ancestors had been prominent chiefs on the island of Hawaii. His great-grandfather was Keaweaheulu, an adviser to Kamehameha the Great; he had claimed descent from a chief brought by the priest Paao from Tahiti to rule the Big Island in legendary times. The family was linked to the royal house of Kauai when in 1863 David married the personable Kapiolani, granddaughter of Kamehameha's rival Kaumualii.

"The Merry Monarch," as he was called, was a lively paradox, at once kingly and democratic. The attempts of his dynasty to restore personal rule ended in the destruction of the monarchy, but while it lasted, Kalakaua was always the leading actor in a reign which at times resembled a Viennese operetta.

His figure was burly and his sidewhiskers imposing. He had practised public speaking and was adept at winning votes under the universal suffrage amendment passed in 1874. He could speak and write well in both English and Hawaiian, and had been editor of a newspaper, *Hoku i ka Pakipaka* (*Star of the Pacific*). His court was a musical center; he himself composed the words of "Hawaii Ponoi," the national anthem. He was a friend to literature; in 1888 his name appeared as author of *Legends and Myths of Hawaii*, edited by R. M. Daggett, the first important book in English dealing with these old tales. His company was enjoyed by such writers as Robert Louis Stevenson and Henry Adams.

Stevenson, who spent six months in the islands in 1889, called the king "the finest gentleman I ever met" and "a very fine intelligent fellow," but added, after Kalakaua had lunched on the writer's yacht *Casco*, "what a crop for the drink! He carries it, too, like a mountain with a sparrow on its shoulders." Adams, who had an audience with the king in 1890, noted that he "talked of Hawaiian archaeology and arts as well as though he had been a professor." C. W. Stoddard wrote: "Oh, what a king was he! Such a king as one reads of in nursery tales. He was all things to all men, a most companionable person. Possessed of rare refinement, he was as much at ease with a crew of 'rollicking rams' as in the throne room." John Cameron, who as master of a steamer running to Kauai often found His Majesty seated among his retainers on mats on the afterdeck, termed him "easy to approach and difficult to leave; unfailingly genial; kind to high and low alike; beloved by his subjects. . . . It was not strange, I think, that many adventurers took advantage of Kalakaua's liberality and joviality to intrigue for their own miserable ends."

The king introduced modern yachting into the islands, and his boathouse on the waterfront was a popular resort for sporting bloods. The first telephone line installed on Oahu was a private wire from the palace to the boathouse. There the evenings were given largely to playing poker, and many tales are told of Kalakaua's delight in his favorite game, at which entertainment was provided by a troupe of hula girls. One sea captain wrote of a session at the boathouse which lasted forty-eight hours; the players were a lawyer, a naval officer, a king, and a butcher. The most widely told story concerns the time when Kalakaua was apparently cornered by Claus Spreckels, the California sugar tycoon. Spreckels held four aces, but the Merry Monarch faced him down and scooped the pot. "Five kings beat four aces any time," he said. "I have four kings in my hand, and I am the fifth one!"

Kalakaua's reign started auspiciously. He made a royal progress among the islands, greeting his subjects and promising to work for their welfare. Before the first year was out, he went himself to the United States to help promote the signing of the long-deferred reciprocity treaty that was to make sugar the real king of the Hawaiian Islands. He left on the steamer *Benicia* on November 17, 1874, for San Francisco, was given a royal reception in that city, and crossed the continent in a palace car built for President Grant, who greeted him in Washington with full honors. Never before had the king of any country visited the United States, and as a Washington writer noted, "A becoming kingly dignity without pride, pretense, or ostentation gained him universal admiration." He was presented to both houses of Congress and afterwards visited New York and New England — including Boston, where the *Thaddeus* party had set out, and New Bedford, home port of many of the whale ships. Kalakaua returned to his capital on the U.S.S. *Pensacola* on February 15, 1875. Two months later, he joyfully ratified the reciprocity treaty offered by the American government.

The agricultural boom that followed gave the crown a chance to obtain an income almost sufficient to meet the growing extravagance of Kalakaua, and his use of the constitutional power to appoint new cabinets at will enabled him to put into the government more than one minister bent on feathering his own nest. By these methods, adventurers of the type of Celso Caesar Moreno and W. M. Gibson tried to put through grandiose schemes that were not always defeated by the legislature.

Kalakaua now dreamed of doing what no king had ever done before — to make a tour of the world. He appointed as regent his sister Liliuokalani, who had been named heiress to the throne after the death of Prince Leleiohoku in 1877. Accompanied by his chamberlain, Colonel C. H. Judd, and his attorney general, W. N. Armstrong, who was to seek arrangements by which emigrants from foreign countries might be found to work in the expanding cane fields, the king set out in January, 1881. His valet Robert, a decayed German baron who was an accomplished linguist, went along as interpreter.

The party first went to San Francisco, and there took a steamer for Japan. The mikado, Mutsuhito, extended a magnificent welcome to his royal visitor. Kalakaua was the first king of a western, Christian nation ever to set foot in the isles of Nippon. The Japanese government, which had declined a treaty with Hawaii in 1860, had signed one in 1871 and by now was well aware of the crossroads kingdom so often visited by their ships. Kalakaua was himself not averse to strengthening ties with the Orient; indeed, at a private interview with the emperor he proposed an alliance of marriage between his six-year-old niece, the lovely Princess Kaiulani, and one of the imperial princes of Japan. At a grand banquet given toward the end of his stay, Kalakaua in his gorgeous uniform was presented by the emperor with the star and cordon of the Order of the Rising Sun. Surprised but undaunted, he invented on the spot the Order of Kamehameha, and promised to forward to the mikado the Grand Cross of the order as soon as this decoration could be manufactured in Paris.

Kalakaua continued his tour through China, Siam, India, Egypt, and the great capitals of Europe; and everywhere he was royally entertained and honored. His return to Honolulu at the end of October gave another occasion for a triumphal celebration by his subjects.

The pomp and circumstance of foreign courts had given many new ideas to Kalakaua Rex. He had a chance to display some of them at his coronation, which had been authorized by the legislature in 1880, although no previous Hawaiian ruler had ever been crowned. Before he left England Kalakaua had ordered, for himself and his queen, two golden crowns set with precious jewels.

On February 12, 1883, the ninth anniversary of Kalakaua's election, the coronation was held. Its purpose was to symbolize the position of the royal family as the ruling dynasty, and to bring Hawaii to world attention. The fine new Iolani Palace, whose cornerstone had been laid with Masonic rituals in 1879, was the scene of the glittering ceremony. It was truly an international event, witnessed by official representatives of the United States, Great Britain, France, Germany, Sweden and Norway, Japan, Portugal, the

Netherlands, Belgium, Denmark, Mexico, and Russia. Some of the Kamehameha family stayed away, disliking this ostentation, but eight thousand others gathered in front of the outdoor pavilion to witness the coronation.

The ritual was a combination of old ceremonies of Hawaiian chieftainship and the use of the crowns, scepter, and sword of state that had been made in Europe. Kalakaua was robed with a cloak of Kamehameha I, made of five thousand tuft feathers of the o-o bird, as he stood beside the *puloulou* or tabu stick (a seven-foot tusk of narwhal) and the kahili, the feathered staff of power. Then, with a Napoleonic gesture, the man who had been elected king placed upon his head and that of his consort Kapiolani the royal crowns.

The jeweled regalia was never worn again. But years later, on the night the Hawaiian monarchy was overthrown, an officer of the Provisional Government discovered some of his men dicing in the palace basement. The stakes were gems pried from Kalakaua's crown. Most of the jewels were recovered, but an Irish sergeant later said that he had sent a big diamond to his girl in Indiana, explaining that it was just a Hawaiian stone. It is not known whether his sweetheart ever found out that she possessed the largest diamond in the crown of Kalakaua Rex.

"The King Can Do No Wrong"

Two days after the coronation, the celebrated statue of Kamehameha the Great that still stands in front of Aliiolani Hale was unveiled by Kalakaua. But the ideals of civic virtue personified by the statue were to be forgotten by the governmental regime in the palace across the street, where Walter Murray Gibson, the recreant Mormon, became the power behind the throne.

Since 1880, Gibson had so played upon Kalakaua's aspirations as to institute a corrupt rule comparable to that of some United States cities in the same Gilded Age. One of the first acts of the legislature of 1882 was to convey to Claus Spreckels a large tract of crown lands at Wailuku, Maui, to settle a claim he had purchased from Princess Ruth for $10,000. The prohibition against furnishing intoxicating liquor to natives was repealed, with dire consequences to the people. Another bill led to the minting of the silver coins in San Francisco which in 1884 were put into circulation bearing the bust of Kalakaua; on this coinage deal, Spreckels made a profit of $150,000.

In 1884, some Reform Party members were elected despite heavy government patronage of their opponents, and they barely defeated such villainous schemes as a graft-ridden "national bank," a bill to set up a lottery, and a bill to license the sale of opium. This last bill was passed two years later, and gave the government the right to sell an opium monopoly for $30,000. Among the more trivial scandals of the Gibson administration were the sale of public offices, misuse of royal privilege to defraud the customs revenue, illegal leasing of lands to the king, neglect of the roads of the kingdom, and the sale of exemptions to lepers, who might thereby escape being sent to Molokai.

Kalakaua's interest in reviving native customs and traditions opened him to charges that he was "licensing sorcery and the hula and sacrificing black pigs" and had founded a society "for the propagation of idolatry and sorcery." It was the Hale Naua or House of Ancient Science, a secret society combining aspects of Masonry with the rites of pagan chiefs. According to its charter from the privy council, it was organized forty quadrillions of years after the foundation of the world and 24,750 years from Lailai, the first woman. W. D. Alexander believed that it was intended "partly as an agency for the revival of heathenism, partly to pander to vice, and indirectly to serve as a political machine." Kalakaua also founded a "Hawaiian Board of Health" which his critics termed an organized body of kahunas, or medicine men.

Kalakaua's jubilee was celebrated on November 16, 1886, his fiftieth birthday, with a grand *hookupu* or gift-giving. Each of the guests brought a present suitable to his station. Premier Gibson led off with a pair of elephant tusks on a koa-wood stand with the inscription: "The horns of the righteous shall be exalted." The police department, more practical, offered a bank check for $570. The ensuing jubilee pageantry and hula performances lasted more than a week.

Casting about for other worlds to conquer, Kalakaua, spurred on by Gibson, decided to make himself Emperor of Polynesia. Such an idea had often been urged by Charles St. Julian, who from 1853 to 1872, under various titles, had served in Sydney, Australia, as Hawaiian commissioner to the other islands of the Pacific. Kalakaua realized that Samoa, Tonga, the Carolines, and the Gilberts had not yet been annexed by other powers, and in 1873 he appointed the captain of a labor-recruiting schooner, A. N. Tripp, as commissioner to broach the idea of a protectorate over the Gilbert Islanders. In the fall of that year he sent to twenty-six nations a document proclaiming Hawaii's "primacy in the family of Polynesian States."

To implement this Monroe Doctrine of Oceania, Kalakaua sent John E. Bush as envoy extraordinary to the islanders of Polynesia. Bush was welcomed at Apia, Samoa, in January, 1887, by Chief Malietoa, the British-backed main contender for supremacy there. The chief was flattered to receive the Grand Cross of the Order of the Star of Oceania and to be entertained by the Bush delegation. On February 17 a convention was signed to form a political confederation between Hawaii and Samoa.

To make a show of his naval power in the Pacific, Kalakaua hurriedly fitted out a British steamship, the copra-trader *Explorer*, at a cost of $50,000. With the name translated as *Kaimiloa*, this vessel was armed with four muzzle-loading six-pounders and two Gatling guns. The crew was made up mainly of boys released from the Honolulu reform school. Even before the *Kaimiloa* sailed, a riot broke out on board that led to the dismissal of three officers.

When the "Hawaiian Navy" reached Samoan waters in June, trouble was still brewing aboard. Early in July, the drunken gunner tried to blow up the ship, and the German gunboat *Adler* had to restore order. R. L. Stevenson, who was in Samoa soon after, may have been reminded of events in his book *Treasure Island* when he wrote: "The *Kaimiloa* was from the first a scene of disaster and dilapidation; the stores were sold; the crew revolted; for a great part of a night she was in the hands of mutineers, and the Secretary lay bound upon the deck."

Kalakaua's grandiose dream collided, however, with the aims of Prince Bismarck, who since 1884 had been trying to find a place in the sun among the islands of the South Pacific. The colonial policies of Germany and Great Britain might have given an excuse for intervention at home in Hawaii, where a revolution was simmering. Gibson's attempts to make political capital of racial prejudice, added to his machinations in the cabinet, foretold trouble.

Scandals and mismanagement had alienated most of the haole residents as well as many of the natives. Early in 1887 a secret organization called the Hawaiian League had been formed to fight for a more liberal constitution. Hundreds of islanders joined, and it soon turned out that two factions could be found inside the League. One advocated the overthrow of the monarchy, the setting up of a republic, and annexation by the United States. The more conservative wing were in the majority. They felt that Hawaiian independence should be maintained but that the king's powers should be limited by a more democratic constitution; and should the king refuse, they were ready to overthrow him as a last resort.

The League members obtained arms and were ready to fight if necessary to obtain their rights. The immediate occasion for the Revolution of 1887 was the disclosure of a disgruntled rice merchant named Tong Kee, alias Aki, who said that he had paid a bribe of $71,000 to cabinet officials for an opium monopoly in the kingdom, but that the license had been given to the Chun Lung syndicate, who had paid $80,000. At this news, one man advocated a march on the palace by the Honolulu Rifles, the armed militia of the League. Instead, the aroused citizenry held a mass meeting on June 30 in the armory on Beretania Street. Unanimous resolutions were passed demanding that the king dismiss his cabinet and other officials concerned, and that he pledge himself never again to interfere in politics.

This display of popular strength avoided bloodshed. Most of Kalakaua's troops had deserted him, and the battery of field guns he had bought in Austria on his world tour for $21,000 was of little value in defending him from his subjects. Hurriedly he appointed a new cabinet, which drew up a liberal constitution that he signed on July 6. Gibson had been arrested on July 1, but was allowed to escape on a California-bound ship the day before the signing of the "Bayonet Constitution," as the king's sister called it. The strong-willed Liliuokalani was attending Queen Victoria's Jubilee in England, and swore that, had she been at home, Kalakaua would never have signed away his high powers.

One of the first acts of the Reform ministry was to withdraw the Bush embassy and recall H.H.M.S. *Kaimiloa* from Samoan waters, and on its return the ship was junked, along with Kalakaua's dream of winning for Hawaii the "primacy of the Pacific." The chief result of his attempt to build an atoll empire was the introduction into Hawaii of grass skirts from the Gilberts to adorn the palace hula dancers. Nor did the enterprising Aki ever get his bribe money back. The king's debts amounted to a quarter of a million dollars. His trustees refused to pay the Aki claim, and the supreme court decreed that, under the constitution, the king could not be sued.

The ousting of Gibson made possible the renewal of the reciprocity treaty. Negotiations had been stalled because Congress felt that the United States was not getting any advantages from the deal, and that the Hawaiian plantations were competing with mainland industry. The Senate on January 20, 1887, inserted an amendment to read that the renewal, as an extra concession, should give the United States the "exclusive right to enter the harbor of Pearl River, in the Island of Oahu, and to establish and to maintain there a coaling and repair station for the use of vessels of the United States." Taking into consideration the international complexities of the time, the Reform cabinet accepted on the condition that "Hawaiian sovereignty and jurisdiction are not impaired." The treaty was concluded before the end of the year, and reciprocity held sway until the end of Hawaiian independence. During all that time the American government never made any move to use its treaty rights in the Pearl River Harbor.

The Constitution of 1887 made a few changes in the law of the land. Cabinet ministers could not be dismissed by the king except in accordance with a vote of the legislature. The king's veto of a bill could be overridden by a two-thirds vote of the legislature. Nobles were to be elected by voters who were men of property. The right to vote was extended to resident foreigners of American or European birth or descent if they took an oath to support the Constitution.

Kalakaua, chastened but resentful, discovered that he still had some power left — mainly the veto of legislative acts — which he handled skillfully. He made use of the widening rifts in the Reform Party and in the cabinet. Most of the native Hawaiians were irked at the subordinate position given them by the new constitution and were aggrieved that Kalakaua, their highest *alii*, had been stripped of his authority. Opposition to the Reform administration led to bloodshed in 1889 in the insurrection headed by Robert W. Wilcox.

Wilcox had been taken to Europe by ex-premier Moreno, along with several other young Hawaiians, to be educated at public expense. He had been recalled in 1887 by the Reform cabinet, and immediately began plotting to use his knowledge of military science, acquired in Italy, to overthrow the new regime. At dawn on the morning of July 30, 1889, resplendent in his Italian cadet uniform, Wilcox at the head of about a hundred and fifty armed followers surrounded the government buildings and set up artillery.

Kalakaua retired to his boathouse, leaving orders to allow Wilcox to enter the grounds but not the palace, which under these instructions the head of the royal guard refused to surrender to the rebels. The cabinet acted quickly, summoned volunteers, and the revolutionists, after firing a blast of shrapnel at the Opera House, were driven to take refuge in a large bungalow on the palace grounds. Sniped at all day by a band of sharpshooters made up mainly of haole residents, the Wilcox forces at last flew a white tablecloth from one of the bungalow windows. They had surrendered hastily when Hay Wodehouse, son of the British consul general, had tossed some dynamite bombs on the galvanized iron roof, using his skill as a catcher on the local baseball team. The uprising had failed, with seven revolutionaries dead and a dozen wounded.

Strangely, when Wilcox was tried for treason, he stated that he had led the revolt to help the king regain his old prerogatives. He had planned to take possession of the palace and have the king proclaim a new constitution. His plea that he had Kalakaua's approval for treason led to his acquittal by a native jury on the grounds that "the king could do no wrong."

Unwearied, Kalakaua still maneuvered to draw upon the large numbers of the population that might still support his aims. He was aided by the formation of a party among the Hawaiians called the Hui Kalaiaina, which hoped to restore the Constitution of 1864. The weakened Reform Party did not obtain a majority in the legislature of 1890, and its cabinet was forced to yield to a compromise cabinet on June 13.

When the session closed in November, Kalakaua was a sick man. Hoping his health would improve, he left for San Francisco on the United States cruiser *Charleston*. He was further weakened by a tour of southern California, where he was feted by municipal authorities of Los Angeles, San Diego, and Santa Barbara. His return to San Francisco was marked by further festivities that he was reluctant to refuse. His symptoms were those of Bright's disease. He passed away in the Palace Hotel on January 20, 1891.

The king's love of novelty persisted even on his deathbed. Four days before the end, a crude recording machine was set up at his side by an agent of the Edison Phonograph Company. Weakly, slowly, he spoke in Hawaiian into the mouthpiece. "We greet each other. We shall perhaps hereafter go to Hawaii, to Honolulu. There you will tell the multitude the things you have heard me say here." Kalakaua Rex is still audible, on that first phonographic record of the voice of a king.

The Queen Who Lost Her Throne

THE SHORT REIGN OF H.H.M. LYDIA LILIUOKALANI, "THE SALT Air of Heaven," was filled with tumult. Economic distress led to political enmity, and democratic ideals collided with the queen's violent hostility to the "Bayonet Constitution" and with her determination to restore absolutism to the Hawaiian throne. The result was *pilikia* — trouble.

No cables connected the islands with the outside world in 1891, and the first sign of the death of the king was the appearance of the *Charleston*, rounding Diamond Head with her yards cockbilled and her flag at half-mast. After a ceremonious lying-in-state that would have pleased the ceremonious king, the body was entombed at the Royal Mausoleum, and his sister became queen of Hawaii.

The imposing new sovereign was fifty-two years old on her accession on January 29, 1891. A Chicago newspaper woman, Mary H. Krout, two years later described her face as "strong and resolute. The features were irregular, the complexion quite dark; the hair was streaked with gray, and she had the large, dark eyes of her race. Her voice was musical and well modulated . . . and she spoke remarkably pure and graceful English. Her manner was dignified, and she had the ease and the authoritative air of one accustomed to rule."

Two years younger than Kalakaua, she had like him studied at the Royal School. Shortly after she was born, she had been adopted by the parents of Bernice Pauahi, and reared as part of the social circle near the throne. Twice she had served as Kalakaua's regent during his absence. Her ideas were similar to his but her will was stronger, and her desire to restore the old *alii* authority to the crown led to the downfall of that crown. The wise restraint of her husband, John O. Dominis, was lost when he died seven months after her accession.

The depression that fell over the islands during the reign of Liliuokalani resulted from the McKinley Tariff of 1890, which wiped out the advantages that Hawaiian sugar had held in the United States market over sugar produced in other foreign countries. The uncertainties of the Kalakaua reign had alarmed the sugar planters who were now the economic backbone of the kingdom. Annexation to the United States would offer stability and fulfill what seemed to be the destiny of the Hawaiian Islands, and possibly give island sugar the benefit of the two-cents-a-pound bounty offered to American growers under the tariff. But annexation would almost certainly put an end to the use of Oriental labor on Hawaiian plantations.

The Annexation Club, a small secret organization composed of haoles who felt that this step offered the only hope for stable government, was formed in Honolulu in the spring of 1892. Revolution was in the air. In the legislative session of that year, a long battle was waged by Liliuokalani and her advisers to overthrow the Constitution of 1887 which she had taken the oath to maintain. The royalists also succeeded in passing a lottery bill and an opium-licensing bill. The queen signed these bills and appointed a cabinet from her own party. She had also prepared a new constitution, resembling that of 1864; she proposed to appoint members of the upper house of the legislature, and she would exclude from voting all foreigners not married to Hawaiian women.

Liliuokalani planned to proclaim this new constitution by royal fiat immediately after the legislature was prorogued at noon on Saturday, January 14, 1893. She felt that the cabinet should sign the document, but knowing the angry temper of the community, they refused, and one of the members warned her that to promulgate it would be a "revolutionary act." Late in the afternoon the queen announced to the crowd outside the palace that her bestowal of a new constitution would be postponed for a while.

That same afternoon a Committee of Safety was organized to take action. It was comprised of about half a dozen Hawaiian subjects, mainly of American blood, and about the same number of citizens of the United States, Great Britain, and Germany. Dominated by members of the Annexation Club, the committee decided that the monarchy must go. A mass meeting was held on Monday, at which resolutions were adopted denouncing the action of the queen and authorizing the Committee of Safety to do whatever was needed "to secure the protection of life, liberty and property in Hawaii." Meanwhile, Liliuokalani had become alarmed and had issued a statement that no change in the constitution would be made except by lawful amendment.

The promise came too late. On Tuesday, January 17, the Committee of Safety gave the word. The queen was defended by her household guards and the police, altogether not more than a hundred and fifty men. The revolutionists had recruited only a few more than that many volunteers. At their request, John L. Stevens, American minister, had arranged with Captain G. C. Wiltse of the United States cruiser *Boston* to land troops in Honolulu for the protection of American lives and property. The city was filled with alarms and rumors, and residents sent their women and children to Waikiki for safety.

The conspirators met under cover of darkness and offered the command of their forces to John Soper. He refused to accept unless supreme court judge Sanford Ballard Dole — born at Punahou in 1844 and reared on Kauai — would head the movement. Dole was summoned and at first was reluctant. He agreed that the manifest destiny of the islands was annexation to the United States and that Liliuokalani should be deposed. But he suggested that her niece Kaiulani — daughter of Princess Likelike and a Scottish merchant, A. S. Cleghorn — should be made queen under a regency. Others pointed out that Kaiulani had been educated in England and that her guardian, the British businessman Theophilus H. Davies, was not pro-American. Dole went home to ponder, and decided to accept the presidency of the executive council of the revolutionists.

The committee finished organizing itself the next day. Three o'clock was set as zero hour for taking possession of Aliiolani Hale, the government office building. Men were sent to collect the hidden arms to be used by the Dole forces. The queen's marshal, aware of these plans, sent a force to defend the building. About a hundred Hawaiians were gathered on the steps of the Opera House nearby, and police were waiting across the street from the offices of W. O. Smith to arrest Dole and his committee when they should emerge.

At two-thirty a shot was fired that sounded the knell of the Hawaiian monarchy. John Good, in charge of a wagonload of ammunition leaving E. O. Hall & Sons' hardware store near Fort and King Streets, was attacked by a force of policemen. He fired his revolver and winged a man who was grabbing the reins. The wagon dashed off and escaped, but the rest of the police and the crowd at the Opera House ran to the scene of commotion. Unarmed and unmolested, Dole and his friends walked into Aliiolani Hale and took possession from a few alarmed clerks. Their forces then seized the treasury and the archives, and from the steps read a proclamation abrogating the monarchy and setting up a Provisional Government until annexation could be arranged.

The "P.G.," as it came to be called, at once demanded that

Liliuokalani surrender her authority. Perhaps having in mind the upshot of the Paulet annexation, she did so, under protest, stating that she "yielded to the superior force of the United States." This wording was based upon the fact that Minister Stevens had acted quickly to land the marines. He was, in fact, very friendly to the annexationist group, and he was prompt in extending formal recognition to the Provisional Government. A month later he was to write to the American secretary of state: "The Hawaiian pear is now fully ripe, and this is the golden hour for the United States to pluck it."

The troops from the *Boston* remained ashore, and on February 1 the American flag was raised over the islands to proclaim a protectorate. A Japanese warship was in Honolulu harbor, and a British ship was on the way. The ministers of the P.G. daily expected a countercoup by the royalists. Representatives of both sides went to Washington to plead their cause. The five P.G. commissioners quickly obtained a treaty of annexation which was signed on February 14 and immediately submitted to the Senate by President Benjamin Harrison.

The lame-duck Republicans had to give way on March 4 to the Democrats, however, and the incoming president, Grover Cleveland, had his doubts about Hawaii. He withdrew the treaty and sent a special commissioner to investigate the revolution. James H. Blount arrived in Honolulu on March 29 with a letter from Cleveland to Dole stating that "in all matters affecting relations with the government of the Hawaiian Islands, his authority is *paramount*." Three days later, Blount ordered Admiral J. S. Skerritt to haul down the American flag, embark the troops, and withdraw the protectorate. Blount collected information until early in the fall, when he left to write his report. His final impression of Hawaii was not a pleasant one for this former colonel of a Georgia regiment in the Civil War. Bandmaster Berger, with the best of intentions, led his men at the gangplank to speed Blount's departure with the rousing strains of "Marching Through Georgia."

The report of "Paramount Blount" aroused indignation in the islands. He seemed to be prosecuting a case against those who had petitioned for annexation to the United States, and he whitewashed the queen to such a point that, in a message to Congress, Cleveland was led to denounce the "lawless occupation of Honolulu under false pretexts by United States forces." A cartoon in a New York paper showed the President singing: "She's my Lili, I'm her Gro. . . . Liliuokalani is my sweetheart."

The new minister who arrived in Honolulu in October was Albert S. Willis. He carried orders to unscramble the omelette and put Liliuokalani back on the throne. Willis secretly explained to her that as a condition she would, of course, grant full amnesty to the revolutionists. She replied that such clemency was a matter for the privy council and cabinet, but that the legal penalty was death, although she might favor confiscation of the traitors' property and their banishment.

The P.G. version was that she had demanded the beheading of all concerned. Against Willis they stood pat. President Dole stated that his government would "refuse compliance with the extraordinary demand of Mr. Willis." The main question in their minds, as worded by Miss Krout, was: "Shall what now exists — society, wealth, comfort, in which even the poorest shares — be dissipated by hands incapable of administering law and order; or shall it be transferred to those who created it, and who, in saving their own, must save with it that which yet remains to the natives?" They refused to restore the monarchy, denied the truth of Blount's report, and said that Washington had no right to meddle with the internal affairs of the Hawaiian Islands. What if Honolulu Harbor was jammed with the gunboats of three nations? Dole and his supporters wagered that American ships would never fire on Americans to prop up a foreign throne; and they were right. Congress at last decided that the United States should observe a "hands-off-Hawaii" policy, and Cleveland could do nothing more.

While the deposed Liliuokalani meditated on her woes, the

P.G. went ahead. Despite its concentration on United States-Hawaiian relations, it found time to make improvements in internal and local conditions, to repeal the opium and lottery laws, to set up a National Guard, and to pass an act providing for a constitutional convention. This last piece of legislation paved the way for the birth of the Republic of Hawaii.

Laboratory of Democracy

COULD THERE BE A RUN OF *alalauwa* IN HONOLULU HARBOR? SHOALS of this delicious little red fish, which readily snaps at a hook, occasionally throng the island waters. Their arrival is thought by the natives to presage the death of a high chief. On the afternoon of Thursday, January 3, 1895, many Hawaiians were seen rambling toward a certain pier at Kakaako. But they carried no fishing poles, and when they saw they were observed by the Republic's police they went back to their homes.

Government officials believed that the rumored counterrevolution of the monarchists had come at last. They suspected that an attempt to land guns and ammunition at the harbor had failed, but that another effort would be made to start an uprising and take over the city of Honolulu. It was odd that the U.S.S. *Pennsylvania* had sailed off, leaving no American forces near Oahu for the first time in twenty years.

Near dusk on Sunday, a telephone call led police to inspect the house of Henry Bertlemann under Diamond Head. A shadowy group in a canoe shed started firing, and Charles L. Carter, who had lightheartedly gone along to offer his aid, fell mortally wounded in the breast. He was the first casualty in the most serious skirmishing in the islands since the days of Kamehameha the Great.

Arms had been brought from the mainland in the American schooner *Wahlburg*, transshipped to the island steamer *Waimanalo*, and then secretly buried in the sand of Kahala beach. The news that the rebels were digging up the hidden rifles disrupted evening services at Central Union Church. The men poured out and soon a citizens' guard patrolled the streets, protecting strong points and cutting off supplies. Martial law was declared. Next day the rebels, driven inland by shells fired from Kapiolani Park and from the tug *Eleu* off Diamond Head, scattered and retreated up the valleys behind the city. Their last stand, led by Robert W. Wilcox, was broken at Moiliili on January 7. This inveterate firebrand was captured several days later in a fisherman's hut at Iwilei.

Firm action had ended the last attempt of the royalists to regain power. About two hundred persons were arrested for complicity, including the ex-queen and her nephew Prince Jonah Kuhio Kalanianaole. A small arsenal of arms and dynamite bombs was uncovered at sedate Washington Place. Comfortably confined in an upper room of her former palace, Liliuokalani signed a formal abdication, and as plain Mrs. Dominis took allegiance to the Republic of Hawaii.

All the prisoners were tried for treason or lesser offenses by a special commission, and nearly all were found guilty. Heavy sentences were imposed, but no heads rolled in the sand. President Dole, backed by public opinion, urged a policy of clemency. The death sentences were commuted to imprisonment, and the pardoning power was used so liberally that all the condemned were free again within a few months after the rebellion was over. The spirit of sportsmanship was well expressed by Prince Jonah. After Hawaii was annexed by the United States, he said to his brother, Prince David Kawananakoa: "You lead the Democrats, David, and I'll start up the Republican Party in Hawaii!" Jonah was elected Delegate to Congress in 1902 from the Territory of Hawaii and served in those halls for twenty years.

Innovations and Immigrations

THE REVOLUTION OF 1895 WAS ONLY ONE OF THE PROBLEMS THAT had to be dealt with by the Republic of Hawaii. Sanford Dole, whose long, white, forked beard made him look more patriarchal than his fifty years, had become President of the Republic on July 4, 1894. Counting the P.G. period, he was to sit at the head of the island government for more than a decade; for, although the country was annexed in 1898, he held the reins until the territorial government was set up in 1900, and as its first governor served until November 23, 1903. Back around 1886, Dole had published, as an anonymous pamphlet, a three-act play called *Vacuum*, which had satirized Kalakaua under the title of "Skyhigh Emperor of the Coral Reefs and Sand Banks of the Big Blue Sea," surrounded by rascally ministers named Palaver, Calabash, Mango, and Bananagan. Now, during the "Dole decade," this lanky, Hawaii-born son of New England parents had a chance to show the world what a common-sense government might do for the island people.

Eighteen elected delegates — including five native Hawaiians — met with the executive and advisory councils of the Provisional Government on May 30, 1894, as a constitutional convention. A draft of the proposed document, chiefly the work of Dole and Lorrin A. Thurston, was debated and thoroughly amended before its adoption on July 3. The result was a combination of Hawaiian and American ideas, and, although not allowing universal suffrage, gave the framework for an honest and efficient administration until the time when Hawaii could be admitted as an integral part of the United States. The Republic was soon recognized by all the foreign powers with which Hawaii had diplomatic relations.

Toward the turn of the century, the dreamy, lotus-eating era of the Pacific paradise had by no means passed away; but the modern world was making inroads on the Hawaii which Stoddard had depicted as the land where it was "almost always afternoon."

The city of Honolulu was still growing, and the age of invention had arrived. The first steam fire engine was brought to Honolulu in 1879. On July 21, 1886, Iolani Palace Square was illuminated by electric bulbs under whose glare Kalakaua reviewed his troops. Two years later, electric street lighting was introduced, superseding gasoline lamps; and in the same year ground was broken for a mule-drawn street railway, predecessor of the pioneer electric-railway line begun in 1900.

Only two years after Alexander Graham Bell patented the telephone in 1876, a line was strung by Charles H. Dickey between Kahului and Wailuku on Maui, and within a few years a phone system, both urban and rural, was operating on Oahu. "Telephones are probably more numerous here," wrote a Honolulan in 1889, "than in any city in the United States with a like number of inhabitants." Two rival concerns consolidated in 1894 as the Mutual Telephone Company. Four years later there were thirteen hundred phones on Oahu.

The first stamps under the Postal Union were issued in 1882, and a parcel-post system in co-operation with the United States was started in 1889. That same year, the first section of an inter-island undersea-cable system was laid between Maui and Molokai.

The first automobile had a trial spin in Honolulu in October, 1899, reaching a speed of fourteen miles an hour. Early in 1900 about twenty electric autos for public hire were imported, but the company went bankrupt and they lay rusting among the weeds because nobody could think of a use for them. These "devil dragons," as the Chinese called them, had frightened animals and children as they raced along at ten miles an hour, and people preferred the old-fashioned carriages or double-seater hacks; automobiles either exploded or broke down and had to be towed home. Despite this bad start, other cars were brought to the islands, ancestors of the hordes that create the highly civilized traffic jams of today. On Oahu alone there are now more than a hundred thousand passenger cars, and on the crowded highways may be seen license plates from all the forty-eight states.

Roads were improved and bridges built. Engineers began laying out small-gauge rail lines. B. F. Dillingham and his associates obtained a franchise for the Oahu Steam Railway in 1888, and its roadbed reached Ewa within a year. When Kalakaua died, railroads were in operation not only on Oahu but on Maui and Hawaii, snaking through the fields or crossing deep gulches on spiderweb trestles.

Communications with the outside world were still slow at the century's end. "Boat day" was a gala occasion. Warned by a telephone call from Diamond Head Charlie, whose job was to spot the approach of vessels from his cottage on the old crater, most of the townsfolk would hurry wharfward, laden with flower garlands, to meet newcomers and hear the latest talk. Reporters would board incoming steamers off-port, grab bundles of newspapers — even searching passenger cabins for stray pages — and rush back to the office, to sit up all night reducing the columns to "telegraphic brevities" more than a week old. But messages by Marconi wireless could be sent among the islands at the turn of the century, and by 1902 the Pacific cable from San Francisco brought the world's tidings to Honolulu's breakfast tables.

Shipping was a booming business. The government in 1877 had ordered the 382-ton wooden steamer *Likelike* built in San Francisco for interisland runs. This vessel and the old *Kilauea* were soon purchased by Samuel G. Wilder, whose Wilder Steamship Company began operating a growing fleet. The Inter-Island Steam

Navigation Company was organized in 1882, and by 1890 these two lines, which were to merge in 1905, were running a total of fourteen steamers, large and small. Many blue-water vessels were required to haul thousands of tons of sugar to market. Most of it went in steamers, but they did not have a monopoly, and the tall masts of schooners and square-riggers were to be seen in island ports until the end of the century.

One of the greatest problems for the Dole government was that of immigration and the labor supply. The complexion of the island population had changed greatly during the latter half of the century. By 1890 more than half these people had been born in other countries. Why did they come? And whence did they come?

Most of them were brought by the government to work on the ever-expanding plantations; and they came from certain overpopulated lands as immigrants to these isles of promise. The story of immigration to Hawaii goes back even earlier than 1863, when Wyllie wrote: "Unless we get more population, we are a doomed nation." At first the hope was held that natives of other Pacific islands could be brought in to continue the Polynesian stock. A scheme was broached in 1852 for transporting to Hawaii the entire population of Pitcairn Island, last refuge of the *Bounty* mutineers, but the plan fell through. Ten South Sea Islanders came to work on Koloa Plantation in 1859, and the missionary packet *Morning Star* brought fourteen Marquesans to Honolulu in 1865. Other attempts were made — John Cameron tells of bringing a cargo of South Sea "blackbirds" in 1881 — but in all, only about 2500 Pacific Islanders were recruited, and most of them returned home when their indentures expired.

Importation of labor from China had been suggested as early as 1816 by Dr. Scheffer. Under the auspices of the Royal Hawaiian Agricultural Society, the first contingent of nearly two hundred men and boys came in January, 1852, on the British bark *Thetis* from Amoy, on five-year contracts. About a hundred more arrived on the same vessel later in the year. By 1866 a total of thirteen hundred had been brought, mostly males; four hundred of these had come from San Francisco. Some of the laborers eventually went back to China; but many stayed and married Hawaiian girls, who discovered that John Chinaman was a fine catch as a foreign husband. He was a good provider; he was thrifty with his money, but liked to dress his family in pretty silks and brocades, and insisted upon regular health habits and a sound diet. He usually did the shopping, cooked the meals, and even fed and bathed the children; and to top all this, his Hawaiian wife found that she had no mother-in-law nearer than Canton.

Such families saved money earned in the fields, and many of them moved to the towns to start small businesses. By 1890 Chinese were entrenched in all trades, especially draying and hack-driving, wholesale and retail merchandising, butchering, and restaurant operation. Today many persons of Chinese blood are found in all lines of endeavor, the professions as well as agriculture and business.

Some planters expressed dissatisfaction with "coolie hands," and the need to find other sources of labor led at the end of 1864 to the founding of a government Bureau of Immigration. This agency appointed Dr. William Hillebrand to go to China and send in enough laborers to fill immediate needs, and then to investigate other countries, such as India and Malaya, that might export workers. Hillebrand concluded that China was still the best source; but the problem stuck in his mind, and when some years later he returned to Europe, he did not forget his old assignment. His researches in botany had taken him to the Madeira Islands. There he found an offshore folk that, he thought, would fit in well in Hawaii; and he arranged that a band of them should emigrate there in 1878. Thereafter many a shipload of Portuguese families came from the Atlantic islands to make their homes in the Pacific; by the end of the century the total reached eighteen thousand. They took to plantation life with zest and became eager citizens; but the cost of bringing them from Europe was high.

Chief source of imported labor in the latter part of the century was Japan. A band of 148 laborers had been brought from there in 1868, but thereafter no more of these nationals arrived until 1885, when the living cargo of the *City of Tokyo* was landed to begin a wave of Japanese immigration which, stimulated by the reciprocity treaty, became a torrent.

The Wilson Act passed by Congress in 1894 ended the bonus to American sugar growers and restored the tariff, so that Hawaii's benefits were regained and the labor question again became urgent. By then Japanese immigration had been encouraged to the point where fears were expressed that Hawaii might soon become a colony under the mikado. In 1896 Japanese comprised no less than a fourth of the population. Measures were taken during the three years 1895-1897 to reduce Japanese entries and encourage those from China, but during that time the number of Japanese still exceeded the Chinese by more than two thousand.

The immigration of Japanese after 1894 was no longer controlled by the convention of 1886 and was conducted by Japanese companies chartered in Japan. Hawaiian officials charged in 1897 that these companies were evading the restrictions imposed, and they refused admission to some twelve hundred immigrants on the grounds of fraud. The Japanese government now entered the controversy, and in May the cruiser *Naniwa*, under Captain Heihachiro Togo (later to be victor over the Russians at Tsushima Strait), brought demands to indemnify the companies involved. Having recently defeated China on the battlefields, Japan was the leading Asiatic power, and in June, a few days after Hawaii and the United States signed the annexation treaty, Japan protested that annexation would upset the *status quo* in the Pacific and endanger the rights of Japanese subjects in Hawaii. Finally Japan withdrew the protest, but still continued to press claims for indemnities for alleged injustices to Japanese subjects. After the annexation resolution was approved by Congress in 1898, the American government made strong suggestions that all disputes between

Hawaii and Japan should be settled before the new territory yielded its sovereignty. Hawaii proposed arbitration, but Japan's conditions were unacceptable, and at last, without admitting that its position was wrong, the Dole government paid an indemnity of $75,000 to satisfy the claims in full.

Territory of Hawaii, U.S.A.

THE TRIUMPH OF THE REPUBLICANS WITH THE ELECTION OF McKinley in 1896 aroused the high hopes of the annexationists. A new treaty was signed at Washington on June 16, 1897, and was sent to the Senate on the same day. It was approved by the Hawaiian Senate, and signed by President Dole on September 10. But it could not come up for action until the regular Congressional session met in December. Those interests that had been against the reciprocity treaty were able to forestall favorable action, so that the required two-thirds majority of senators could not be obtained. Thus it was decided to use a different method of annexation — one that had been followed in the case of Texas. This method was to pass joint resolutions, which would require only a simple majority vote in each house. The Senate resolution was introduced on March 16, 1898, and the one in the House on May 4.

Something happened between those dates — the outbreak of the Spanish-American War. On May Day, Admiral Dewey's fleet was victorious over the Spanish squadron in Manila Bay, and troops were rushed to support him. Pearl Harbor had not been developed under the lease of 1887, and Hawaii might easily have maintained a neutral policy. But Dole offered on May 10 "the unreserved alliance of Hawaii," and Honolulu threw open its harbor to the transports filled with American soldiers on the long voyage to the Philippines. The "boys in blue" were given a Hawaiian welcome (the first Red Cross group in the islands was formed at this time to serve them).

The war turned the tide in favor of annexation. The House passed the resolution on June 15; the Senate passed it on July 6, and President McKinley signed it the next day. Great excitement greeted the news when it reached Honolulu by the S.S. *Coptic* on July 13. At last Hawaii would be permanently linked to the fortunes of the United States of America!

The sovereignty of the Republic of Hawaii was transferred in a brief ceremony on August 12. On a platform on the steps of Iolani Palace, which had been named the Executive Building, President Dole and his cabinet met with Harold Sewall, United States minister, Colonel J. H. Barber of the United States Army, and Rear Admiral J. N. Miller of the Navy, before a crowd of thousands of citizens and foreign observers. Out of respect to the former queen, many Hawaiians stayed away. Sewall presented a copy of the joint resolution to Dole, who then delivered sovereignty to Sewall for the United States. At a signal just before noon, the Hawaiian flag was lowered to the strains of "Hawaii Ponoi" and American banners broke out from the three towers of the Palace and from the Judiciary Building across the street, while shore batteries and the U.S.S. *Philadelphia* boomed a twenty-one gun salute.

The islands were now a part of the American Union, but questions of national policy connected with the aftermath of the war with Spain delayed the designing of a new form of government. For two years longer, Dole and his fellow officials carried on, operating under two different constitutions at once, subject to the approval of the White House.

The most vital problem to be faced in the latter days of the Republic was an outbreak of bubonic plague. Five cases, all fatal, were reported on December 12, 1899. The news sounded worse than the cholera epidemic of '95. All schools were closed and public gatherings, even church services, were forbidden. Most of the cases were found in the jerry-built slums of Honolulu. Board of Health officials and volunteers patrolled the suspected areas, and quarantine and disinfection methods were tried. Although the true connection between rats and the "black death" was not clearly known, it was suspected, and rat-control was practiced. But as the mortality toll mounted, a meeting of physicians concluded that as long as "Chinatown" existed, it was a menace to the health of the entire community. The worst sections should be burned to the ground.

The fire department had done good work in incinerating infected premises, but on January 20, 1900, when the Kaumakapili block was fired, a rising wind carried sparks out of bounds. Explosions burst out when the fire reached stores of kerosene or thousands of firecrackers in the shops. The National Guard and American soldiers raced to fight the flames and to channel the refugees streaming away from their blazing tenements, and miraculously, no lives were lost. Fire Engine No. 1 was a mass of twisted metal. Before night, thirty-eight acres of houses, from Kukui Street to the waterfront, and from Nuuanu to River Street, had been burnt to ashes and more than four thousand residents were homeless.

Even this fiery purge did not wipe out the plague, and not until April 30 was the quarantine lifted from the crowded port. Out of eighty persons stricken, seventy had died. The loss by fire and disruption of business was tremendous, and more than half a million dollars was spent by the government to fight the disease. One good effect was to call public attention to the need for sanitation and decent living conditions for all the people of the community.

Hawaii became an incorporated territory of the United States on June 14, 1900, when Sanford B. Dole was appointed its first governor and the Organic Act went into effect. This was the Congressional act signed by President McKinley on April 30, which set up the territorial government under which Hawaii has operated for more than half a century. Its structure resembles that of many state governments, but there are several important differences. To begin with, the Congress, having created the territorial government, can also abolish it and substitute some other form, such as commission rule or even a military administration. Congress also has the right to amend or invalidate any territorial law, although it has never exercised this right.

Under the Organic Act, the principal executive officers of the Territory of Hawaii, the governor and the secretary, were appointed by the President, who also named judges of all courts of record (territorial supreme court and circuit courts, and a Federal district court). Heads of various territorial departments were appointed by the governor. District magistrates were appointed by the chief justice of the supreme court of Hawaii. The legislature consisted of two houses — senate, fifteen members, and house of representatives, thirty. Subject to Congressional approval, it could pass laws on substantially the same subjects as do state legislatures. One delegate to Congress, elected by the people, was a member of the United States House of Representatives who could introduce bills but who could not vote on any bill.

All persons who had been citizens of Hawaii at the time of annexation were, under the Organic Act, made citizens of the United States. Thus the ordinary people in the islands were granted more political power than they had ever before enjoyed. For more than twenty years the Hawaiians and part-Hawaiians formed an absolute majority of the electorate, and for another decade they outnumbered any other racial group of voters. Thus, those of Hawaiian blood for many years dictated the choice of men who sat in the territorial legislature.

At first, the strong brew of democracy went to the heads of the solons who met in the remodeled Iolani Palace. Although Republican and Democratic party organizations had been formed previous to the first election under the Organic Act, a Home Rule Party also ran, under the slogan of "Hawaii for the Hawaiians." Candidate for delegate to Congress under the Home Rulers was the untiring revolutionary Robert W. Wilcox. He was elected, and the same party also won a strong majority in each house of the legislature. Filibustering was common, and this first session was one long and irritable debate on trivialities. It came to be labeled the "Lady Dog

Legislature," because for the first twenty-four days it discussed a bill to reduce the tax on canine females.

Experience, however, soon revealed the folly of blind prejudice and trust in reckless leadership. "Now the meetings are usually quiet and orderly," wrote a young lady visitor to the legislature in 1901, "and never at any time degenerate to the level of the fist fights, and flinging ink bottles at each other, which I have seen with my own eyes at the Capitol in Washington." When Wilcox sought re-election in 1902 he was defeated by the Republican candidate, Jonah Kuhio Kalanianaole, nicknamed "Prince Cupid," who continued to serve as Hawaii's delegate in Washington until his death in 1922. The Home Rule Party declined thereafter and disappeared after the 1912 campaign. Although Dole was critical of the attitudes of the first two legislatures, only a few years later one of his successors, Walter F. Frear, wrote in complimentary terms of the efficiency and businesslike attitude of the legislators who were working with him. Many a session in Iolani Palace was severely criticized by the electorate and one or two of them might have supplied material for a dramatist in search of rich comedy. Yet the legislature's achievements during a half century compare favorably with those of most state bodies on the mainland, and their debates resulted in many statutes designed to handle a number of knotty political and social problems in America's laboratory of democracy in the Pacific.

The creation of county governments to decentralize the administration was soon demanded, especially by residents of islands other than Oahu. One such bill was passed as early as 1901, but was killed by veto, and other acts were passed in 1903 and 1905. This last one was declared constitutional and, in July of that year, five county governments were set up. A law was enacted in 1907 creating a municipal administration for the "City and County of Honolulu," which included the entire island of Oahu, and this replaced the Oahu County government at the opening of 1909. The clear division of functions and financial responsibilities between the territorial and county frameworks was never made, however, and controversies continued as twentieth-century needs of government expanded. Irritation was aroused especially when the legislature passed laws mandating the counties to make payments or perform acts which the localities did not wish to accept.

Financial problems arose early. Extra money was needed because the old customs revenues of the Republic were now collected by the Federal government, which did not assume all the obligations to which that source of funds had been applied. The added expense of the county governments also required the finding of new avenues of taxation. The first prominent innovation was the passing of a territorial income tax in 1901. Some of the states had experimented with such a law, but Hawaii pioneered in the successful enactment of an income tax more than a decade before the Sixteenth Amendment to the United States Constitution was passed in 1913. During the first half century of American rule, the collection and expenditure of tax monies became big business. Tax receipts in the territory in 1901 (including those of the Federal government) were $2,140,297; expenditures were $2,818,382. In 1953, tax collections reached $218,276,913; of these 62.5 per cent were Federal, 35 per cent were territorial, and 2.5 per cent were county collections. Cost payments in the same year merely for the territory and its subdivisions totalled about $135,000,000. Government is the biggest employer in Hawaii; in 1954, about 38,000 civilians worked for Federal, territorial, and county agencies — some six thousand more persons than were found on the average payrolls of the sugar and pineapple industries combined!

A Rainbow of Races

AMERICANIZATION OF HAWAII'S PEOPLE WAS THE WATCHWORD AFTER the islands were annexed to the United States. Many persons were not optimistic that this aim could be achieved, because so much of the population was made up of people from Asia, and because there was no large class of small farmers tilling their own lands. The Oriental aliens were barred by law from becoming American citizens. Their children born in the islands were citizens under the Organic Act and the United States Constitution. Could they be made Americans in spirit as well?

These critics felt that Americanization would not work on people of non-European origin. They believed that the only answer was to bring into the islands many Americans from the mainland or else people from Europe who would become naturalized. It was assumed that many of the newcomers would obtain homesteads and get to be middle-class farm owners, raising a variety of crops and livestock. Thus, immigration and homesteading were early considered to be the two chief instruments for Americanization in Hawaii.

Right after annexation, prospects in the sugar industry looked so bright that plantations expanded, and a great demand for more labor was thus created. Chinese immigration had been stopped by the annexation resolution, which also abolished the old contract-labor system. Some workers were brought in from Europe, but the broad stream still flowed from Japan. During the last two years of the century, about thirty thousand immigrants arrived from that country. Although many of the earlier entrants had returned to Japan, the census of 1900 showed that Japanese comprised almost two fifths of the entire population of 154,000 people. Hawaiians and part-Hawaiians comprised about one fourth; Chinese, about one sixth; and Portuguese, about one eighth. Fewer than half the group were citizens (62,022 by birth and 1199 by naturalization), and less than five per cent were of Anglo-Saxon blood.

Efforts to induce residents of the States to settle on the public lands of Hawaii never met with much success. More hope was held for importing workers from other countries. The legislature in 1905 set up a Board of Immigration to bring in persons "capable of becoming American citizens," and received much financial support from the sugar industry. From Portugal and Spain, between 1906 and 1913, about 13,000 people were brought in, but many of them were lured away by the attractions of California. Nor did many of the 2121 Russians brought in by the Board of Immigration remain very long in Hawaii. Several thousand Puerto Ricans were imported by the planters, but the results were not happy.

A wave of immigrants from Korea began on January 13, 1903, with the arrival of the S.S. *Gaelic* carrying 101 persons. By April, 1905, almost eight thousand had arrived. Thereafter, the emperor of Korea ordered the stoppage of emigration from his country because a project to send laborers to Mexico caused trouble. The Korean community was augmented between 1911 and 1924 by the arrival of "picture brides," who helped to even out the sexes, and to establish families whose children are active in all phases of Hawaiian community life today.

A few Filipino families were brought to Hawaii in the *Doric* in 1906, and until after World War II many workers from the Philippines were imported by the sugar planters or came individually. In all, about 125,000 of them entered as laborers, and enough have remained to fill many jobs, not only in the fields but also in service trades. Since the Philippine Republic was founded in 1946, the largest number of those applying for naturalization in Hawaii are from that country, although a number of Orientals previously barred from citizenship have seized the opportunity offered by the McCarran-Walter Act of 1952 to take out papers.

Japanese immigration continued to provide the largest share of entrants. More than 77,000 came in the first decade of the new century, and although in the same period about an equal number returned to Japan or went to the mainland, about 18,000 Japanese babies born in the islands swelled the list of residents. The inflow of male Japanese was checked by the so-called "Gentleman's Agreement" of 1907, although picture brides continued to be admitted until the Immigration Act of 1924 excluded all Orientals. The process reached its peak when in 1920 Japanese comprised 42.7 per cent of the island population. The Japanese group was large enough to maintain its own identity and was slow to assimilate. Kimono wearers could be seen on the streets until World War II. But after December 7, 1941, the vast majority of nisei threw their devoted efforts into the American fight for democracy, and since that time have been marrying outside their group almost as briskly as have other ethnic stocks. Like other immigrants, the Japanese were not always willing to remain on the plantations, but branched out into small-scale agriculture, fishing, and shopkeeping, and have won esteem as skilled machinists, carpenters, and masons. Today they are finding places in the professional and managerial positions, and more than most other groups are eager to take advantage of all the educational facilities offered under the American way.

Homesteading as a path to Americanization was tried through the years. But in Hawaii, unlike the western states of the mainland, there were no large areas of new land that could be offered for cultivation by pioneer families. The Great Mahele had granted *kuleana* tracts to the common people and had allowed other residents to buy small plots; but as time went on, most of these were absorbed into larger holdings. The trend has generally been toward large-scale agriculture, although many efforts have been made to build up a mass of small holders raising varied crops. As far back as 1884, legislator S. B. Dole had helped to enact a law "to facilitate the acquiring and settlement of homesteads." But those who were willing to patent such lands and till their own soil were few. The Organic Act tried to prohibit the leasing of public lands by corporations and to restrict leases to five years, but in 1908 Congress raised the limit to fifteen years. The temptation to sell or sublet "homesteads" to large plantations hampered the movement. A commission reported to the legislature in 1946 that "the majority of homesteaders have proved themselves to be mere speculators or investors."

Another ideal — to get Hawaiians and part-Hawaiians out of the slums and settle them on small farms — was behind the Hawaiian Homes Commission Act passed by Congress in 1921. This worthy rehabilitation project has had its ups and downs caused by divided opinions, lack of irrigation water, and the not unexpected failure of the taro-patch Hawaiian to transform himself suddenly into a replica of a Western dirt farmer. However, at the end of World War II about four thousand Hawaiians lived in homestead communities.

Neither immigration nor homesteading, the record shows, has done much to effect the Americanization of the islands. Yet all the sociologists and Congressional investigators of recent years seem to agree that in all important aspects, Hawaii is a truly American community. The history of the territory in the twentieth century, including two world wars, has demonstrated that Orientals as well as Europeans can learn to be effective and loyal citizens of the United States of America.

Trite but true it is that Hawaii has become a Pacific melting pot, in which folk of a dozen national origins have become intermingled in a new amalgam. Here can be found an attitude of race tolerance unequaled anywhere else in the world. This spirit of "racial *aloha*" has been nurtured by the community, where to reveal prejudice is to commit political suicide. "Jim Crow" attitudes are treated with pity or disdain.

The ethnic salvation of Hawaii has been the fact that there can be no single and simple line of racial discrimination. Leading citizens today may carry as many as four or five blood strains. Miss Hawaii of 1953 was lovely Dorothy Leilani Ellis, of English-Chinese-Japanese-German-Hawaiian-Irish-Scottish ancestry. The attempt to keep records of national groups in the population is rapidly running into higher mathematics, as the various combinations of seven main stocks are multiplied over several generations. The usual scheme of classifying a child by the race of his father is unrealistic. A girl born of a Chinese father and a Filipina mother, for example, would be put down as Chinese; but if she should marry a person of Japanese ancestry when she grew up, her children would be listed as Japanese.

The hues of Hawaii's racial rainbow are becoming more and

more intermingled each year, and since World War II — which hastened the process amazingly — the proportion of inter-race marriage has run about forty per cent. The sociologists foresee, as a result, that although the Hawaiian and part-Hawaiian segment is still expanding faster than any other group, and the Oriental proportion has steadily declined since 1920, a truly polyracial population is in the making. Japanese, Caucasian, Filipino, Chinese, Korean — all are still prominent stocks in the community. But as all these people continue merrily to intermarry, there will emerge a growing "cosmopolitan" type welded of manifold blood combinations.

The immigrants of yesteryear, eager to take advantage of the opportunites offered by the American standard, have bettered themselves; and their children and grandchildren are as thoroughly American — as capable, as well educated, as patriotic, and as law-abiding — as are the descendants of European immigrants on the mainland United States. Among them the American pattern predominates in politics, religion, business and industry, and social life. The "neo-Hawaiians" of today — alert, healthy, and smiling — are an outstanding proof of the power of American ideals to build citizens even on islands far from the continental coast.

Cosmopolitan Campuses

HAWAII WAS VISITED BY AMERICANS EVEN BEFORE THE UNITED States had won its freedom. Since that time, the island people have become progressively more American in their aspirations. President Lincoln wrote of the Hawaiian Kingdom in 1864: "Its people are free, and its laws, language and religion are largely the fruit of our own teaching and example." Many agencies have been at work to instill Americanism in these islands: schools, churches, libraries, Young Men's and Young Women's Christian Associations (the first Y.M.C.A. building in Honolulu was dedicated in 1883), Boy Scouts and Girl Scouts, clubs and social organizations of many kinds. Athletic sports and contests have helped; on Hawaiian teams, young people of polyracial origins learn to work together and to respect each other's individual worth and sportsmanship.

By far the most important influence has been education. "Illiteracy in the islands among native-born citizens," concluded the 1946 Congressional subcommittee, "is almost non-existent. Hawaii has well-equipped schools throughout the territory. . . . The standards of instruction, according to the United States Chamber of Commerce, are the same as on the mainland and higher than those in many states." A fifth of Hawaii's tax dollar is spent on public education.

A decade before annexation, a steady advance was begun toward achieving the American ideal of universal, compulsory, nonsectarian, and tax-supported education. All English-language government schools were by 1888 free to students without tuition payments. In the same year, teacher-training classes were begun and teachers' conventions were revived. American textbooks had been used in public schools for some years, and already about forty per cent of the teachers were Americans. Under the Republic, education was restored to its early important place under a separate Department of Public Instruction, and English was made the required classroom language. The Honolulu Normal and Training School was set up in 1896 for the production of skilled teachers. The kindergarten movement in the islands was also born in these years. Secondary education was begun with the founding of Honolulu High School (now McKinley High School) in 1895.

The public schools had achieved such a high standard by 1900 that the framers of the Organic Act provided that the existing system should remain in force under the American flag. During the period of territorial rule, school enrollment expanded many-fold and the needs of personnel, buildings, and finances have at times been acute; but wise legislators, administrators, and parents have steadily worked to keep Hawaii's schools up to date. Adult education under the State Board of Education is brought to thousands through evening classes in various localities.

Private schools have continued their illustrious history in the islands, and about a hundred and fifty of them are found there, ranging over all grades from preschool through high school. Punahou School has now been turning out pupils for more than a century. Two institutions begun by the Anglican Church under the monarchy are still in operation: Iolani School for boys and St. Andrew's Priory for girls. An extensive Catholic system has grown up since the days when Ahuimanu School was started on Oahu in 1846 to fulfill a promise extracted by Captain Mallet from Kamehameha III. Its functions as a boys' academy were taken over by St. Louis College, organized in 1880; a girls' school, Sacred Hearts Academy, opened in September, 1909. Other parochial schools are found on Oahu and other islands. The heavily endowed Kamehameha Schools, nonsectarian and founded under the will of Bernice Pauahi Bishop to educate young people of Hawaiian ancestry, opened the boys' division in 1887 and the girls' division in 1894, placing stress on vocational studies. Under careful trusteeship, the original bequest of the heiress of the Kamehameha family lands has grown to a present worth of about $15,000,000. A noted private high school for boys and girls is Mid-Pacific Institute, the successor of several Protestant schools which merged early in the twentieth century. The chief predecessor of Mid-Pacific was Mills School, which dated back to 1892, when Mr. and Mrs. Francis Damon, former missionaries to China, began giving lessons in their Honolulu home to Chinese boys from rural districts of Hawaii.

Higher education is offered by the University of Hawaii, the only state university in the Pacific Ocean area. It was organized in 1907 as the College of Agriculture and Mechanic Arts, and opened in the fall of 1908 with five students and a faculty of twelve. The name was changed in 1911 to the College of Hawaii, and the following year it moved to its present site at the mouth of Manoa Valley, three miles from the center of Honolulu and two miles from Waikiki Beach. The name was finally fixed as University of Hawaii in 1920. It is open to all qualified persons regardless of sex, racial ancestry, or nationality, and its courses, which include those for Master of Arts and Doctor of Philosophy, are accredited by the Western College Association.

For the past few summers, about a thousand students from mainland colleges have flown to Honolulu to obtain credits and enjoy Hawaii as registrants in the university's summer session. Student life on the "Rainbow Campus" differs little from that of college folk anywhere. The university has an energetic all-year athletic program and its teams compete in football, track, and water sports with various colleges in the States. About a fourth of the regular student body of five thousand is of Caucasian ancestry, but it reflects the island citizenry by including such stocks as Japanese, Chinese, Hawaiian, Korean, Filipino, Chamorro, Puerto Rican, Samoan, and various intermixtures thereof. Students are proud of their origins, and on festival days present colorful pageants and dances reminiscent of customs found in many parts of the Pacific and its borders. Yet their real loyalty was expressed by a college lad from the States who was showing a friend the gaily costumed line of campus beauties who were competing for titles as queens of various racial groups. "Sure, they look different," he said, "but they're all American as hell."

Treasure from
Soil and Sea

"THEY DON'T KNOW WHAT THEY'VE GOT!" JACK LONDON SAID OF THE American public when, arriving at Pearl Harbor on the first leg of his yachting trip in the Pacific in 1907 in the 43-foot ketch *Snark*, he and his wife Charmian began a four-month tour of the Territory of Hawaii.

Previously, this ex-hobo, war correspondent, Klondiker, socialist, and prolific author had thrice glimpsed the islands; but now he had time to ransack the beauties of the region and try to open the eyes of mainlanders to the charms of their Pacific possession. He reveled in the company of people of high and low degree. He learned to bestride a surfboard at Waikiki, and rode with Louis von Tempsky on a Maui ranch. He was amazed that so few Americans came to view such a world wonder as that titanic crater, the House of the Sun. And before he sailed off for the South Pacific he concluded: "The

Hawaiian people are poor boosters . . . when it comes to describing what Hawaii so beautifully and charmingly is."

When London returned twice in wartime 1915, to spend most of that year in the isles he loved, he added: "Because they have no other place to go, they are just beginning to realize what they've got." American readers were to learn, through his stories and articles, the thrills of Hawaiian life. He helped a globetrotting newspaper man, Alexander Hume Ford, to revive and popularize the royal sport of surfriding — an activity that led to the founding of the Outrigger Canoe Club at the spot at Waikiki where the Londons had camped in a tent in 1907. He also aided Ford in founding the Pan-Pacific Union, which had its first international conference on Balboa Day, September 25, 1916, an organization designed to spread a "hands-around-the-Pacific" attitude of friendliness and co-operation.

The people of Hawaii responded to London's outspoken feeling of *aloha*. Some of them thought that he made too much melodrama of the leper motif, even though he tried to give a factual picture of the Kalaupapa settlement and stated that "the horrors of Molokai, as they have been painted in the past, do not exist." But before his death the following year, "Keaka Lakana" had well earned the proud title of *kamaaina* (old-timer); and on his desk was found an unfinished novel about race relations in Hawaii. By then, people both in the islands and on the mainland were beginning to realize what they had in Hawaii. The lure of its scenery was pointed out on a national scale, and tourism was starting to supplement the income from sugar and pineapples. Hawaii National Park, volcanic home of the rare silversword plant, was created in 1916; its total area of 270 square miles spreads on two islands, Hawaii and Maui. Nowadays, the tourist trade is Hawaii's "third industry," worth more than $800,000,000 to the economy.

Raising Cane Is Big Business

THE FIRST TWO INDUSTRIES, OF COURSE, ARE SUGAR AND PINEAPPLES. These two products account for the lion's share of Hawaii's market dollar.

"Grow diversified crops!" was the cry raised in 1898 and many times thereafter, when it seemed that the territory was dangerously staking its future on a very few staple products. But to base island agriculture on a variety of crops was more easily said than done. For one thing, cultivable land amounts only to seven per cent of Hawaii's total area. On this land it was found impossible to grow both "money crops" and crops to furnish all the food needs of the people. If the land is used for concentrated production of sugar cane and pineapples, then Mr. and Mrs. Hawaii have money to buy imported supplies from other regions, where such foods can be raised more cheaply. True, livestock and diversified crops worth $35,000,000 annually in the wholesale market are produced these days. But no staple for outside consumption has been discovered that can rival coffee, pineapples, and sugar.

After the McKinley Tariff took away protection of Hawaiian products, a flurry of experimentation began. Tea planting, from seed brought from Ceylon, was tried at Kona in 1892. A company for growing sisal from "century plants" was started in 1893, but labor costs of making cordage were found to be too high to rival those of Yucatán. Rubber trees were introduced in the twentieth century, and the raising of cotton and rice was revived — but labor costs were still prohibitive. A good quality of tobacco was developed, but growers did not have enough capital to survive the depression of the 1930's. Recently, export of toothsome macadamia nuts and fresh papayas, as well as splashy orchids and other flowers, has brought in a good income. The most recent authority, Perry F. Philipp, concludes: "There probably exists now a wider range of cultivated crops in Hawaii than in any other place of comparable size." But diversified agriculture on the mainland pattern has not worked out.

Sugar and pineapple, then, are the main crops by which Hawaiian sunshine is transmuted into payroll dollars. The two go well together; for just as swampy taro land was not suitable for sugar cane, which brought into cultivation forest, pasture, and arid soil good only under irrigation, so it was found that pineapples did not compete with cane areas but grew best on high, cool plateaus where heavy rainfall was not needed.

Raising sugar and pineapples cannot be called "farming" in the mainland sense, for both demand widespread operations under complex setups utilizing all the latest discoveries of science and engineering. Only about a tenth of the cane crop, for instance, is grown by small landholders, and most of them send their harvest to big mills for grinding. Improvements in milling technology have had to be made, to attain maximum extraction and to handle the vast tonnages grown (to get a ton of sugar, seven to twelve tons of cane must be run through the mill). Since it takes two years to grow a sugar crop, much capital is needed. Large investments in heavy equipment for planting, cultivating, harvesting, and transporting the product are demanded. In the face of rising costs, the island plantations of the twentieth century could never have survived had they not been truly "factories in the fields" run by managements that have used every bit of the magic of modern technology and integration.

Research has been the salvation of the sugar industry. The Hawaiian Sugar Planters' Association, organized in 1895, soon started an experiment station to handle such problems. The H.S. P.A. now spends $1,750,000 a year on research, which brings back many times that amount in benefits through discoveries and improved efficiency. Breeding of high-yield varieties has shown fine results. As much as a hundred tons of cane can be grown on one acre, with an average above eighty; raw sugar per acre averages more than ten tons, with records close to eighteen tons.

The research program has also shown spectacular results in soil chemistry, fertilizer use, land and water conservation, and weed control. The battle to protect the juicy green leaves of the cane from insect foes has been waged for generations. One defense was to develop pest-resistant varieties, but the most dramatic gains have been made by importing parasites to prey upon the invaders. A tiny "leaf hopper," probably from Australia, sneaked into the fields around 1900, and within four years had chewed up three million dollars' worth of cane. Could a creature be found that was a natural enemy of the hopper? After intensive search, two scientists brought back from Queensland a parasite that laid its eggs in the insect's body. Other enemies — such as *Cyrtorhinus*, brought in about 1920 — helped to check the ravages of the hopper, but it was never completely wiped out. A similar method of fighting bugs with bugs was used against the pestiferous cane borer, which lays eggs in the growing stems, on which the grubs later gorge themselves. After scientists spent years searching in the Orient and East Indies, a borer-eating tachinid fly was found which was imported alive to Honolulu and used ultimately to reduce the borer depredations by about ninety per cent. Similarly, the *Scolia* wasp of the Philippines was brought in to control the *Anomala* beetle, whose offspring grow fat chewing the root systems of the cane stalk. Importation of new insects into Hawaii is, of course, carefully guarded; to know the bad effects when one mean breed gets loose, one has only to recall the ruin of many island food crops when the Oriental fruit fly dodged quarantine a few years ago.

To keep down insects, a large toad that relishes even scorpions and centipedes was imported from Puerto Rico in 1932. The offspring of the first hundred specimens of *Bufo marinus* have been settled in all island localities, and their giant appetites have done much to cut down the insect population. Not so successful was the importation of the mongoose in 1883 from the East Indies, by way of Jamaica, West Indies, to tackle the rats infesting the cane fields. Descendants of the first thirty-six pairs spread over the islands, but the mongoose showed little interest in eliminating rats and became more than a nuisance on its own account.

Raising sugar cane has been the main industry of Hawaii for more than a century. When the output hit 150,000 tons in 1895, one planter remarked that this was undoubtedly the maximum that the islands could ever achieve. Ten years later, the tally was 426,000 tons; in 1915 it was 600,000; and in 1932 the first of the million-ton crops was harvested. The early boom days came between 1895 and 1905, when much new acreage was put into cane. No less than fifty-six plantations were found on the seven islands in those years — twice as many as nowadays, when most acreages have been absorbed into large corporative operations. After the war with Spain ended, Hawaii had to meet the competition of sugar growers in other new possessions such as Puerto Rico and the Philippines; moreover, Cuba was given tariff preferences. Yet the promise of tariff protection after annexation led to enthusiastic trading on the revived Hawaiian stock exchange, where many fortunes were made and several were lost.

A syndicate of Hawaiian producers in 1904 obtained control of a sugar refinery at Crockett, California; from this beginning has grown the world's largest refinery, run by the California and Hawaiian Sugar Refining Corporation, owned by a group of Hawaiian plantations. Only one refinery is to be found in the islands. Most of the raw sugar is still shipped to the mainland, usually not in bags, but in "bulk loading" of freighter hulls.

Politics has continued to be linked with sugar. A Democratic administration entered the White House in 1913, and when in October of that year the Underwood Tariff placed sugar on the unprotected list, the wholesale price dropped to 2.28 cents a pound. The outbreak of World War I caused a jump in demand, however, and when the tariff was repealed in April, 1916, sugar was such a strategic article that the Food Administration set the base price and controlled distribution. Since the labor supply in Hawaii was reduced by needs of the armed forces, hundreds of schoolboys worked in the fields to keep sugar flowing to a wartime world. When controls were removed in 1920, the wholesale price zoomed to 23.5 cents a pound, and the final deflation did not come until 1923. The resulting reorganization to gain efficiency was beneficial, and the industry was able to face with courage the greater depression of the thirties.

The sugar growers were struck a bad blow, however, by the Jones-Costigan Act of 1934. Its intention was to forestall overproduction, but congressmen from sugar states succeeded in getting minimum quotas for mainland beet and cane output, meanwhile lumping the American territory of Hawaii along with island possessions and foreign countries as producers who might supply any leftover demand. The result of this discriminatory law was a slump and a loss of ten per cent of Hawaiian sugar acreage.

A quota was granted under the Sugar Act of 1937, which recognized Hawaii as a domestic producer, and the industry operated under this scheme throughout World War II. The unfairness of the Jones-Costigan Act had made the business leaders of Hawaii keenly aware, though, of how fully they were under the rule of Congress so long as they remained inhabitants of a mere territory, and this realization gave a big impetus to the movement for full statehood for Hawaii. The quota theory was continued in the Sugar Act of 1947, which allotted to Hawaiian growers a tonnage which is about one fourth that of all sugar grown under the Stars and Stripes, and which fills 14 per cent of America's sugar bowl.

The sugar industry is one important way in which Hawaii's people earn a share in the national economy. The marketing of its annual crop brings home about $150,000,000. Stock in the producing companies is owned by almost fourteen thousand persons. Its sixteen thousand employees in 1958 received wages of $56,000,000; they are paid the world's highest year-round agricultural wages, averaging about $13 for an eight-hour day. Improvement in efficiency and in machine use enables the sugar industry to turn out the same tonnage today as it did a decade ago, with sixty per cent as many workers. The backbreaking labor of the early days is quickly being replaced by machine methods. Nobody is sorry.

Pineapples by the Million

THE FLAVORSOME PINEAPPLE HAS WON ITS TITLE AS THE BASIS OF Hawaii's second industry. This development came largely since annexation; in that time the value of the annual "pine" crop has risen from almost zero to more than a hundred million dollars.

Nobody knows who brought the first pineapple to Hawaii. Marín the Spaniard experimented with this fruit in 1813, and it was sold to ships in the whaling era. During the Gold Rush a small, sour variety grew wild at Kona; these were picked while still unripe and sent to Honolulu, to be transshipped to California. They usually spoiled in transit, and Captain John Kidwell, a settler from Devonshire, planted a few acres of slips on Oahu to help shorten the journey. Seeking a fruit larger, juicier, and sweeter than that of Kona, Kidwell chose the Smooth Cayenne variety that grew in Jamaica, and around 1884 imported a thousand slips of this type, which is the grandfather of the staple cannery variety of today. Small plantations were set out in Manoa Valley and in the Pearl Harbor region; but the new variety spoiled even more quickly than the old. Canning seemed to be the answer and was tried by Kidwell in 1892, but too many technical difficulties soon brought discouragement. An initial export shipment in 1895 of 466 cases of two dozen each, produced by the Hawiian Fruit Packing Company, was the beginning of the industry that now packs each year no less than half a billion cans of pineapple products. Yes, half a billion.

Annexation brought removal of customs duties on fruit and gave an impetus to growers. The industry of today dates from 1900, when a band of farmers from southern California homesteaded around Wahiawa, Oahu, and began raising several kinds of crops, including pineapples. The problem of cutting down on hand labor was solved by planting the prickly rows of pines with seven-foot lanes between them, so that horse-drawn implements could be used for cultivation. An abandoned cannery was hauled from Pearl Harbor and set up at Wahiawa, scene of new attempts to preserve the fruit.

A leader in the adolescent industry was James D. Dole, a distant relative of the Republic's president who had come from Boston in 1899. He realized that its future lay in developing an export trade in canned pineapple of high quality. Dole secured some capital and on December 4, 1901, organized the Hawaiian Pineapple Company, whose first crop was packed in 1903. Methods were improved, so that cans no longer exploded on the wharves, aboard ship, and even on grocery shelves. In the Iwilei district of Honolulu the company set up in 1906 a plant which is now the largest fruit cannery in the world. Topped by a water tank in the form of a giant pineapple, the factory is a favorite touring spot for thousands of visitors to Oahu.

Pineapple fields began to spread on the uplands of most of the islands, and production boomed. The first million-case pack was attained in 1912. Ten years later, the Hawaiian Pineapple Company bought nearly all the land on the island of Lanai, the former Gibson stronghold, and developed a harbor, a city for workers, and a vast plantation whose crop was hauled by barges to Honolulu. By that time, pineapples had become a large corporative industry similar to that of sugar; indeed, the pine growers were able to learn much by studying the history of sugar in the islands. Co-operation was demonstrated to be even more necessary than in sugar, for the main problem came to be one of sales rather than production. The pineapple growers doubled their pack during each of the two years 1906-1908, for example, and in the following February found themselves with about three fourths of the previous year's product still unsold. Advertising was the answer, and the Hawaiian Pineapple Growers Association, founded in 1908, began a successful campaign to popularize what had too often been considered a luxury fruit.

Similar drives, financed by the growers, have brought Hawaiian pineapple to every table in America. The islands have always been able to turn out more canned pineapple than the market can normally buy, and although recipes for new uses are continually invented, expansion is limited by prices of competitive canned fruits such as peaches, and canned and frozen juices of several sorts.

Scientific study of pineapple problems was begun in 1914 when the H.S.P.A. staff did contract research on various insect pests. The future of the industry was threatened in 1920 by the wilt disease, and a world-wide search was begun for parasites that might control the mealy bug that, it was discovered, caused this plant plague. (An emulsified oil spray, as it turned out, was the answer to the wilt problem.) A plot was leased at Wahiawa in 1922 for trial plantings, and from 1924 to 1926 an experiment station, forerunner of the thriving Pineapple Research Institute of today, was organized with headquarters at the University of Hawaii. The P.R.I., which grew out of a producers' co-operative association formed in 1932, spends a million dollars on research annually.

Benefits derived from modern technology have been almost as spectacular in pineapple as in sugar. Almost all the special-handling equipment used in growing, harvesting, and packing pineapples has been invented in Hawaii. The ingenious "Ginaca machine" was devised in 1913; at one-hundred-a-minute speed it cuts off the shell and removes the core at one swoop, leaving a smooth cylinder of yellow fruit ready for slicing and canning. In the field, an iron-sulphate spray first demonstrated in 1916 supplies iron to plants grown where this element is not provided by the soil in usable form. Tarred mulching paper was an idea borrowed in 1924 from the sugar growers; young plants are started in holes made in yard-wide paper carpets whose use controls weeds, holds soil moisture, and retains warmth. Hormone sprays were developed to hasten or retard ripening; but three fourths of the crop still has to be harvested in July, August, and September. Most operations have now been mechanized; even the harvesting is done with an immense machine which passes down the rows and fills its giant bins with fruit that is cut, trimmed, and tossed on a conveyor belt by walking men armed with large knives. Often the work goes on at night, and presents a startling picture when several of these monster machines, decked with blazing lights, crawl over the starlit hills, gathering pineapples for the dinner tables of the world.

The islands have about 73,000 acres covered with pineapple fields, whose terraced rows of spiky, steel-gray clumps are over-burdened at harvest time with green-and-gold spheres of ripe fruit. Two crops are obtained in four years, and despite competition from other tropical regions, Hawaii supplies more than half of the global consumption of pineapple products. Between three and four hundred million pines are picked annually. Eight companies operate a total of fourteen plantations, and nine canneries process the fruit. In a recent year these turned out eighteen million cases of canned fruit and more than fourteen million cases of canned juice. Many tons of fresh pineapples are shipped to the mainland, along with fresh-frozen chunks and frozen juice concentrate. Nothing is wasted, not even the shell, which is made into cattle fodder; other by-products include citric acid, alcohol, and natural sugar reclaimed by a new ion-exchange process. Even the plant stems are used to make commercial enzymes. Agricultural employment runs to 4000 year-round and 1500 seasonal workers; manufacturing operations call for about 5000, and during the busy season another 10,000 are hired, including housewives and young people on vacation from high school or college. Wages run between $1.16 and $2.01 an hour, with an average of $1.39.

If cane is king in Hawaii, pineapple is surely queen. Together these industries overshadow all other businesses, many of which depend heavily upon their operations or upon the dollars they bring into the islands from the world's marketplaces. Banks, agencies, trust companies, brokers, and other financial organizations key their dealings to sugar and pineapple prices. Shipping lines, air lines, and telephone and radio communications have been fostered by these industries. Skilled in constructing sugar machinery, the Honolulu Iron Works has grown to impressive size and has installed sugar mills from the Philippines to Cuba. A commercial-fertilizer factory and a can factory have been built to serve the needs of the staple exports. A large part of the tax incomes of both the territorial and Federal governments in the islands comes from sugar and pine growers and their employees. Any marked disturbance of these basic industries would be heavily felt not only among the people of Hawaii but among those of the continental United States.

The omnipresence of sugar and pineapples is visible to anyone riding over the roads of Hawaii. The income from their production is the lifeblood that courses through the arteries and veins of the community's economy.

Fishermen in Blue Sampans

THE FISHING INDUSTRY OF HAWAII, ON THE OTHER HAND, IS PARA-doxically small. The value of the commercial catch annually is only about four million dollars. A large portion is one or another kind of tuna, canned at a modern plant at Kewalo Basin in Honolulu. All year long, the islands are surrounded by schools of food fishes of many varieties, but the small size of the Hawaiian fishing boats, and the lack of navigational experience of their operators, usually limit them to a cruising radius of three hundred miles. The boats do not go out unless prices are high, and locally caught fish often costs more per pound in the market than mainland beefsteak. Long-term research by Pacific Ocean Fishery Investigations, financed by the Federal government, is designed to help the fishermen of the Central Pacific to reap greater catches from the well-stocked ocean around them.

Fish was a main part of the Hawaiian diet in olden times, and about six hundred kinds of food fishes are found in island waters.

Nearly all of these were caught by the natives with methods devised by them; most of the ancient methods are still used, and although modern skill has invented new means of luring the finny tribe, even commercial fishermen have learned much from studying the age-old skills of Hawaii Nei.

The fishermen of today cruise in "sampans," which may be seen any time at Kewalo Basin. These craft are built locally and are usually painted light blue. They have high prows, low sterns, and a shallow draft to enable them to skim over reefs; they are powered with diesel engines and carry modern refrigeration machinery.

Two kinds of sampan are operated. The larger ones, carrying a ten-man crew, are designed to take "aku" (skipjack or ocean bonito), a light-meated tuna. Schools of these fish — each one averaging about ten pounds, although some run as high as forty — are plentiful in Hawaiian waters during the spring and summer months. The method used to take them is similar to that used by the natives observed by Captain Vancouver in 1793. The aku cannot be netted; each must be hooked individually. When a school offshore is sighted by watching the cloud of screaming sea birds that prey upon it, the sampan cuts across the head of the school and slows down, and live bait in the form of fingerlings called *nehu* is tossed overboard. Then all the crew, including the cook and engineer, stand on the flat, round stern and begin fishing like mad.

They use stiff, ten-foot bamboo poles, and lines on which are small, feathered, barbless hooks. At first the voracious aku snap at the unbaited hook, for they will strike at anything on the surface, particularly when a stream of water is sprinkled on the lure from pipes on the sides of the sampan. Boating a slippery aku is a fine art. It comes sailing through the air on the unbarbed hook and is hugged by the pole-wielder's left arm; then the hook is flipped from the fish's mouth back into the water, and the fish is dropped on the deck. When the frenzy dies down, live bait must be used on the hook, and the catch must be brought to gaff, so that the rate is slowed. But when the aku are first biting, one man can haul ten or fifteen aboard in one minute, and a boat might take ten tons of aku within an hour.

Smaller sampans, usually called "ahi" boats, may range for a thousand miles and stay out for days at a time. They operate flag lines as much as a mile long, to which are attached pendants dropping to depths of a hundred fathoms. Hooks are baited with frozen fish, or else the crew use aku to catch mackerel, which in turn become bait for the ahi (the prized yellowfin tuna or albacore). These vessels catch larger fish than the aku boats, but not so many of them; they bring in not only ahi but most of the marlin, swordfish, *ono* (whose name means "delicious"), dolphin or *mahimahi*, ulua, and other food fish found in local markets.

The Paradise of the Pacific is a paradise for the sport fisherman. For the benefit of the fresh-water Walton, trout are stocked in high streams on Kauai and Hawaii, and bass and bluegill in reservoirs on Oahu. But salt-water angling, for which no license is required, flourishes the year round. Cumbersome boots and other clothing are not needed, for one can fish in swimming togs from a sandy beach or off the rocks, or else from a boat supplied with all the gear necessary to take a record-size marlin under the rules of the International Game Fish Association.

Every fisherman has his own favorite methods and types of equipment; but one can have many hours of fun just dropping a hand line from a boat or wharf, or using a bamboo rod for still-fishing, whipping the surface, or casting. Mullet are found close to shore in calm waters, and along the edges of harbors and inlets people may be seen sitting for hours on individual stilt-seats built over the water, patiently angling for this elusive fish. Hooking a mullet is a tricky sport that requires skill and experience; some experts use a jig-line with a spring of piano wire and a tiny hook. Inshore fish of many varieties may also be speared, or taken by nets. The picturesque circular throw-net, weighted around the edge and cast from shore over a school of fish descried in the water, is usually considered typical of Hawaii, but it was introduced into the islands from Japan as late as 1890.

The sandy beaches of the islands, on most days of the year, are dotted with fishermen casting with jointed rods equipped with reels, hoping to hook a hundred-pound ulua (jack crevally) or a sixteen-pound *oio* (bonefish). Most popular for casting and bottom fishing is the incurved *oio* hook, evolved from an ancient Polynesian design, which does not snag on coral; it has been modified by the addition of a ball eye and a barb.

Spear-fishing, a livelihood for the ancient Hawaiians, is an underwater sport that has been revived and has attracted many fans in the past few years. The "skin diver" needs only rubber swim fins, tight-fitting goggles or face mask, cotton gloves, a spear, and a companion near by in case of need. Barbed metal rods with one or more points are used for throwing into a school of fish or for underwater action. Two kinds of "spear guns" are favored in the islands. One of these is fired by pulling the spear straight back on a heavy rubber band attached to a short length of bamboo which encircles the shaft. The other is also powered by a strip of rubber, but the spear is fired from a metal socket attached to a wider metal tube from which projects a trigger. The lucky spearman threads his catch by a wire needle to a fifteen-foot line hooked to his waist, with the other end tied to a wooden float, a glass ball, or a dry coconut. Some hardy underwater fishermen stow their catch inside their swim trunks, but now and then a shark, trying to snatch a bite, may startle the swimmer with his pants thus laden.

Spear-fishing at greater depths is possible with the Aqua-Lung. To the wearer's back is strapped a cylinder of compressed air which is fed to the diver through flexible tubing at automatically regulated pressures. The expert "frogman" can descend a hundred feet and stay down for half an hour in this way, and thus harvest huge catches of fish, eels, lobsters, crabs, sea urchins, giant turtles, and octopus.

Trolling near shore from a skiff powered with an outboard motor is another popular thrill. Either hand lines or else rods with reels are used, baited with spoon, plug, feather lure, or live fish. Deep-water trolling under charter-boat skippers is a regal sport at which amateurs often have a chance to set records. The best hunting grounds are the Waianae coast off Oahu, the Kaiwi Channel, the Hana coast of Maui, and the famed Kona coast of Hawaii. In these waters a hooked fish is seldom attacked by sharks, and the sportsman thus has a good chance to boat it, no matter how long he takes to bring it to gaff.

Speaking of sharks, specimens from eight families of them are known to cruise in Hawaiian waters, but a person can swim there for ten years without spotting a single dorsal fin cutting the waves around him. The strange-looking hammerhead shark has a bad reputation, but feeds mainly on the sea bottom. More to be dreaded are the tiger shark, the blue shark, and the fearsome great white shark of Hawaiian legends, which may reach a length of forty feet. Aside from commercial boats hunting sharks for flesh and liver, those who know sharks best are the spear-fishermen. They recommend that, if a cruiser of the depths really wants a fish you have, it is wise to give it to him. Don't swim into a cave in the coral when one is about — he may see your waving legs and mistake them for something edible. In self-defense, the diver may jab the shark on the snout with a spear, or fire at his gill openings — the rest of his body is armored in a horny hide that can sandpaper one's own skin.

So few people have been pestered by sharks that the head of the Fish and Game Division once stated: "Being bitten by a shark in Hawaiian waters is akin to being struck by lightning" — and lightning flashes very seldom in the skies over the islands. No clear case of an attack on a living man was recorded in late years until December, 1952, when Gervacio Solamo, captain of the sampan *Rainbow*, was setting nets in the water around his vessel a mile off the Waianae shore of Oahu. A twenty-foot shark, attracted by the live bait scattered around the nets, in a feeding frenzy took off the left arm of the victim, who died soon of shock and loss of blood. A fortnight later, several giant sharks became entangled in nets in shallow water off the Honolulu Airport, and one of them, a thousand-pound sand shark, was captured and sold to make fish cakes, an Oriental delicacy. On the fourth of July, 1953, another fisherman, who fell off his sampan near Niihau, was bitten in the calf of his leg but was rescued before the shark could do greater damage. And late in the summer of that year, a fifteen-year-old lad who was spear-fishing near the spot where Solamo died was attacked and fatally bitten in the thigh.

More than sharks, some swimmers dread the barracuda; these fast, sharp-toothed fish grow sometimes to a length of five feet and can give a nasty bite. And even veteran divers shudder at the thought of what might be done to an unprotected limb by a painted moray eel, or worse, a six-foot white eel with teeth as long as a man's thumb. Also to be feared is the sting ray, a round fish with a long, whiplike tail armed with a saw-edged spike which is able to inflict a painful wound. On Christmas Eve, 1951, a giant "stingaree" invaded Kuhio Beach at Waikiki and after an hour was herded into shallow water and killed by lifeguards with spears. It was found to be eight feet long and five feet wide, and it weighed about three hundred pounds.

Whales may still be descried, in season, sporting and spouting off Diamond Head. An incident recalling the fate of the celebrated ship *Essex* took place at two in the morning of February 4, 1936, when the Dollar Line steamer *President Pierce* collided with something in the dark. Its progress was strangely slowed, and at dawn off Waikiki, officers saw a forty-foot sperm whale lodged on the liner's bow. When engines were reversed, the body sank at once, flooding the waves with oil and filling the air with a pungent odor reminiscent of try-pot days on the decks of the whale ships of olden times.

The Territory and the Nation

THE PEOPLE OF HAWAII BEGAN IN 1900 TO WORK FOR AN HONORED place in the life of the nation. Much progress was achieved by the territory during its first half-century as an integral part of the United States. Population trebled under American rule. The people earned a niche in the national economy; the latest per capita figure for personal income in the islands is $1740, which is higher than that for any of thirty states. The island folk became eager customers for mainland goods; they spent $800,000,000 for these goods in 1958. Hawaii was converted into the westernmost fortress of American military might. Sea transport between Hawaii and the rest of the world was improved by the founding of new shipping lines. The air age arrived in the Pacific skies. And the Hawaiian people fought for America in two world wars. They had been sheltered under the Stars and Stripes; and in return they gave generously of the things they had, strove to earn a proud position in the national scene, and began to work toward the acceptance of Hawaii by the Union as its Fiftieth State.

Building the Bastion

A SNAPSHOT TAKEN ALMOST ANYWHERE IN HAWAII AFTER 1900 would probably have included the figure of at least one soldier, sailor, marine, or defense construction worker. Since that time, the islands have grown to be America's foremost military bastion in the Pacific.

President McKinley by proclamation in 1898 and 1899 had reserved several land areas on Oahu for naval and military establishments. The first garrison troops were an infantry regiment and a battalion of engineers who arrived in August, 1898, to set up a temporary post, Camp McKinley, near Diamond Head. First of the permanent posts was Fort Shafter, on the outskirts of Honolulu, which was to become the Army's headquarters in the territory. Some of its buildings were finished and occupied in 1907. Before World War I, two rings of forts were set up as harbor defenses. To the east were Fort Armstrong at the entrance to Honolulu Harbor, Fort De Russey at Waikiki, and Fort Ruger behind Diamond Head; to the west, guarding the dredged-out entrance to Pearl Harbor, were Forts Kamehameha and Weaver. In the same years, on the Leilehua plateau of central Oahu was established Schofield Barracks, first occupied in January, 1909, which finally grew to be the largest permanent Army post under the flag.

Naval development took many years of work. Although the United States had held the right since 1887 to make a fleet base in the spreading lochs of Pearl Harbor, creation of the Naval Station, Honolulu, as it was called, was not authorized by Congress until 1908. The channel was further deepened and widened, and millions of yards of mud and coral were dredged from the mooring areas inside the harbor. Then the project ran into trouble.

Construction of a gigantic drydock had been started in 1909. The Pearl Harbor waters, said the old Hawaiians, were the sacred haunts of the queen of all the sharks, but ceremonies of propitiation were forgotten by the busy naval engineers. Work went on for several years, but the shark queen was only biding her time. In February, 1913, the foundation of the $4,000,000 drydock suddenly collapsed, letting in the sea. Navy investigators, after study, reported that hydraulic pressure had caused the catastrophe, but more than one person nodded and remembered the wrath of the shark goddess.

The project, resumed with new plans, was completed in the summer of 1919, and this time the dock stood; it is famed as the only one of its kind built on a coral foundation. The naval base was, however, far from complete; during maneuvers in 1925 and 1928, only a few battleships could find berths in Pearl Harbor. Although wharves, shops, and other spreading buildings had been completed around the base, they were only the beginning of a vast development to come. Between wars, and especially after 1931, work went on to transform naval facilities in and around Pearl into a fortified haven that would easily hold the entire Pacific Fleet.

An early disaster still remembered was the loss of the submarine *F-4* on March 25, 1915. When the *F-4* left Honolulu Harbor with three other subs of its class, the hulk of the U.S.S. *Bennington,* a "hoodoo ship," was towed across her bow; and this evil omen was recalled when the *F-4* promptly sank in the fairway with the loss of all twenty-one of her crew. For months, shifting currents, choppy seas, and snapped cables defeated salvage operations, and not until August 29 was the hull finally hauled from its watery tomb, three hundred feet down.

World War I did not call for much naval action in Hawaiian waters. At the outbreak in 1914, the German cruiser *Geier* and some smaller vessels, pursued by the Japanese battleship *Hizen,* took refuge in Honolulu Harbor and remained interned there under parole. On February 4, 1916, the *Geier* and half a dozen other steamers were set on fire by their crews, but American bluejackets and marines saved the *Geier* from destruction. It was then found that every German ship in the harbor had been sabotaged by its crew, even though the United States was not yet at war with Germany.

The people of Hawaii contributed their energetic share to winning World War I. Almost a thousand men from the islands served in the Army or Navy, and a substantial number of names are found on the roster of those killed in battle or dead of wounds received in action.

As early as 1914 a War Relief Committee was named, which later merged with several similar groups to form the Hawaiian Chapter of the American Red Cross, organized after America entered the conflict. People of all races and faiths joined in war work, contributing money, preparing hospital supplies, and volunteering for service in many organizations both on the home front and in the war areas of Europe and Siberia. Everybody labored for food conservation and production; the populace joined with the rest of the nation in having meatless and wheatless days and in repeating the slogan: "Food will win the war!" Actual or threatened shortages of such staples as fish, rice, and taro did affect many people.

Large steamship lines have grown up in the twentieth century to serve the needs of Hawaii. At the beginning of the century, more than half the sugar crop was hauled around Cape Horn to refineries on the eastern seaboard of the United States. Two lines owed their origins mainly to this trade. One was Matson Navigation Company, founded in 1901 by Captain William Matson of San Francisco and associates. The other was American-Hawaiian Steamship Company, which between 1900 and 1914 constructed twenty-two steel cargo vessels suitable for freighting sugar. These all had names like *Californian*, *Nebraskan*, and *Texan*, and in the first decade of the century ran steady schedules between Honolulu and New York, by way of the Straits of Magellan. The steamers cut in half the records of the windships, and reduced average time between New York and San Francisco to sixty days. A later American-Hawaiian route transshipped cargo on a railroad across the Isthmus of Tehuantepec in Mexico, but conditions in that country after 1913 caused a return to the Cape Horn route. But the Panama Canal was a boon to Pacific shipping. The first cargo to pass through the Canal was a bargeload of Hawaiian sugar, which was ferried through on May 18, 1914, even before the route was formally opened.

Matson began catering to the passenger trade between the West Coast and Honolulu when in 1910 the little ship *Wilhelmina* began the run, foreshadowing the primacy of the big white liner *Lurline* today. Since December, 1922, many round-the-world tour ships have put in at Honolulu.

Hawaii has become a crossroads of the sky as well as of the sea. The first air flight in the islands was made by a civilian when, on the last day of 1910, Bud Mars took off from the Moanalua polo field. Early aviators such as Tom Gunn, a Chinese, barnstormed in 1913 on several of the islands, giving exhibitions. The first civilian flying school was started in Honolulu in 1921.

Military aviation began in 1917, when the Army set up a flying center at Fort Kamehameha. When the value of air warfare was demonstrated in World War I, both Army and Navy air bases were built to protect Oahu. Luke Field was put into operation by the Army on Ford Island in Pearl Harbor; later it was turned over to the Navy. Next to be founded was Wheeler Field, adjacent to Schofield Barracks; the third was Hickam Field, today the largest and most important. Navy and Marine fields were built at Kaneohe, on the northeast side of Oahu, and at Barber's Point.

The armed forces pioneered in transoceanic flying. Two Navy planes under the command of John Rodgers made in September, 1924, the longest one-day flight up to that time when they took an admiral on an inspection tour from Honolulu to Hilo and back. The following year, Rodgers headed the first flight from the West

Coast to Hawaii. Three Navy seaplanes started on August 31, 1925, but two turned back, while Rodgers and his companions in the *PN 9-1* pushed on. Naval ships were stationed a hundred miles apart along the ocean route, and all seemed well; but then the radio of the *PN 9-1* went silent, and for nine days nothing was heard from its crew. They had made 1992 miles in twenty-five hours, but had run out of gas two hundred miles short of Pearl Harbor and lacked power to operate their radio. Floating on the water for 218 hours, they drifted toward the northwest. By burning wood from the edges of the lower wings, they managed to distill fresh water to drink. Planes and surface vessels searched for days, but at last it was a submarine that spotted the seaplane off Kauai. The *PN 9-1* was towed into Nawiliwili, and thus completed the first flight from California to Hawaii.

A few months after Lindbergh flew the Atlantic, the first non-stop flight to Hawaii ended in the early morning of June 29, 1927, when Army lieutenants Lester J. Maitland and Albert F. Hegenberger, less than twenty-six hours out of Oakland, California, put down their trimotor Fokker monoplane, *Bird of Paradise*, at Wheeler Field.

The first civilian flight ended with a crash landing when, on July 15 of the same year, Ernest L. Smith and Emory B. Bronte, who had flown their Travelair monoplane for twenty-five hours, ran out of gas and plunged their craft into a clump of keawe trees on Molokai, landing unhurt.

A month later, a number of flyers taking part in "the first transoceanic flight race in history" were not so lucky. They were competing for two prizes, one of $25,000 and the other of $10,000, offered by James D. Dole, then president of the Hawaiian Pineapple Company. Out of eight planes starting at Oakland on August 16, two smashed in taking off, two were forced to turn back, and two others disappeared in the Pacific. Only two entries finished the "Dole Derby." First in this longest overwater race up to that time was the monoplane *Woolaroc*, piloted by Arthur C.

Goebel and navigated by William Davis; their time was 26 hours and 18 minutes. Second was Martin Jensen, the only Honolulan in the race, with his navigator Paul Schluter in the *Aloha;* they overshot Oahu and had to circle back, landing with only four gallons of gas in the tank. Then anxious days passed, while the people of Hawaii waited for news of two planes that had not arrived. One was the *Golden Eagle,* owned by the San Francisco publisher George Hearst, which was considered the fastest craft in the race; pilot Jack Frost and navigator Gordon Scott were never heard of again. Most tragic was the loss of the biplane *Miss Doran,* named for its 22-year-old passenger Mildred Doran, who with her crew, Augie Peddlar and Vilas R. Knope, also vanished into the blue Pacific. Three days later, William Erwin and A. H. Eichwaldt in a rescue plane told of going into a spin; then silence closed down. Altogether, the Dole Derby cost the lives of ten persons — three in preparing for the flight, five during the race, and two in search efforts.

Air-passenger service among the islands began on November 11, 1929, when Inter-Island Airways (now Hawaiian Airlines), founded by Stanley C. Kennedy, made its first commercial flight from Honolulu to Maui and the Big Island (Hilo Airport had been dedicated in February, 1928). On the next day the first flight was made to Kauai. Eight-seater Sikorsky amphibian biplanes were used, and passengers were paddled out from the dock to the plane in outrigger canoes. In those days, the names of passengers and pilots were published in the newspapers before each flight. Between runs, the seaplanes were used for sightseeing over the city. In 1934 the line was awarded an interisland airmail contract. It was the first United States airline to operate daily freight schedules. Today, Hawaiian Airlines and its lively rival, Aloha Airlines, founded in 1949, provide more than fifty interisland flights a day with clocklike regularity. Among the millions of passengers carried by both lines over the channels among the islands, not one life of passenger or crewman has been lost in an accident. Convair planes holding forty-four passengers shuttle among the sixteen airports on the main islands like buses in other regions, and taking to the air seems to come naturally to island residents.

The trans-Pacific sky trail to the Orient was blazed when on April 17, 1935, the Pan-American China Clipper flew from the West Coast to Honolulu. The first regular flights, carrying mail, began in November, and a passenger license was granted a year later. After establishing regular schedules to the Orient via Midway, Wake, and Guam, the same company, early in 1937, made the first commercial flight from Honolulu to New Zealand, via Kingman Reef and Pago Pago. Recently, use of the "jet stream" in midwinter has enabled Clippers to fly nonstop the 3800 miles between Tokyo and Honolulu in less than twelve hours. Today, Honolulu International Airport is a humming center for eight scheduled trans-Pacific airlines that connect the city with the air network of the earth. The capital of Hawaii is less than nineteen hours by air from the capital of the United States.

Air-freight lines running among the islands carry more than a thousand tons a month. They have flown stud bulls, race horses, giant marlin, fresh vegetables, and scenery for Hollywood movies made on island locations. A "seafood special" flies fresh marine delicacies to Honolulu from French Frigate Shoals, 460 ocean miles away.

The Early Struggle for Statehood

CHARLES J. MCCARTHY IN 1918 SUCCEEDED WARTIME GOVERNOR Lucius E. Pinkham, and took the lead in getting the territory back on a more normal basis. McCarthy also did something about the idea of applying for statehood.

As far back as 1903, the legislature had petitioned Congress for admission as a state, and many subsequent legislatures had made the same request. But McCarthy believed that Hawaii's progress during two decades as a territory, along with her record in the war, demonstrated that her people were ready for statehood. He therefore recommended to the 1919 legislature the adoption of a memorial to Congress, pressing for this recognition. As a further measure, Delegate Kalanianaole on February 11, 1919, introduced in Congress the first of a long succession of bills to grant statehood to Hawaii; another was introduced by him in the early months of the Sixty-sixth Congress. But these bills were merely referred to the committee on the territories, for local support was not sufficiently strong at this time.

Most people in Hawaii recognized that there might be some delay in attaining statehood status. They did not worry about the prospect of delay. What disturbed them was the fact that many mainlanders, including Congressmen, looked upon the islands as a mere colony rather than as an incorporated territory only one stage removed from statehood. Hawaii was subject to all taxes and other general contributions imposed on the states, and annually paid into the Federal treasury many millions of dollars, sums larger than those paid by many of the states; but Hawaii was excluded from the benefits of Federal laws giving appropriations to the states for good roads, education, child welfare, and other improvements.

Governor Wallace R. Farrington in 1923 called the attention of the legislature to this situation and declared, "A vigorous campaign should be conducted to restore territorial prestige and position in the Federal scheme of appropriation and administration." The legislature responded by enacting what was called "Hawaii's Bill of Rights." This act asserted the territory's right to the same treatment from Congress as that received by the individual states. When this plea was formally presented, Congress recognized the justice of the claim by passing in 1924 a law extending to Hawaii the benefits of various appropriation acts already passed. But later appropriation bills had to be watched by the delegate to make sure that provisions were inserted so that their benefits would apply to Hawaii.

At this time the island people were also concerned about the possibility that they might be governed by "carpetbaggers" who would be appointed from outside the territory. Congress lent a friendly ear and in 1921 amended the Organic Act by making a residence of three years in the territory a prerequisite to appointment to most territorial and Federal positions.

The principle of home rule now seemed to be accepted, and although statehood bills were regularly dropped into the Congressional hopper, most people appeared to be content with Hawaii's status in the nation. Governor Lawrence M. Judd, appointed in 1929, had barely been settled in Washington Place when the stock-market crash gave warning of the depression of the 1930's. Judd had the unpleasant duty of initiating drastic cuts in salaries and other territorial expenses, and of dealing with the problems of widespread unemployment. The people grappled with the rigors of the depression years, until they were rudely awakened to the fact that their status in the nation was still precarious and could be upset by a wave of feeling in Washington.

Two quite unrelated and dissimilar episodes of the early thirties revealed to the people of Hawaii their utter dependence on the wishes of Congress in all matters concerning their form of government and its administrative details. One of these was the passage of the Jones-Costigan sugar-control act of 1934, which clearly discriminated against the rights of the sugar producers in Hawaii. The growers brought suit in the supreme court of the District of Columbia. The judge decided against the complainants and ordered the suit dismissed; he admitted that Hawaii was an integral part of the United States, but announced that Congress had plenary power to legislate for the territory and could discriminate against it if the lawmakers saw fit to do so. An appeal to the United States Supreme Court was dropped when a compromise was made with the secretary of agriculture, who administered the act; but to the citizens of Hawaii the lesson was clear that under territorial status, Congress could give and also could take away.

A more shocking demonstration of Hawaii's position in the nation was the aftermath of a crime of violence — the notorious "Massie case," which made the headlines in September, 1931. An assault was made by a band of Honolulu hoodlums upon the wife of a young naval officer. At the trial of the youths indicted for the assault, the jury was so baffled by uncertainties in the evidence that it was unable to agree on a verdict. While a second trial was pending, one of the defendants was taken and killed by a party made up of the young naval officer, his mother-in-law, and two sailors. The slayers were tried and found guilty of manslaughter; a sentence of ten years' imprisonment pronounced upon them was commuted by the governor to one hour.

Lurid treatment of the case in the nation's newspapers, which underlined what seemed to be a carnival of crime in placid Hawaii, threw a spotlight on local law enforcement. At the request of the Senate in Washington, Seth W. Richardson, an assistant United States attorney general, made an investigation in Honolulu. He found no evidence to justify the wild rumors circulated on the mainland, but his report did reveal some laxity and inefficiency in the administration of criminal laws and some defects in the machinery of justice. Citizens of the territory had been previously aware of these deficiencies; Governor Judd in 1930 had appointed a crime commission, whose report had been the basis for some legislative acts in 1931. In 1932 and 1933, under pressure from the agitation that followed the Massie case, the Hawaii legislature passed other corrective laws.

Richardson recommended several changes in existing laws and in the law-enforcement organization. He also recommended removal of the "anticarpetbagger" requirement. Bills to carry out these ideas were introduced in Congress in April, 1932. Other bills were drafted providing for the setting up of a commission form of government in Hawaii, in which the Army and Navy would have some ruling powers. None of these bills was enacted into law, although when Franklin D. Roosevelt became President in 1932, one of his first acts was to request Congress to grant authority to appoint a nonresident as governor of Hawaii. The bill did not pass, and home rule was saved for the while. But the impact of the Jones-Costigan Act and the Massie case aroused many thoughtful citizens of Hawaii from their indifference toward the ultimate goal of statehood.

Delegate Victor S. K. Houston at the end of 1931 had introduced in the House a statehood bill in the usual form of an enabling act, but his bill, drowned out by the Massie case uproar, died in committee. Although much unfavorable publicity for Hawaii resulted from the case, the broad result was that many people on the mainland, and especially Congressmen, obtained a clearer picture of many aspects of life in the territory. President Roosevelt visited Hawaii in 1934 — the first President to do so — and, although he did not commit himself on statehood, his administration was thereafter more friendly to its people.

Delegate Samuel W. King introduced a statehood bill at the opening of Congress in January, 1935, and succeeded in getting the House committee on territories to appoint a subcommittee to visit the islands in October on a tour of investigation. It reported that it "fouhd the Territory of Hawaii to be a modern unit of the American Commonwealth, with a political, social, and economic structure of the highest type." Further study was deemed necessary, however, and two years later another visiting Congressional committee, made up of twelve senators and twelve representatives, held hearings in October. This group reported that Hawaii had "fulfilled every requirement for statehood heretofore exacted of territories," and that it was entitled to "a sympathetic consideration of its plea for statehood." To measure the possibility of opposition to the idea in Hawaii, the committee suggested the holding of a plebiscite. The territorial legislature followed this suggestion, and the question "Do you favor statehood for Hawaii?" appeared on the ballot in the general election of 1940. Although this was an unfavorable time for such a plebiscite, because of growing tension between the United States and the Japanese Empire, which was leaning heavily toward the Rome-Berlin axis, the people of Hawaii voted more than two to one in favor of statehood.

The overshadowing argument faced by most advocates of statehood during the 1930's was the question: "Should war break out, especially against an Asiatic power, would the Oriental residents of Hawaii remain loyal to the United States?" That question was decisively answered when, on December 7, 1941, a shower of bombs and aerial torpedoes on Hawaii plunged the United States into World War II.

Remembering Pearl Harbor

EVERYBODY WHO LIVED THROUGH THE "DAY OF INFAMY" ON OAHU can give a detailed and stirring account of everything he saw and did that fatal Sunday. The greatest defeat in American history aroused the battle spirit of Americans everywhere to mobilize, under the slogan "Remember Pearl Harbor!", the greatest warpower the world had yet known.

Smoke from the ruins of naval and air installations signaled to the people of Hawaii that they must dedicate themselves now to a long struggle for victory against fascism around the earth. These people, already on a defense footing, helped to win that ultimate victory. Thereafter, no one familiar with their war record could doubt that the region where America was first attacked was a vital part of the United States. Rising from the ruins, Pearl Harbor became the headquarters for the Pacific war, and all the islands became staging areas for the long march of westward conquest. The people of Hawaii bent all their strength toward the war effort, both on the home front and on far battlefields.

Unalerted to the stealthy attack launched from the Japanese fleet two hundred miles north of Oahu, the island lay open to enemy planes. The first dive-bombers struck Pearl Harbor at 7:55 A.M., part of a unit that also struck the Army planes on Hickam Field and the Navy PBY's on Ford Island. Another bomber force came in from the north and smashed the unmanned Army fighter planes lined up wing-to-wing on Wheeler Field, near Schofield Barracks. The second wave over the Harbor was made up of forty torpedo bombers, which launched their deadly missiles at the main Pacific fleet moored along Battleship Row. In their wake came fifty horizontal bombers, followed by forty-five fighters that would shoot down any American planes lucky enough to get in the air, and would riddle any unbombed installations left on Oahu.

The second wave of 171 aircraft striking an hour later was hardly needed. In the first fatal quarter-hour, the Japanese had wiped out or paralyzed almost the entire air strength of Oahu. In that time they had also achieved most of their main objective — to knock out the Pacific Fleet of the United States before the war began. The new-model aerial torpedoes exploded against the sides of the big battlewagons. Bombs crashed into the decks, ammunition magazines blew up, and several ships were thrown on their sides by the force of the blasts. Only one or two ships managed to get under way in the channel before the second wave of dive bombers went in at 8:50 A.M. to deal the finishing strokes.

The attack from the air crippled American naval power in the Pacific for many weeks thereafter. The price paid by the Japanese was not heavy; they lost twenty-nine aircraft, one fleet submarine, and five midget subs (one of these was sunk outside the harbor by the United States destroyer *Ward* at 6:45 A.M. by the first shots fired in the war by Americans). The American losses were staggering. All eight battleships were put out of action. Two of them, the *Pennsylvania* and the *Maryland*, were restored to duty fairly soon by the energetic workers of the bombed shipyards, and the *Tennessee* was repaired shortly thereafter. The *Oklahoma* and the *Arizona* were total losses. Three other ships, through almost superhuman endeavors, were finally restored to sea service. Three cruisers — *Raleigh*, *Helena*, and *Honolulu* (a ship which had first visited its namesake city only two years before) — were badly damaged, and three destroyers were wrecked. The lives of 2323 men of Army and Navy were taken, and total casualties in killed, wounded, and missing from both services were estimated at 3435.

The armed guardians of America had been dealt a treacherous blow, and even as bombs were dropping in Honolulu and radios blared "Take cover! This is the real McCoy!", the civilian defenders rushed to help them. The people avoided panic, refused to be stampeded by false rumors, and set in motion the machinery of civilian defense. Local doctors and nurses hurried to tend the rows of casualties at Pearl Harbor and at the Honolulu emergency hospital. Some twelve hundred doses of plasma were drawn from the life-giving blood bank started by the community early in 1941.

Only a few scattered bombs fell on Honolulu, but some damage was done by spent antiaircraft shells from the guns of the city's defenders. One explosion went off near Iolani Palace, and a heavier one beside Washington Place, the governor's residence. Ironically, one part of the city where damage was greatest was a downtown section where many Japanese lived; of the first thirty-six civilians killed by shrapnel and by fires caused by explosions, twenty were of Japanese blood. About three hundred civilians were wounded, and at least sixty lives were lost on December 7.

Under the Hawaii Defense Act, which had been passed by the legislature in special session in October, Governor Joseph B. Poindexter at 11:30 A.M. on December 7 proclaimed an emergency period. That afternoon, at the instigation of Lieutenant General Walter D. Short, he issued a proclamation invoking martial law, suspending the writ of habeas corpus, and requesting the commanding general to exercise all the normal powers of the governor of Hawaii. Next day General Short set up offices in Iolani Palace and began issuing directives that affected every aspect of Hawaii's life for the duration of the war. Under martial law, Army officers occupied all courtroom positions, including that of judge. Civil government had ceased to exist, and despite vigorous efforts by many citizens after they were sure that the islands were no longer liable to further attack, the courts were run by the military for more than four years. Not until February 25, 1946, long after the war ended, did the Supreme Court of the United States repudiate the action of the Army and hold that the reign of martial law imposed upon the citizenry of Hawaii had been unconstitutional, since the territory was an integral part of the United States.

The only combat against an armed enemy on Hawaiian soil was fought far from Oahu, on a secluded islet; and the defenders were men and women who demonstrated again that in Hawaiian veins flows the blood of warriors.

Niihau, often call the "Forbidden Island" because it is privately owned and most visitors are not welcome there, is only fifteen miles by water from Kauai; but for most purposes it might just as well be a thousand. This island, only about five by twenty miles, has no source of fresh water other than rain clouds, and hence can support no more than two hundred inhabitants. It was purchased in fee simple from Kamehameha V in 1864 for $10,000 by the Sinclair-Robinson family. These Scottish people left New Zealand in their own full-rigged ship, loaded with household goods, farming tools, and valuable sheep. On their way to resettle in British Columbia, they stopped in the Hawaiian Islands for water and fresh food — and in Niihau found the little empire they sought. Today descendants of the original purchasers live on neighboring Kauai and send a weekly sampan to bring supplies to Niihau and keep it in touch with the outer world.

Niihau is one large, water-bounded ranch, on which rove cattle, sheep, turkeys, and Arabian horses. Most of its inhabitants are Hawaiians who are self-sufficient and live as much as possible by the old ways. There is no jail on Niihau, no general store, no telephones, autos, police force, movies, or liquor shop; people find most of their social life at church. News travels slowly to and from Niihau; unofficial election returns in 1954 were flown from there to Kauai by carrier pigeon.

Thus, when bombs fell on Oahu, Niihau, lying something more than a hundred miles to the westward, was one of the few places in the world that did not get the news. But about 2 P.M. on December 7, its pastoral peace was broken by the arrival of a Japanese plane trying to get back to its carrier. It made a crash landing on a rocky slope, and its dazed pilot was met by Howard Kaleohano, a Hawaiian, who noted that the plane was pocked by bullet holes. He called as interpreters the only two Japanese on the isle — Shintani, an alien, and Harada, an island-born citizen who had been brought over the previous year to tend the bees. Questioned, the aviator admitted that Oahu had been attacked. Kaleohano took the man's papers, maps, and gun, and hid them well, to await the arrival next day of the weekly sampan from Kauai. The launch did not arrive, because of wartime restrictions.

On Friday afternoon the aviator, aided by Harada armed with a shotgun, escaped from his guards. He sent Shintani with $200 to bribe Kaleohano to produce the hidden papers. Kaleohano refused and then, suspecting that matters were serious, he galloped with a band of other cowboys the fifteen miles to Kii. There on the channel shore they built a big fire to signal to Kauai that trouble was loose. At midnight, Kaleohano and four others began a sixteen-hour trip across the water, rowing against rough seas to carry the word that the enemy was running wild.

The pilot and Harada spent the night in a campaign of terror. They stripped the downed plane of its machine guns, set them up in the street of Puuwai village, and threatened to shoot every soul unless Kaleohano gave up the papers. They captured a villager named Kalimahuluhulu and sent him with a message to Mrs. Harada, but the man doubled back. Then he persuaded middle-aged Benjamin Kanahele to join him in a raid. The two sneaked up behind the Japanese, swiped their machine-gun ammunition, and lugged it off into the woods. Women and children of the settlement spent the night in caves, except for one elderly Hawaiian lady who ignored the pilot's threats and calmly went on reading her Bible. When a search of Kaleohano's house failed to reveal the papers, the two Japanese burned it down. In desperation, they also burned the crippled plane.

Early on Saturday, the Japanese captured Kanahele and his wife, and sent him off to look for Kaleohano, who was now offshore in a whaleboat. Mrs. Kanahele was held as hostage, and her 51-year-old husband, worried about her safety, soon came back to protect her. The duped aviator then threatened to kill them both as an example. Kanahele vainly appealed to Harada to turn on the flyer and disarm him. When the aviator's back was turned, husky Kanahele tackled him. Mrs. Kanahele grabbed at his gun arm, but Harada pulled her away, and the weapon barked thrice. Kanahele was shot three times — in chest, hip, and groin.

"Then," said Kanahele later, "I got mad." Despite his wounds, he seized the Japanese as if he were a struggling sheep, and broke his body against a stone wall, crushing the skull. His wife grappled with Harada, who, fearful of Kanahele's vengeance, turned the gun on himself and committed hara-kiri.

The attempt to take over one of the islands by modern force of arms had been defeated by a barehanded Hawaiian couple. Admiring citizens, on hearing the story of the "Battle of Niihau," told each other: "Never shoot a Hawaiian three times — he will get mad at you!" The month the war ended, Benjamin Kanahele was awarded the Purple Heart and the Medal for Merit in a ceremony at Fort Shafter, while the band played "They Couldn't Take Niihau Nohow." A year later Kaleohano, the smart cowboy, was awarded the Medal of Freedom.

V-J Day and After

WORLD WAR II BROUGHT TENSE MONTHS AND YEARS TO HAWAII AS the global struggle wore on. Those were times of curfew and nightly blackouts; of censorship of all mail, cables, and telephone calls to the mainland; of bomb shelters, OCD wardens, and air-raid sirens; of gas masks for all civilians, school children, and infants; of evacuation centers, gun emplacements, and barbed-wire barricades on lovely beaches. Buildings were hastily disguised, and the women whose trade had been making flower *leis* turned to making camouflage nettings and artificial shrubbery.

Submarine warfare had begun on December 8, and at the end of the month Japanese subs shelled, without much effect, the ports of Hilo, Nawiliwili, and Kahului. On January 28, the army transport *Royal T. Frank* was torpedoed in Hawaiian waters, with a loss of twenty-nine lives.

Effectiveness of blackout regulations was nullified toward the end of April, 1942, when Mauna Loa erupted, emitting a glow that could be seen by the enemy for two hundred miles at sea. After the crushing defeat of the invading Japanese fleet off Midway Island early in June, citizens of Hawaii breathed somewhat easier, and buckled down to achieving a proud war record. Many of the men and women entered the services; a total of more than 36,000 residents, of all racial ancestries, were enrolled in the armed forces. The islands themselves became headquarters for the Pacific war, a staging area for many attacks, and a spacious training school for invasion landings, jungle combat, soldier survival, and gunnery. Hawaii was a supply center, a prisoner-of-war area, and a rest and recreation region for war-weary men. About a million persons of the armed forces, it is estimated, passed through Oahu during World War II.

It was obviously impossible for residents to open their homes to more than a fraction of these visitors, but Hawaiian hospitality was organized to supplement the entertainment offered by movies, USO and Special Services shows, bars, and the honky-tonks of Hotel Street. Civilians visited convalescents, aided the Red Cross and other agencies, and opened to service men the churches, libraries, concert halls, Honolulu Academy of Arts, and other civic buildings. The Honolulu Community Theatre worked closely with USO Camp Shows, began putting on plays three weeks after December 7, and in all gave 250 free performances before a total audience of 150,000 service men on Oahu.

The people of Hawaii contributed much more than their quota in war-bond purchases; total subscriptions to all seven loans reached more than $200,000,000. They sought war jobs to supplement the labors of imported workers (at one time defense workers from the mainland numbered more than 82,000). The main task of the residents, however, was to continue the agricultural production of the islands, since both sugar and pineapples were considered by the government to be essential crops. Sugar plantations, at a time when their output was rationed for war needs, kept production at a high level despite losses in land area, manpower, and heavy equipment. In almost all high schools the week was reduced so that students could volunteer for work in the fields.

The colorful story of Hawaii in World War II has been related in Gwenfread Allen's fact-filled volume, *Hawaii's War Years*. Not since the days of Captain Cook and Kamehameha the Great had such a revolution been wrought in island life; and thereafter the people of Hawaii could never forget that they were part of an immense nation, made up of folk from many states and localities, working together for the common good. No longer was Hawaii merely an offshore tourist haven; it was the hub of an immense wheel of American expansion into the world's largest ocean. The war made clear forever that Hawaii's future was an indissoluble part of the future of the United States of America.

The loyalty of Hawaii's Japanese population was clearly shown. Right after the "blitz" of December 7, a number of Japanese suspects were rounded up by men from military intelligence and the F.B.I. Some two hundred consular agents scattered around the islands were among those placed in custody; but in contrast with the wholesale displacement of Japanese populations on the West Coast, the proportion of residents of Hawaii held for investigation was low. The number actually interned and sent to camps on the mainland was only one per cent of the adult Japanese population in the islands. Fears of fifth-column activities turned out to be unfounded. During a Congressional investigation in 1946, both Army and Navy intelligence officers testified that "not a single act of sabotage was committed by any resident of Hawaii before, during, or after the attack on Pearl Harbor." Far from plotting sabotage, many of the Japanese residents gave energetic aid in the conduct of the war both on the home front and abroad.

The war had a profound effect upon the Japanese in Hawaii in bringing them more strongly toward participation in the broader life of the community. Their patriotic activities gave them new respect at home, and they took well-earned pride in the valor of their sons who served in the American Army on battlefields in both Europe and the Pacific. A final count of Hawaii's war casualties shows that 80 per cent of those killed and 88 per cent of those wounded were of Japanese ancestry, even though baseless fears of the loyalty of Hawaii's nisei kept most of those of military age out of service for some months after the outbreak of the war.

Some 1500 of the nisei had, however, been inducted into the Army through Selective Service previous to the outbreak, and in the summer of 1942 about 1300 of them left for Camp McCoy, Wisconsin, to train as the 100th Infantry Battalion. In September of the next year they entered Italy at the Salerno beachhead. Nine months later, after having won fame as the "Purple Heart Battalion" because of their heavy combat casualties, they were incorporated into the newly arrived 442nd Regimental Combat Team, composed of nisei volunteers from Hawaii and the mainland United States. By V-E Day that regiment had been designated by military experts as "probably the most decorated unit in United States military history." The story of the events which led to the Army's decision to use nisei troops, and of the battle record which they made, is dramatically told by Thomas D. Murphy in *Ambassadors in Arms*. The "Go For Broke" spirit of the fighters of the

442nd was shared by the more than 18,000 A.J.A.'s (Americans of Japanese ancestry) who were in the armed forces by the war's end. During its later stages, many of Hawaii's Japanese served in the Pacific theater, largely as interpreters who, in many engagements from Guadalcanal to Okinawa, risked their lives to intercept information on enemy movements. The nisei servicemen of World War II proved beyond doubt President Roosevelt's dictum: "Americanism is a matter of mind and heart; Americanism is not, and never was, a matter of race or ancestry."

The end of the war came soon after the explosion over Hiroshima of the first atomic bomb used in warfare. The unofficial jubilation that broke out on August 14, 1945, at the news of Japan's imminent collapse was the greatest celebration in Hawaii's history. Peace was again a reality.

One result of the war was an upsurge of demands for greater self-determination among the workers of Hawaii. The "paternalism" of earlier business management was on the defensive. Even before the war, huge defense contracts, often carried out by large mainland firms, had broken down the old monopolistic control by interlocking directorates. The greatest challenge to Big Five predominance was the rise of organized labor. A charter to a typographical union had been granted as early as 1884, but until the middle 1930's the "horizontal unions" had never gained a strong foothold in the islands. At that time, as an aftermath of the 1934 waterfront strike in San Francisco, unionization began under the sponsorship of the maritime unions of the West Coast, and spread under the militant leadership of the International Longshoremen's and Warehousemen's Union.

During World War II, pressure of war duties and blackout restrictions made further organizing efforts impossible. Moreover, the military government issued orders which froze both wage rates and mobility of workers, who could not change their jobs without permission. Labor smarted under such emergency controls, and the end of the war brought, in line with the mainland pattern, a wave of strikes demonstrating its demand for a greater share in the gains available in the postwar world.

The most destructive strike in Hawaiian history came in 1946, when the C.I.O. called out 28,000 workers on thirty-three sugar plantations. Mills ceased grinding, irrigation ditches lay untended, and workers lost millions in wages as the strike dragged on from September 1 to November 14. At the end, wages were increased at a cost to the sugar industry between $10,000,000 and $17,000,000. One important result of the strike was the great impetus given to mechanization of plantation work, to balance expensive increases in labor costs and disturbances in production.

Hawaii has caught up on the labor front, benefiting by most of the legislation passed by Congress since 1933. Recent estimates of union membership in the islands run to 25,000 for the I.L.W.U., which includes most of the sugar and pineapple workers, and 6000 for members of A.F.L. locals. Most employees of the state and the counties are found in the ranks of the Hawaiian Government Employees Association, with 9,500 members, and the United Public Workers with 2000.

The terrifying maritime strike of the summer of 1949, when for 178 days the longshoremen's union prohibited shipping between the West Coast and Hawaii, pointed up the inability of a mere territory to act to protect itself at such a time. This was the longest major maritime tie-up in American history. Efforts in Honolulu to break the impasse failed when it was revealed that the national government was uninterested in keeping Hawaii's lifeline open. This strike was one more reason for the increased intensity of the drive for statehood after 1945 — an effort in which most people in the islands united.

The Achievement of Statehood

Right after the war, Delegate Joseph R. Farrington, who had succeeded Samuel W. King when the latter went back into the

Navy during the conflict, worked to get favorable action on the statehood bill he introduced in Congress. A subcommittee of the House Committee on Territories under Henry D. Larcade, Jr., arrived in the islands in January, 1946, and carried on the most searching investigation yet made of the territory's qualifications for statehood. They returned with a recommendation that the Committee on Territories give immediate consideration to legislation to admit Hawaii as a state. The movement was supported in a state-of-the-Union message by President Truman on January 21, 1946, but no further action was taken until the opening of the Eightieth Congress in January, 1947.

On the first day of the session, Delegate Farrington introduced H.R. 49, designed like previous bills to enable Hawaii to become the Forty-ninth State. The House Committee on Public Lands met in Washington in March to consider this and ten other identical bills. On the basis of all the thousands of pages of testimony accumulated to this time, the measure was passed by the House on June 30, by a vote of 197 to 133, and was forwarded to the Senate.

An investigation requested by the Senate Committee on Interior and Insular Affairs and carried on by Senator Guy Cordon in the islands in January, 1948, concluded its 500-page report with the words: "Hawaii has met the requirements for statehood. . . . It is able and ready to accept the social, political, and economic responsibilities of state government as well as the advantages. As a state, it could more effectively manage its own affairs and contribute to the welfare of the nation. As a nation, the United States, by granting statehood to Hawaii at this juncture in history, could demonstrate to the world that it means what it says and practises what it urges when advocating true democracy for all peoples." The committee voted, however, to defer action until the members could make trips to Hawaii for further study.

A move by Senator William F. Knowland to get the bill out of committee for a floor vote was defeated. Senator Hugh Butler, committee chairman, made a private investigation in Hawaii in the fall of 1948. He concluded that statehood should be deferred until Communism in the territory could be brought under control. His was the only unfavorable report ever made by a Congressional committee, and later he became one of the foremost champions of the statehood cause.

The Eighty-first Congress convened in 1949, and the Hawaii Statehood Commission established two years earlier began preparing a more vigorous campaign. One hundred years had now passed since a newspaper in Lowville, New York, had published on May 1, 1849, a two-column editorial advocating annexation and statehood for the Hawaiian Islands. Now, in 1949, the territorial legislature passed Act 334, authorizing the holding of a constitutional convention. Its purpose was to try another avenue for achieving statehood should the enabling-act procedure fail. Hawaii decided to follow the precedent of fifteen other territories which entered the Union after having drafted a constitution previous to admission as a state.

Sixty-three delegates began on April 4, 1950, their task of writing a constitution for the State of Hawaii. They formed a good cross-section of the community, and had been chosen at a nonpartisan election at which more than 80 per cent of the registered voters cast their ballots. The convention lasted 110 calendar days, and all committee meetings were open to the public, press, and radio. Verbatim transcription of proceedings was made by use of electronic tape recording. The resulting constitution, rooted in the special needs of the community, is unlike that of any other state, although all such documents were carefully studied by the delegates. Many of its features reflect the best current thinking in political science. One provision calls for reapportionment of representatives, a reform badly needed. A bicameral legislature is provided: a Senate of twenty-five members, serving for four years, and a House of Representatives of fifty-one, serving for two years. The State Constitution of Hawaii was ratified by the people by better than a three-to-one vote.

An enabling act passed the House in March, 1950, for a second time, by an overwhelming majority of 262 to 110. On June 29 the Senate Committee on Interior and Insular Affairs, after public hearings, reported favorably on the measure. Four days later, the Korean attack broke out. In the last few weeks of the special session toward the end of 1950, opponents of the bills to grant statehood to Hawaii and Alaska forestalled a vote. The Alaska bill was withdrawn to make way for other measures, and the advocates of Hawaiian statehood were forced to start over again.

In the Eighty-second Congress, bills to grant statehood to both Alaska and Hawaii for the first time reached the Senate floor, but a 45 to 44 vote in February, 1952, sent the Alaska bill back to committee and the Democratic leadership decided not to call up the Hawaii bill. In the Eighty-third, a group of Southern Democrats in 1954, fearing that Hawaii might elect Republican Congressmen, avoided a showdown by making a party issue of linking Hawaii and Alaska in a single bill, which was unable to emerge from the powerful Rules Committee.

Joseph R. Farrington died at his desk in Washington in 1954 — a martyr, many people felt, to his devotion to the cause of the Hawaiian statehood. When, despite a Democratic triumph in filling other offices, his wife Betty was elected in November, 1954, to succeed her husband — the first woman delegate sent to Congress from the islands — many observers felt that the voters had given a clear mandate to pursue the fight. She termed Hawaii the "lighthouse of democracy in the Pacific" on January 25, 1955, before hearings on a Hawaii-Alaska joint statehood bill, which on February 16 passed the House Committee on Interior and Insular Affairs by a resounding 19 to 6 vote. But in May, the House of Representatives voted 218 to 170 to send the statehood bill back to committee.

In 1957 a statehood bill failed to pass Congress for the twenty-second time since 1903. In the closing weeks of the Eighty-fifth Congress, Alaska was voted into the Union. John A. Burns, a Democrat who had been elected delegate from Hawaii in 1956, was advised not to press for statehood until the ensuing session.

By that time, press and public had assumed that, with Alaska in the Union, there would be no further question concerning Hawaii's qualifications. These popular assumptions swept away final opposition in Congress. The enabling act was passed by the United States Senate on March 11, 1959, by a vote of 76 to 15 and by the House of Representatives on the twelfth by an overwhelming 323 to 89. A spontaneous celebration broke loose in the islands a few moments after the triumphant word was telephoned from Washington.

A final barrier had to be hurdled. The enabling act signed by President Eisenhower on March 18 required that the citizens of the proposed state should vote approval of all three propositions on a plebiscite. The hopes of the people were demonstrated by a "yes" vote approving statehood by a majority of seventeen to one!

An election held on July 28 — at which no less than ninety-three per cent of the registered voters cast their ballots — established a slate of officials which represented the varied forces in the new state. Territorial governor William F. Quinn, Republican, was elected the first state governor, and his party also held a majority in the state senate, although the house of representatives was predominantly Democrat. To Washington went two Senators: Oren E. Long, a Kansan who had formerly served as territorial governor, and Hiram L. Fong, a successful lawyer of Chinese parentage. Hawaii's first Congressman was Daniel K. Inouye, a young Japanese-American who had lost an arm in combat in World War II. Senator Fong and Representative Inouye, first persons of Oriental ancestry to be seated in the United States Congress, were living proof to the world that American democracy still was a dynamic force, which did not stop at the edge of the American continent.

President Eisenhower signed a proclamation on August 21, 1959, admitting Hawaii to the sisterhood of states. Several weeks earlier, the first giant jet passenger plane had arrived in Honolulu on a scheduled flight from San Francisco in less than five hours. Times had indeed changed since Captain Cook's sailing ships had first revealed the Polynesian island paradise to the outer world!

The Life of Long Ago

"HAWAIIAN HOSPITALITY" IS NOT AN EMPTY PHRASE. WELCOMING the visitor is a custom ingrained in Polynesian nature, and a man of ancient Hawaii who let a stranger depart hungry from his door would suffer public shame. Guests were supposed to carry away with them all the remains of a feast; otherwise it would seem that they were dissatisfied with what was provided. Doors were never locked in the old days. While the family was away, they expected other travelers to stop in and partake of the food and water left in the home for that purpose.

Questioning a stranger about where he came from, where he was going, and whether he would return was considered mere politeness. If one household had a visitor, a neighbor would soon drop in to find out how long he would remain. The entire village then rallied to entertain him, and food would appear on the table throughout his stay. Usually a field of taro and vegetables was cultivated by the villagers in common, and any family could draw upon the communal supply when there was need.

A household was likely to have a deluge of visitors when the crops were abundant, and visitors were considered foolish if they left while the food supply still held out. Foreigners who did not understand this custom were often dismayed. John Nicol, a sailor who married a native girl and settled in the islands at the end of the eighteenth century, discovered to his annoyance that his bride's entire family arrived to share his bed and board, and he finally had to evict his hungry in-laws with a club.

The tradition of hospitality is merely one of dozens of customs that still survive in the islands from the days before the haole came. Less than two centuries ago, the islands were inhabited by a race of Stone Age people who enjoyed a high culture developed in their oceanic environment and marked by many amenities and charming folkways which should be remembered in our more frenetic age. Everywhere in Hawaii today are reminders that these islands were discovered and cultivated by a people with a long history, a ripened social system, and a deep knowledge of farming and fishing and craftsmanship. They were a robust, intelligent, and laughter-loving race that sang and danced and feasted and worshiped their gods under a wide sky. The Hawaiian culture had its grimmer side, but many of their ideas are still joyfully remembered and celebrated today, by the newer inhabitants of Hawaii Nei as well as by the descendants of the Polynesian voyagers in the Pacific of days long ago.

The Polynesian Columbus

THE ANCESTORS OF THE HAWAIIANS WERE A SEAFARING PEOPLE WHO came originally from westward, and probably had their origins in southern Asia. Of Caucasian stock, they were skilled voyagers who discovered and populated all the inhabited islands of the Pacific in the "Polynesian triangle" that runs from Hawaii on the north down to

New Zealand on the south, and eastward as far as Easter Island. These Polynesians, whose name is coined from the Greek words meaning "many islands," migrated through unknown centuries of sailing expeditions, probably using the scattered isles of Micronesia as way stations, and mingling their blood with that of the Malaysian peoples of southeast Asia during the generations of travel.

We have no need to believe that the Polynesians were related by blood or culture to the peoples of ancient America. True, the prevailing winds of the central Pacific come from the east; but there are seasons when the westerlies blow, and it is known that the Polynesians were able to make many long voyages from west to east. The only clear link between Oceania and the New World is the presence throughout Polynesia of the sweet potato, a South American tuber. Either the Polynesians made at least one trip to South America and brought back this plant, or else some Indians brought it to the islands. The celebrated voyage of the raft *Kon-Tiki* daringly proved that people from the South American continent could have sailed or drifted to a shore of Oceania in past times. But the "sweet-potato mystery" will probably never be solved.

The true discoverer of the Hawaiian Islands was not Captain Cook, but the unknown Polynesian Columbus who, around the eighth century A.D., first sighted these lands from his ocean-going canoe. At a time when our European ancestors were hugging the shores of their narrow seas, the "Vikings of the sunrise" were navigating the expanses of the world's largest ocean, and performing feats of seamanship never equalled by any other "primitive" peoples.

Their voyages were made in hollowed-log canoes, fitted with outriggers and with lateen sails of woven coconut or pandanus fiber. Often double canoes were used, lashed together with flooring between the two hulls, on which shelters were built to protect the stores of supplies. The voyagers might have to spend a season on an arable island along the way, to plant and harvest a crop. Seasons were important to these daring sailors, for the westerly winds blew only at certain times of the year. At these times, fleets of exploring canoes would set out, each one about five miles apart, keeping in touch by signals. They would then sweep the ocean until new lands were sighted or until the winds turned and blew them home again.

How did these navigators, lacking the compass, find their way about the Pacific? They guided their craft by the sun, clouds, winds, waves, and currents. Sometimes they could descry an atoll by the reflection in the sky of its mirroring lagoon. They followed the tracks of migratory birds. Mainly they traveled by the stars. The Polynesian helmsman could recognize and name more than a hundred and fifty stars and planets, knew which of them belonged in the same parallel of latitude, and could foretell their changes in position from month to month. On any cruise he would note all stars and landmarks so that he could find his way back home.

On a voyage of migration, from sixty to a hundred persons could exist for weeks on a large canoe, which might be a hundred feet in length. The Polynesians, as is well known, did survive long spells at sea. From Tahiti to Hawaii, for instance, is a distance of some 2500 miles; yet canoes using only sails and paddle power accomplished such a journey many times. Their craft often made a hundred miles in one day, and their crews were trained to live for a month at sea without dying of hunger or thirst. On the voyage that first populated Hawaii, women and children must have been taken along, and also live animals — pigs, dogs, and chickens. Seeds and plant cuttings must also have been shipped, for the coco palm, the banana, and the breadfruit trees were brought to Hawaii by human means. After the fresh stores were eaten, the seafarers lived on dried foods — pandanus flour, cooked breadfruit and sweet potatoes, preserved fish and shellfish. The animals were fed on scraps and on dried coconut, and they might be cooked and eaten on the way, for fires could be burned in the canoe on a bed of sand. Fish and birds could be caught at sea. Water was carried in gourds or in bamboo pipes.

Yet the early voyages were not luxury cruises. The brown-skinned discoverer of the Hawaiian Islands, the most isolated large group in the Pacific, could not have known that there was any land at all in these latitudes, and only by good luck would he have sighted shore in that vast bowl of sea and sky. Perhaps more than one shipload of Polynesian emigrants perished in storm or wreck, or died mad with thirst without catching a glimpse of the promised land. But at least one far-wandering couple did come ashore in Hawaii, to become the Adam and Eve of the new oceanic paradise.

For a period of some two hundred years after about 1100 A.D., there was a lively traffic between the Hawaiian group and Tahiti. The era of voyaging then came to a close, and for some centuries — until the coming of the ships of Cook — the Hawaiians lived in isolation from the broader world that they knew only through their oral traditions. The population grew and rival chiefs fought to enlarge their domains. The larger islands — Hawaii, Maui, Oahu, and Kauai — were often held as "kingdoms" ruled by families of chiefs. The smaller islands might for a time maintain their independence, but more often they were conquered by their larger neighbors. Now and then an ambitious "king" tried to bring all the group under his rule, but none succeeded in uniting the islands in the days before the white man brought his new ships and new weapons.

Ancient Hawaii was ruled by a feudal system of a sort similar to that found in Europe during the same centuries. At the top were the *alii*, chiefs or nobles who were warriors and lived on the produce of the people. Rank was hereditary, and women as well as men could inherit high position. Some chiefs of Hawaii were of such high parentage that they found no peers except their own sisters with whom to marry — a practice not found elsewhere in Polynesia. Hawaii had a famed College of Heralds to judge all claims to inherited title.

The high chiefs were attended by councilors, by taxgatherers and stewards, and by the kahuna class — priests and specialists in the professions. This priesthood furnished experts in oracles and divina-

tion, in location and construction of temples, in supervision of
housebuilding and canoe making, in predicting the weather, and in
practicing the art of healing. They might also indulge in sorcery and
cause sickness or "pray a person to death."

The mass of the people, called *makaainana*, were farmers, fishermen, canoe builders, bird catchers, adz makers, and the like. These
commoners, although dependent on the *alii* class, were not serfs, and
could join another chief if their lot was too harsh. There was also a
class of wandering beggars, and a few hereditary slaves called *kauwa*.

Through many seasons of warfare, petty kingdoms arose, covering
a part of one island or extending to several islands. The king was
called the *alii-aimoku*, and attained his supreme position through a
combination of natural ability and inherited rank. He was usually
assisted by a chief priest, *kahuna nui*, and by a prime minister, *kalai-
moku* or "island carver," whose duty it was to divide up the royal
lands. Many agents of the king, called *konohiki*, carried out his
orders for levying troops, constructing public works, and collecting
taxes. Constables called *ilamuku* acted as police to enforce laws and
tabus.

The duty of the *alii* class was mainly to furnish leadership in
war; the *makaainana* served as soldiers and also supplied the neces-
sities of life from the sea and the land. If a king was defeated in war,
all his chiefs would be removed from power too, and there would
be a new deal all around in land titles, for government was closely
associated with ownership of land.

Gods, Kings, and Kahunas

IN THEORY, A NEW KING OWNED ALL THE LAND IN HIS REALM, AND
after setting aside what he wanted for himself, he parceled out the
remainder to his loyal followers, who became governors, regional
chiefs, or owners of estates. At the death of a chief, his lands reverted
to the king.

All lands were held on terms of obedience to the feudal superior and payment of taxes to him. In time, the taxes for a certain tract of land came to be fairly standard; in a letter written by William Richards in 1841 the annual royal tax on an *ili* or estate was said to be "a hog, a dog, a fish net, a fishline, a cluster of feathers, and twenty kapas [sheets of bark cloth], a part of which were square for bedclothes, and a part long and narrow for female dress."

The king could call out everyone to perform any sort of labor he needed; and the workers, as part of their rent, ordinarily cultivated their landlord's patches one day out of five.

The people were expected to offer their landlords the first fruits of sea and soil and to present gifts on other occasions. They also had to support the chiefs when they went traveling about the country with their retinues. At any time, the king or chiefs could seize anything they wanted. The commoners who produced the wealth of the land probably were able to keep only about one third of the total; the rest went to the nobles and priests, in return for their protection. But, since the goods were perishable and wealth could not be stored up in money, there was no reason, before the coming of the white traders, for the rulers of the people to take more goods than they could themselves consume.

The absolute powers of the chiefs and priests were somewhat tempered by *noblesse oblige*, by public opinion, and by custom. Rules of land tenure and water rights were well established, as was the absolute power of a man over his children. Criminal laws and property laws of a primitive sort were also administered by courts held by the chiefs and also by the priests. Those accused might have to undergo ordeals to prove their innocence; but they were entitled to plead their own cases and to appeal to a higher court. The rank of a litigant, of course, might affect the decision, nor was justice free of graft or obtained as a matter of course.

Robbery, especially of the goods of a chief, was a recognized offense, and often was punished by death. But in times of disorder or war, all rules went by the board, outlaw gangs roamed about, and banditry and murder were rife. At such times, a man's survival depended on his own courage and cunning; and the individualism of our pioneers was not unknown in ancient Hawaii.

The religion of the premissionary days was founded on a reverence for the manifestations of nature, and ceremonies were performed to set up and preserve proper relations between man and the powers that surrounded him. Although a Supreme Being was supposed to rule over the universe, there were many other gods that symbolized the many objects and aspects of nature, which had to be invoked or placated.

The island pantheon was, in fact, somewhat overcrowded; one chant speaks of "the four hundred thousand gods." The four Polynesian gods most fervently worshiped in Hawaii were Kane, father of living creatures, and identified with sunlight, fresh water, and the forests; Ku, fierce god of war, to whom human sacrifices were made; Kaneloa, ruler of the land of departed spirits; and Lono, god of growing things, rain, harvest, sports, and peace, during whose autumn *makahiki* festival a truce from war was joyously celebrated. Pele, goddess of the volcanoes, was respected and feared, especially in the southernmost islands. Certain deities were patrons of particular activities: Hina presided over kapa beating and other women's work; Laka was goddess of the hula schools; and Kuula was the god of fishermen. The gods were considered the ancestors of men, and long genealogies traced descent back to a deity or demigod. There were also many legendary heroes, ghosts, and elves, as well as familiar demons belonging to a particular sorcerer. Trees, rocks, plants, animals, heavenly bodies, and other natural objects might also be deified.

Each family had an ancestral guardian spirit called an *aumakua*, worshiped at the family altar and invoked when help was needed in any enterprise. The main public worship, however, was conducted on the enclosed temple platform called the heiau, decorated by large carved images of the gods, where rites were performed on certain days of each month. The sites of five hundred of these temples are known in the islands. In addition, every activity of Hawaiian life, from the felling of a tree to the planning of a military campaign, would be inaugurated by prayer or a religious ritual.

Two main ideas stand out in Hawaiian religion: "mana" and "*kapu*." Mana is the supernormal power that may be possessed by a person or an object. A man endowed with mana might perform superhuman feats of courage, skill, or magic. He could obtain it by descent from sacred beings, or by observing tabus, offering sacrifices, or uttering prayers and rituals. It was believed that contact between objects or persons possessing different amounts of this spiritual power could be dangerous to the weaker one.

To regulate the handling of such power in the Hawaiian community, a network of prohibitions, called the *kapu* system, grew up. The word is a variant of the Polynesian "tabu," and not only connoted a simple warning like "No Trespassing," but extended to every phase of Hawaiian life. Superficially, the system seems invented to assure autocratic domination of the society by the favored caste; but fundamentally, the idea grew out of a dualistic view of nature which placed on one side that which was sacred — the male principle, light, life — and on the other side that which was common and secular — the female principle, darkness, and death. Whatever was branded as *kapu* was forbidden either because it was divine and therefore to be set aside from what was vulgar and common, or else it was corrupt, and thus dangerous to both the common and the divine. Anything connected with the gods acquired sacredness; hence there were many *kapus* relating to priests, temples, and worship. Since the noble class was descended from the gods, the chiefs — particularly the highest ones — were protected by many *kapus* and in turn had to observe certain restrictions of their own. Women, as allied with the negative principle, underwent many prohibitions.

Some *kapus* might be periodical or temporary, associated with times and seasons; others might last as long as thirty years in the old days. During a season of strict *kapu*, according to William Ellis, "every fire and light on the island or district must be extinguished;

no canoe must be launched on the water, no person must bathe; and, except those whose attendance was required at the temple, no individual must be seen out of doors." At such times, even the animals were not allowed to make a noise; the mouths of dogs and pigs were tied up, and fowls were kept from crowing by putting them under a calabash.

Penalties for violating a *kapu* were severe, death being a common punishment. Ignorance of the *kapu* was no excuse — a person could violate it unknowingly, but he nevertheless must suffer the penalty.

The alliance of chiefs and priests finally came to use the *kapu* system as a main method of government. It was most oppressive upon the common people and upon women of all classes, and was undoubtedly abused many times. Although the system provided a rigid code that tended to preserve the native culture, its abuse led to the abolition of the whole scheme a few months after the death of Kamehameha the Great.

Fingers in the Calabash

THE EARLY HAWAIIANS, UNLIKE THEIR LUCKIER COUSINS OF CENTRAL Polynesia, had to work hard to grow their food. Some crops were raised on the grassy uplands or in forest clearings, where rainfall was abundant. In the lowlands it was necessary to terrace the fields and use irrigation tunnels, dams, ditches, and bamboo pipes. To provide the large amounts of water needed for growing taro, the people developed elaborate systems and a complicated scheme of water rights to enable the sharing of water among the farms.

The chief implement was the o-o, a sharpened stick six to nine feet long, for digging holes. Most of the backbreaking labor of cultivation was done with the bare hands, and the farmer often worked in mud up to his waist. Wisely, he often labored all night in cool moonlight and rested in the heat of the day — a custom that later led to charges of laziness from the unsuspecting foreign observer.

Poi, the Hawaiian staff of life, is made from the starchy root of the taro, one of the most concentrated plants known to man. A square mile of "wet-land" taro, the kind most commonly raised, would supply, according to the calculations of G. W. Bates, enough food to support 15,151 Hawaiians for a year. It was grown in prepared beds like rice fields, with raised borders to keep the roots covered with water. The farmers planted at proper times to have taro maturing throughout the year. The beds were used over and over, so that it was necessary to renew the soil with fertilizers, which included rotted hau leaves, weed mulch, and burned bones.

Sweet potatoes were set out in hills on the dry uplands; the islands of Niihau and Kauai were especially known for their yams. Bananas and sugar cane were planted from cuttings. Gourds were raised from seed in cleared ground, and calabash gourds could be grown in various useful shapes. The mulberry tree from which kapa was made was planted in clumps near the villages.

The ancient Hawaiians had no fortified towns or large villages, and they clustered in hamlets by the seashore or in homesteads near their fields. The climate required only the lightest protection from sun and cold, although in some spots heavy rainfall made a good roof essential.

Captain Cook described the village of Waimea, Kauai, as a collection of thatched dwellings, large and small, scattered without any order, looking like English haystacks, with peaked roofs running almost to the ground. He thought them stuffy and poorly adapted to the climate, but admitted that they were kept remarkably clean, with floors covered with dry grass over which mats were spread for sleeping.

Almost everybody in Hawaii lived in such thatched homes a century ago, although today the "little grass shack" is a thing of the past. No carpenter's guild existed to build houses; the owner and his friends would get together and put up a new dwelling. But many careful preparations had to be made, and plenty of materials had to be gathered and shaped. Then, on a stone platform, a notched frame of forest timbers and rafters was lashed together with cords of sennit or the rootlets of the ie-ie vine. Even had there been metal nails in old Hawaii, this lashing would have been preferable, to give elasticity against the elements. Thatching of pili grass, or sometimes of hala, sugar cane, or ti leaves, was tied in bundles and lashed to battens. The priest supervised every step, and before the owner could move in, the priest trimmed the thatch over the doorway, meanwhile chanting that he was cutting the navel string of the house. A well-built new house might be weather-tight for five to ten years, after which it would need to be rethatched.

Instead of dividing his house into rooms, the Hawaiian built a separate house for each of his main activities. A farmstead might consist of one or two huts and a storehouse, but a person of position might have six or seven edifices for his family needs. These were an eating house for men (*mua*), an eating house for women (*hale aina*), a work shelter for women (*kua* or *kuku*), the common dormitory (*noa*), and a retreat for women (*pea*). There might also be a small heiau for the family altar, and a shed on the shore to cover the canoe. Fire was a serious hazard, and thus the cooking oven was well removed from the houses. Habits of cleanliness were instilled in the people from childhood, and a Polynesian settlement in early times was swept daily with a broom of coco-palm leaves.

The men of old Hawaii not only provided the food for the home, but also did the cooking. Since men and women could not eat together, all cooking was done separately. A further complication was added by the fact that some foods were *kapu* for the women; they dared not eat pork, bananas, coconuts, or certain kinds of fish. When the old restrictions were overthrown in 1819, all the male cooks of the islands must have breathed sighs of relief as the women took over the labor of kneading the family poi.

Meat was scarce, and came only from pigs, chickens and wild birds, and dogs. Vegetables were breadfruit, sweet potatoes and yams, bananas, arrowroot, sugar cane, and greens such as cooked taro tops. Relishes were salt, roasted kukui nuts, dried octopus, and a seaweed called limu. The staples of the diet were fish and poi.

Taro roots contain tiny, sharp crystals that will cut one's tongue, and therefore this vegetable had to be steamed for hours in an underground oven. It was then peeled, pounded with stones into a thick paste on a poi board, and mixed with water to the proper stiffness — "one-finger poi" is thicker than "three-finger poi." The dough could be kept for weeks in a dry state and used from time to time as a sort of C-ration.

Food could be boiled by dropping hot stones in a calabash of water, but the main method of cooking was baking in the oven called the imu, a hole in the ground in which stones were laid in an open fire and covered with grass on which food was spread, bundled in leaves. Then the mass was covered with green leaves and old mats, banked with earth, and steamed until the food became a delicious barbecue. Taro required three or four hours to cook; the rest of the feast was put into the oven later. Meat was also cooked in the imu, and hot stones were put inside the body of a large pig to make sure the meat was thoroughly done. Puddings of coconut, sugar, and arrowroot were baked in packages made of ti leaves.

Seafood of many varieties, including oysters, lobsters, and crabs, was prized by the Hawaiian cooks. Certain fish, such as mullet, were fattened in ponds along the shore. The fish were broiled over coals, or steamed in ti leaves, or boiled in a calabash with hot stones. Contrary to belief nowadays, the people never ate fish raw from the ocean; it was either cooked or else salted and dried in the sun.

The meal was spread outdoors in good weather, and the food was usually eaten cold. The diners reclined around clean mats, decorated with ferns and flowers, on which the meal was laid out. The food was served in large calabashes, and everyone ate from the common supply, daintily dipping his fingers into the bowl. Afterward, fingerbowls were passed around, and all scraps were carefully burned.

Meals were times of gaiety and cheerful conversation, and nothing serious was discussed at table. Sometimes eating would be interrupted while the diners enjoyed a relaxing massage or lomi-lomi. Often they were entertained by songs or by recitals of the deeds of great ancestors.

No fixed times were set aside for eating. If food was plentiful, five or six meals a day might be eaten; often the people would rise in the night for a snack. Conversely, if food was scarce in the neighborhood, the people might go for two or three days without eating, and make up for the lack by feasting later.

The household was furnished with many utensils made by the people. Shapely wooden bowls (*umeke*) ranged in size from small dishes to storage containers seven feet in diameter. The lathe was unknown, but these calabashes, usually circular, and cut with a stone adz from blocks of seasoned hardwood, were beautifully carved with thin walls. Koa was not used in the old days because it gave the food a bitter taste. Ring-shaped mats of *lauhala* were placed under the calabashes to keep them from tipping.

Large dishes and platters were also carved of wood. Dippers, spoons, and cups were made of coconut shells. Gourds were fashioned into water bottles, funnels, dishes, and covers. Large gourds were also used for storing clothing, featherwork, and fishing gear. Fancy designs were sometimes etched on the outside of a gourd container.

A few dishes were made of stone. The largest of these were the shallow slabs in which sea water was put to evaporate to obtain salt. Stone implements were shaped for pounding taro and seaweed, and the kahuna used a mortar and pestle for grinding his medicines.

Refuse containers, such as slop basins and spittoons, were important, for it was believed that if a sorcerer could obtain a person's spittle or fingernail parings they might be used to "pray him to death." The chiefs kept trusted henchmen to bury or empty such refuse into the sea, and the spittoon-bearer was a regular member of the court. Slop basins studded with the teeth of a dead enemy were not uncommon.

Fire was kindled with a Polynesian invention, the "fire plow." A slender hardwood stick was rubbed back and forth in a groove on a softer piece of wood, and then the smouldering dust was fanned on a bit of kapa until the tinder burst into flame.

Outdoor illumination came from torches made of dried kukui kernels wrapped in leaves and mounted on a bamboo pole. Indoors, candles of these kernels strung on a stick were used, or else a stone lamp fitted with kukui oil and a kapa wick.

The Stone Age craftsman of Hawaii lacked metals but had amazing skill in working with tools made of stone, shell, wood, and bone. The chief tool was the hafted adz of shaped basalt. The adz varied in size from those more than a foot long, with which to chop down a tree or hollow out a canoe, down to tiny ones an inch long, for carving the grooves on a kapa beater. Hammers and chisels were also made of stone, and stones of various degrees of hardness were also used like sandpaper. Knives were made of shark's teeth. Awls and scrapers were formed from shells, and files were made of sharp-edged coral. Needles of bone were used in sewing together the edges of sheets of kapa for bedclothes. A workman pierced holes in hard material by means of a rotary drill, consisting of a wooden shaft with a balance wheel. A crossbar was attached by two cords to the top of this shaft, and pumping up and down on the crossbar twisted and untwisted the cords to revolve the shaft. A sharp rock splinter or a sea-urchin spine served as a drill point.

Crafts of Shore and Sea

THE WOMAN'S WORK IN THE OLD DAYS INCLUDED THE REARING OF children, the plaiting of mats, and the making of bedcovers and clothing from the inner bark of the paper mulberry tree. This material was peeled off, soaked in water, scraped, and then beaten into thin strips, which were overlapped to make wider pieces, and built up into layers for thickness. The musical sound of the kapa mallet hitting on a wooden anvil was a familiar part of Hawaiian home life.

The mallet was a square-edged club on which grooves or patterns were cut which gave different textures to the surface of the cloth. "That beaten with the plain side is smooth like paper," wrote C. S. Stewart; "that with the coarse groove has something the appearance of dimity; that with the close, more like corded muslin." The fabric was bleached in the sun or dyed in tones of gray, brown, blue, red, and yellow, and on it delicate designs were stamped with carved bamboo sticks, used as in block printing. Kapa was sometimes decorated with paint put on with a brush made of the chewed tip of a pandanus fruit. Black dye was made from charred kukui nut in oil; other dyes came from plant juices and from colored earths.

The island climate called for few garments. The men wore a malo made of kapa; it was a sort of loincloth tucked under the legs. The women wore a short kapa skirt called a *pa-u*. Either sex might wear in the evening a square shawl called a *kihei*. Kapa clothing might be soaked in coconut oil to make it waterproof; raincoats of matting were also worn.

Styles had to be followed, and a commoner could be executed if he donned the malo of a chief. Ladies of high rank not only wore skirts that were highly decorated, but also used voluminous lengths of material.

The Hawaiians excelled all other peoples in the craft of featherwork, and their helmets and cloaks, made from the tufts of thousands of small birds, were worn only by chiefs and are still museum treasures. A special guild of bird catchers went into the dense forest haunts of the mamo and o-o birds, and trapped them on twigs smeared with a sticky gum. Only a few of the yellow feathers of each bird were plucked, and the bird was then released to grow new ones. The birds were also caught with light nets of fiber, with nooses, and even with the bare hands, after they were enticed by tame decoys or by calls imitated by the fowler.

In making cloaks and capes, a netting of olona fiber was woven, to which the feathers were tied. Patterns of geometric figures were made in contrasting colors of yellow and red, with now and then a touch of black. Of some 140 known specimens of these Hawaiian mantles, no two have the same design. Some cloaks were nine feet across and six feet long, and at least one of them used the feathers of eighty thousand birds. But the value of these royal examples of featherwork has been greatly exaggerated; the highest price ever paid for one of them was only a few thousand dollars.

With his cloak the *alii* wore a helmet of ie-ie fibers on which were woven bright feathers. Most of these helmets had a raised crest and in design somewhat resembled those of Europe, although they were not, of course, modeled on those of the Greek warriors or medieval knights.

A heraldic standard called a kahili was made of feathers arranged in an individual pattern on the top of a tall pole. It was a rallying point in battle, and was also held or carried beside a personage on ceremonial occasions. The poles were made of carved wood or of the bones of defeated chiefs.

The men and women were fond of adorning themselves with shell bracelets, with pendants of boar's tusks, and with anklets made of hundreds of teeth from dogs. The body was sometimes decorated with tattoo marks, although this practice was not so common in Hawaii as in other parts of Polynesia.

The favorite adornment was the *lei,* a necklace or headband made of many kinds of material, which is still the symbol of love and friendship in the islands. The *lei* of early days was a garland of orange ilima, of feathery red ohia, of fragrant *maile* leaves, or of fern. But *leis* were also made of carved, dried kukui shells, looking like polished jet; of yellow pandanus fruits; of various seashells; of beads carved from walrus tusks; and of bright feathers. The most treasured ornament, worn only by persons of high rank, was a whale's tooth, carved in the form of a hook and hung on many fine strings of braided human hair.

The Hawaiians were also highly skilled in using the vegetable fibers of the islands for their needs. They did not know the loom, but plaited and wove and knotted fibers with great cunning. They did not use coconut leaves or husks as much as did their cousins to the south. For basketry and mat-making they preferred the pandanus leaf or *lauhala*, a fiber woven in Hawaii to this day. From it they also made pillows, fans, canoe sails, and sandals.

The finest product of the island weaver was the *makaloa* mat. A sedge growing beside streams furnished stems which were heated over a fire until they became a light brown. The mats were made with a diagonal plait with as many as twenty strands to the inch. One sample in the Bishop Museum covers five hundred square feet.

The aerial rootlets of the ie-ie vine were used to fashion coiled baskets, covers for gourd containers, and helmet frameworks. Ropes and twines were made of the bark of the hau tree, from banana and coconut fibers, from ti leaves, and from certain grasses. But the finest fiber for nets and fishlines, one of the strongest in the world, was made from the inner bark of the olona, a plant of the nettle family growing in the rain forest. After being soaked, scraped, and bleached in the sun, the fibers were twisted on the thigh and rolled into cord of various sizes. It was tough enough to stand years of use in salt water, yet a rather small cord made an excellent fishline or lashing. A quarter of a century after Cook, William Shaler said that the Hawaiians made "excellent white cordage, of all sizes," and added that "for running rigging, there is no better rope."

The Hawaiians were truly amphibious, and traveled freely about their shores in trim canoes. These masterpieces of craftsmanship varied in size from a one-man outrigger, for fishing, to large double canoes, for interisland voyaging. Although the giant vessels of the migration period were no longer needed, warcraft and the canoes of kings might be a hundred feet long, made always from a single log. Koa was the favorite wood for canoes, and logs brought from the forest with proper ceremonies were hollowed out with stone adzes and chisels — fire was never used in making a canoe. After the hull was shaped, the wood was smoothed with lava and coral, rubbed with sharkskin, polished with sand, and finally coated with kukui oil. Burnt kukui nut oil was used to make a black paint; a royal canoe would be trimmed with red.

Double canoes were joined together by lashed spars, arched so that the stage built between the two hulls was well above the water. A single-hull canoe always carried an outrigger to attain stability. This was a long wooden float, usually of *wiliwili* wood, lashed by booms to both gunwales. To the upper edge of the canoe's hull was usually fastened a plank of breadfruit wood six or eight inches high, to keep out the waves, and stem and stern were also covered.

Paddles four or five feet long, with a broad oval blade, were often made of koa wood. It took a hefty man to wield them, and chiefs kept trained crews who did nothing but paddle and sail their big canoes. Many craft were equipped with triangular sails of woven pandanus, trimmed with pennants of kapa, but in the old days they could not sail very close to the wind. The vessels were guided by a long steering oar, and could take off and land on the beach even through rough surf.

The Hawaiians devoted many hours to outdoor sports, developing athletic skill as an asset in war and a relief from daily tasks. Before the days of Captain Cook, about three months in the autumn were devoted to the *makahiki* festival, a sort of island-wide Olympic games dedicated to the god Lono. Thousands of persons would gather to watch bouts of boxing, wrestling, bowling, and javelin-throwing, and gambling on the outcome was so heavy that a man or woman might lose all possessions on a contest, and even life itself.

A sport of chiefs and their wives, called *holua*, was a summer-time toboggan ride on a downhill course paved with stones overlaid with a layer of grass. The sled, twelve to eighteen feet long, had converging runners braced crosswise. These runners were about six inches apart at the top, but only about two inches apart where they touched the ground, and were greased with kukui oil to make them as slippery as possible. The daring riders needed great skill to avoid a bad tumble as they made a running "belly-whopper" take-off, but some were so expert that they rode erect, surfboard fashion. The

304 HAWAII AND ITS PEOPLE

early missionary wife Laura Fish Judd once descended into the depths of Waipio Valley on such a sled. A legend reported by William Ellis shows the hazards of defeating a goddess at *holua*. Kahavari, a champion of the Puna district of Hawaii, won in a contest with Pele without guessing her identity. When he refused to give her his treasured toboggan, she assumed her terrifying real form and chased him downhill to the accompaniment of thunder and lightning, earthquakes, and streams of molten lava. Kahavari escaped by leaping into a canoe, but the spectators, including the brash mortal's entire family, were buried beneath the volcanic flow.

Water sports were then, as now, the most popular, among children and adults alike. Canoe racing, swimming, diving, body-surfing, and surfboard riding were most favored. One type of surfboard was thin and almost flat on both sides; it was about six feet long, and made of breadfruit or koa wood. Another, used by chiefs only, was thicker, tapering, and convex on both sides; this type, usually of *wiliwili* wood, might be as much as eighteen feet long and weigh 150 pounds. The boards were stained black, and after use were dried in the sun, rubbed with coconut oil, and suspended under a roof until needed again. The waves at certain shores, such as Hilo, Lahaina, and Waikiki, are most suitable for this sport.

Surfriding died out almost completely between 1860 and 1910, but thereafter was revived to the point where it is almost synonymous with Hawaiian life and has spread to many parts of the world. Today the sport of Hawaiian monarchs has become the favorite recreation of movie stars, businessmen, and college youths when the waves are running well at Waikiki.

PAU

Appendixes

A. HEADS OF GOVERNMENT IN HAWAIIAN ISLANDS

1. *Native Monarchs*

NAME	BIRTH	ACCESSION	DEATH
Kamehameha I	c. 1758	1795	May 8, 1819
Kamehameha II (Liholiho)	1797	May 20, 1819	July 14, 1824
Kamehameha III (Kauikeaouli)	March 17, 1814	June 6, 1825	Dec. 15, 1854
Kamehameha IV (Alexander Liholiho)	Feb. 9, 1834	Dec. 15, 1854	Nov. 30, 1863
Kamehameha V (Lot Kamehameha)	Dec. 11, 1830	Nov. 30, 1863	Dec. 11, 1872
William C. Lunalilo	Jan. 31, 1835	Jan. 8, 1873	Feb. 3, 1874
David Kalakaua	Nov. 16, 1836	Feb. 12, 1874	Jan. 20, 1891
Liliuokalani	Sept. 2, 1838	Jan. 29, 1891	Nov. 11, 1917

Liliuokalani was deposed and the Hawaiian Kingdom came to an end on January 17, 1893.

2. *President of Provisional Government*

NAME	TERM BEGAN	TERM ENDED
Sanford B. Dole	Jan. 17, 1893	July 4, 1894

3. *President of Republic of Hawaii*

Sanford B. Dole   July 4, 1894   June 14, 1900

Hawaii was annexed to the United States on August 12, 1898, but the territorial government was not established until June 14, 1900.

4. *Governors of Territory of Hawaii*

NAME	APPOINTED BY PRESIDENT	TERM ENDED
Sanford B. Dole	McKinley	Nov. 23, 1903
George R. Carter	T. Roosevelt	Aug. 15, 1907
Walter F. Frear	T. Roosevelt	Nov. 29, 1913
Lucius E. Pinkham	Wilson	June 22, 1918
Charles J. McCarthy	Wilson	July 5, 1921
Wallace R. Farrington	Harding	July 5, 1925
(second term)	Coolidge	July 5, 1929
Lawrence M. Judd	Hoover	March 1, 1934
Joseph B. Poindexter	F. D. Roosevelt	April 2, 1938
(second term)	F. D. Roosevelt	Aug. 24, 1942
Ingram M. Stainback	F. D. Roosevelt	Aug. 24, 1946
(second term)	Truman	April 30, 1951
Oren E. Long	Truman	Feb. 28, 1953
Samuel Wilder King	Eisenhower	Sept. 2, 1957
William F. Quinn	Eisenhower	Aug. 21, 1959

Hawaii became the Fiftieth State on August 21, 1959, when President Eisenhower proclaimed the inauguration of a slate of state officials elected on July 28, headed by William F. Quinn, Republican, first governor of the State of Hawaii.

Governors of the State of Hawaii

William F. Quinn	Elected July 28, 1959	Republican
John A. Burns	Elected November 6, 1962	Democrat
George R. Ariyoshi	Elected November 5, 1974	Democrat
John Waihee	Elected November 4, 1986	Democrat

B. A HANDY GLOSSARY OF HAWAIIAN TERMS

THE HAWAIIAN LANGUAGE WAS FIRST WRITTEN BY MISSIONARIES using a roman alphabet which is completely phonetic; all letters are pronounced.

Only seven consonants are found — *h, k, l, m, n, p,* and *w.* Sometimes included as a consonant is the "glottal stop," an almost inaudible click in the throat, usually indicated in writing by an inverted comma. Omission of the glottal stop may result in changing the meaning of a word. Consonants are pronounced much as in English, except that the *h* is never silent. The *w* is either a lax English *w* or a very lax *v.* After *e* or *i,* almost all speakers use the *v* sound.

Vowels are *a, e, i, o,* and *u,* pronounced as in Latin or Spanish. Any vowel may be either long or short, and vowel length may change the meaning of a word. There are no true diphthongs, but the following combinations are pronounced roughly thus: *ae* and *ai* are like *ai* in "aisle"; *ao* and *au* like *ow* in "cow"; and *ei* like *ay* in "day."

Most Hawaiian words are stressed on the next to the last syllable; some words have an even stress. The spoken language has a lilting, musical softness pleasing to the ear.

The printed literature in the Hawaiian language is large. It includes not only the Bible and many other volumes of translations, but also several shelves of folklore collections and books written by Hawaiian authors in their own tongue.

The following brief glossary should be helpful to the reader of this book and to visitors to the Hawaiian Islands who wish to become familiar with the localisms most often used, for many Hawaiian words have been taken into English and are used freely in the islands.

a-a: jagged lava
aku: bonito
akua: god
ala: road
alii: chief; nobility
aloha: greeting; affection; farewell
aole: no
aumakua: ancestral spirit
auwe: exclamation
awa: fermented drink of pepper root

Beretania: Great Britain

eleele: dark, black

haku: prince
hala: pandanus
hale: place, house
hana: work; to make
haole: white man; stranger
hapa: half, part
hapai: pregnant
hau: a common tree
Hauoli Makahiki Hou: Happy New Year
haupia: pudding of coconut milk
heiau: altar or temple platform
hikie: elevated sleeping platform
hilahila: shame

hoku: star
holoku: gown with long, pointed train
holua: land toboggan
hoomalimali: flattery, "apple sauce"
huhu: angry
hui: group, syndicate
hukilau: "hauling of the leaves," fish-netting party
hula: Hawaiian dance

ie-ie: local vine
ili: small estate
iliahi: sandalwood
ilio: dog
imu: underground oven
ipo: sweetheart

ka, ke: definite article
kahili: cylindrical emblem of feathers topping a pole
kahuna: expert, sorcerer, priest
kala (English): dollar
kalo: taro plant
kamaaina: "child of the land," old-timer
kanaka: man
kane: male
kapa: beaten bark cloth
kapakahi: crooked, biased
kapu: tabu, forbidden
kauka: doctor
kaukau: food

kauwa: slave class
kea: white
keawe or *kiawe*: algarroba tree
keiki: child
ki: local leafy shrub
kihei: native shawl
koa: a hardwood tree
kokua: help, co-operation
kona: west or southwest; a muggy wind
konohiki: landlord, tax collector
kuhina nui: chief adviser to the early monarchy
kukui: candlenut tree
kula (English): school
kuleana: homestead

la: day; sun
lanai: porch or patio
lani: heaven
lau: leaf
lauhala: leaf of pandanus
laulau: food baked in leaves
lehua: see *ohia*
lei: garland for head or neck; necklace
limu: edible sea moss
lio: horse
loa: long; great
lomi-lomi: Hawaiian massage
luau: Hawaiian native feast
luna: boss, foreman

mahalo: thanks
mahele: division
mahimahi: dolphin fish
mahope: by and by
mai: disease
maikai: good

maile: fragrant plant
makaainana: farmer class
makahiki: harvest season, autumn
makai: direction toward the sea
make: dead
malihini: visitor, newcomer
malo: loincloth
malolo: flying fish
mamo: an extinct bird
mana: supernatural power
manele: litter
manu: bird
mauka: direction toward the mountains
mele: song or chant
Mele Kalikimaka: Merry Christmas
menehune: legendary tribe of dwarfs or brownies
moana: ocean
moe: sleep
moi: leader, sovereign
moku: island; division of an island
moo: tract or field
muumuu: Mother Hubbard gown

nani: beautiful
niu: coconut
nui: great, large

ohelo: berry-bearing shrub
ohia: low tree with feathery flower
okolehao: liquor distilled from *ki* root
olona: local fibrous plant

ono: good to eat
o-o: an extinct bird; digging
  stick
opihi: limpet
opu: paunch

pahoa: dagger pointed at both
  ends
pahoehoe: smooth lava
pake: Chinese
palaka: blue plaid cloth
palapala: written word
pali: cliff
panini: cactus
paniolo: Spaniard; cowboy
pau: finished
pa-u: voluminous riding skirt
pikake: peacock; small jasmine
pilau: stench
pilikia: trouble
pipi: beef
poi: paste of pounded *kalo*
  root
popoki: cat

pua: flower
puaa: pig
puka: hole or cavity
pule: religious instruction
punee: couch or day bed
pupu: shell
pupule: crazy
puu: hill

tapa: see *kapa*
taro: see *kalo*
ti: see *ki*
tutu: grandparent

ukulele: "jumping flea"; well-
  known musical instrument
ulu: breadfruit; grove of trees
ulua: a large food fish
umeke: wooden bowl

wahine: female, wife
wikiwiki: hurry up
wiliwili: local tree

C. A NOTE ON SOURCES

A LIST OF THE MATERIALS, PRINTED OR IN MANUSCRIPT, THAT WERE used in the writing of this book would constitute a rather complete bibliography of Hawaiiana that might overburden a volume intended for the general reader. The sources embody my reading on the subject during the past decade, and few works have remained unconsulted. The author of a quotation in the text is nearly always identified. Although it is invidious to name a few workers in a field where many have labored with success, I may say that for the earlier period I have found most valuable the documentary histories by Ralph S. Kuykendall and by Harold W. Bradley.

My chief concern has been to stress social history even at the expense of politics and diplomacy, and I have drawn heavily upon books that reveal the colorful life of the people of Hawaii during past eras. Fascinating details have been gleaned from narratives of voyagers to the islands, memoirs of missionaries and other settlers, biographies, accounts of travelers and other visitors, and sketches by literary persons such as Robert Louis Stevenson, Jack London, Charles Warren Stoddard, Isabella Bird Bishop, and Mark Twain. An extensive social and cultural history of the Hawaiian Islands, of course, still remains to be written.

A. G. D.

University of Hawaii

D. HEADLINE HISTORY OF HAWAII, 1960-1990

1960. The seventh federal census shows the island population as 609,096. Congress authorizes the creation of the Center for Cultural and Technical Interchange between East and West (East-West Center) at the University of Hawaii; grantees come from all fifty states of the Union and from twenty-six countries of Asia and the Pacific to obtain advanced education in Hawaii and travel on the mainland. *February 18.* The state legislature convenes in its first regular session. It adjourns May 2. *May 23.* Devastating tsunami waves strike the islands and kill fifty-seven persons at Hilo; earthquakes rock the Puna district and an eruption pours lava on Kula subdivision. *July 4.* Hawaii's state flag becomes official and a fiftieth star is added to the American flag. *November.* The people of Hawaii have their first chance to vote for president of the United States: on a recount, John F. Kennedy wins over Richard Nixon by a margin of 115 votes out of 184,705. All three Congressional incumbents are re-elected.

1961. *April 20.* The first cable television service is offered by Kaiser-Teleprompter. *June 25.* The Conference of State Governors holds its annual meeting in Honolulu. *July 1.* The two sections of Hawaii National Park become separate entities, Hawaii Volcanoes National Park and Haleakala National Park; on the same day the National Park Service creates the City of Refuge National Historical Park at Kona.

1962. *November.* Governor Quinn is defeated by John R. Burns.

Daniel K. Inouye joins Hiram L. Fong as the first Senate members of Oriental ancestry. Reapportionment brings two seats in the House, which are filled by two Democrats, Thomas P. Gill and Spark M. Matsunaga. For the first time in history, Democrats control both houses of the legislature.

1963. *June 9.* President John F. Kennedy addresses the National Conference of Mayors in Honolulu. The Polynesian Cultural Center opens as an attraction to visitors.

1964. An undersea cable costing $84,000,000 begins operation between Hawaii and Tokyo. *November.* Senator Fong is elected to a full six-year term. Congressman Matsunaga is re-elected. and Patsy Takemoto Mink becomes a member of the House.

1965. The Viet Nam conflict calls the 25th Division and the Marines to the Asian area. A proposed Kauai National Park arouses a mass of controversy. The state community-college system is created.

1966. *April 25.* The United States Supreme Court upholds Hawaii's reapportionment plan based on registered voters rather than population. *November 19.* Live television to and from the mainland is inaugurated.

1967. This becomes the first year during which one million tourists visit the islands. Hawaii Loa College is founded.

1968. Frank F. Fasi becomes mayor of the City and County of Honolulu for the first time, and the neighbor islands elect their first mayors. The legislature meets for the first time in the new Capitol building.

1969. *July 22.* The Civil Aeronautics Board awards domestic Pacific routes to seven airlines from Hawaii to thirty-five mainland cities. *July 26.* The first human beings returning from the moon, astronauts Neil A. Armstrong, Edwin E. Aldrin, Jr. and Michael Collins, arrive at Pearl Harbor aboard carrier *Hornet,* which had picked them up after splashdown of their Apollo 11 craft, *Columbia 3.*

1970. Eighth federal census records island population to be

769,913. Hiram L. Fong is re-elected to the Senate.

1971. Honolulu Rapid Transit, because of a labor dispute, is taken over by the City and County of Honolulu and operated as MTL, Inc. The University of Hawaii Law School is founded.

1972. Direct distance dialing permits callers to bypass long-distance operators on calls from Oahu to the rest of the world.

1973. *April 2.* Hawaii's teachers begin the nation's first statewide school strike in a dispute over pay and working conditions. *April 26.* Hilo suffers an earthquake causing $1,000,000 in damage. *September.* "Roll-on, roll-off" trailership is introduced by Matson Navigation Co. with two ships, *Lurline* and *Matsonia*. First annual Honolulu Marathon is run by 167 contestants.

1974. The forty-year-old sugar act expires and prices soar from 11 cents a pound to 65.5 cents. Hawaii becomes the first state to impose limits on the sale of gasoline during a world shortage; the ban is ended on April 30. *August 12-16.* The American Bar Association holds its 97th annual convention in Honolulu. *November 5.* George R. Ariyoshi is elected first governor of Oriental ancestry.

1975. *June 15.* Sea Flite makes its first scheduled inter-island passenger trip by hydrofoil with the 45-knot *Kamehameha,* but service is discontinued on January 15, 1978. Aloha Stadium is opened. KHVH radio becomes the first Hawaii station to regularly air twenty-four-hour programs from the mainland.

1976. Hawaii takes part in the national American Bicentennial celebrations of the signing of the Declaration of Independence and carries out numerous projects. The sailing craft *Hokulea* makes a voyage to Tahiti and returns to recall the days of Polynesian canoe travel. Hawaiian activists begin efforts to release the island of Kaho'olawe from Navy use. *November.* Senators from Hawaii are Daniel K. Inouye and Spark M. Matsunaga and representatives are Cecil Heftel and Daniel K. Akaka, first Congressman of Hawaiian ancestry.

1977. *September 13.* The world's most active volcano, Kilauea, begins to erupt and continues intermittent outbursts until September 28. An 118-day strike begun by the Ironworkers' Union halts construction on projects throughout the state.

1978. Hawaii celebrates the bicentennial of the arrival of Captain James Cook and two British ships. *July 5.* The third constitutional convention since the first in 1950 is convened; a ninety-day session produces numerous proposals, all of which are ratified by voters in the November elections. *November.* George R. Ariyoshi wins a second term as governor and state senator Jean Sadako King becomes the first woman lieutenant governor in the history of the state.

1979. Despite a strike against United Airlines and grounding of DC-10 planes because of safety problems, almost four million visitors come to Hawaii. *October.* Many international dignitaries attend the dedication of one of the largest infrared telescopes in the world, joining other observatories atop Mauna Kea on the Big Island, where clear skies advance astronomical research. *October 21.* A forty-one-day strike by the lowest-paid unit of the United Public Workers begins and lasts until December 3. *November.* The fiftieth anniversary of inauguration of the first inter-island air service is celebrated.

1980. *November.* Eileen Anderson defeats Frank F. Fasi, mayor since 1968, to become the first woman to head the City and County of Honolulu. Charles Marsland is Honolulu's first elected prosecutor.

1981. The seventy-fifth anniversary of Filipino migration to the islands is celebrated. An eighty-year-old landmark, the Alexander Young Hotel in downtown Honolulu, is demolished to make way for increasing highrise development.

1982. George R. Ariyoshi defeats Republican Andy Anderson and Independent Frank F. Fasi for governor. *November 23.* Hurricane Iwa strikes Kauai with winds as high as 117 miles an hour, causing an estimated $234 million in damage. It is the most destructive storm to hit Hawaii in historic times.

1983. Official population of Hawaii reaches 1,083,000. Ethnic distribution: Caucasian, 24.5 per cent; Japanese, 23.2 per cent; Filipino, 11.3 per cent; Hawaiian and part-Hawaiian, 20.0 per cent. Kilauea Volcano spews lava on the Big Island, first phase of an island-building eruption that continues into the 1990's.

1984. Twenty-fifth anniversary of statehood is celebrated. Frank F. Fasi defeats Eileen Anderson to regain longtime mayoralty of the City and County of Honolulu. All four Congressional votes go to Ronald Reagan.

1985. Visitor count tops five million. Three Honolulu city councilmen are recalled for switching parties.

1986. *January 28.* Space Shuttle *Challenger* explodes after takeoff, killing the entire crew, including Hawaii's Ellison Onizuka. Corazon Aquino becomes president of the Republic of the Philippines; the Ferdinand Marcos family flees for asylum to live in Hawaii. *November.* John Waihee becomes the first person of part-Hawaiian ancestry to be elected governor.

1987. Polynesian sailing craft *Hokulea* completes a two-year "voyage of rediscovery" to demonstrate native navigation methods. "Ho'olako 1987"—the Year of the Hawaiian—is celebrated. Devastating storm on New Year's Eve causes wide damage.

1988. The Hawaiian Maritime Center opens on the waterfront as an oceanic museum and visitor attraction. Despite the closing of fourteen plantations out of twenty-seven in past years, production for 1988 reaches almost a million tons of raw sugar—about the same as in 1959—and yield per acre has increased by one third. *November.* Daniel K. Inouye, in Congress since 1962, is reelected. Spark M. Matsunaga, in the Senate since 1976, dies in office and Patsy Takemoto Mink is elected in his district. Daniel Akaka, in the House since 1976, is unopposed, and Patricia Saiki is elected. Almost unique among the states, Hawaii gives all four presidential votes to Michael Dukakis.

1989. Hawaii becomes the first state to outlaw chlorofluorocarbon refrigerants to help protect the earth's ozone layer.

1990. Kilauea Volcano is the longest running uninterrupted performer on record, continuing destruction in Puna. *November 6.* Daniel K. Inouye is reelected to the Senate, and Neil Abercrombie and Patsy Takemoto Mink are elected to the House. John Waihee defeats Andy Anderson and is reelected governor. The state of Hawaii enters the last decade of the twentieth century with a large multi-ethnic population, a booming economy, and a strong confidence in facing its Pacific destiny.

1992. Hurricane 'Iniki slams the Hawaiian Islands in September, devastating Kaua'i

1993. 'Onipa'a (stand fast) ceremonies mark the hundredth anniversary of the 1893 overthrow of the monarchy, January 17. President Clinton signs a congressional resolution acknowledging the illegal overthrow of the Kingdom of Hawai'i, November 24.

1994. Ben Cayetano is elected Hawai'i's first governor of Filipino ancestry.

1997. $1.3 billion H-3 Freeway opens after a delay of nearly two decades due to environmental and cultural protests.

2000. The United States Supreme Court rules 7-2 that Hawaiians-only elections for trustees of the Office of Hawaiian Affairs are unlawful due to racial discrimination. The legal case, titled Rice v. Cayetano, was instigated by Hawai'i Island rancher Harold "Freddy" Rice.

2002, Nov. 5. Linda Lingle, the former mayor of Maui County, is elected governor of the State of Hawai'i. Lingle becomes Hawai'i's first female governor, and first Republican governor in 40 years.

2003, Nov. 11. The Navy transfers control of Kaho'olawe to the State of Hawai'i.

2003. Federal spending in the State of Hawai'i totals $11.27 billion, including $4.84 billion in defense spending, ranking sixth in federal spending, and second among all states in per-capita defense spending.

Index

MASS MARKET TITLES FROM
MUTUAL PUBLISHING

HAWAI'I
Ancient History of the Hawaiian People to the Times of Kamehameha I $8.95
Remember Pearl Harbor! by Blake Clark $4.95
Kona by Marjorie Sinclair $6.95
A Hawaiian Reader $6.95
Russian Flag Over Hawaii by Darwin Teihet $5.95
Teller of Hawaiian Tales by Eric Knudsen $6.95
Myths and Legends of Hawaii by W.D. Westervelt $6.95
Mark Twain in Hawaii $4.95
The Legends and Myths of Hawaii by Kalakaua $7.95
Hawaii's Story by Hawaii's Queen $7.95
Rape in Paradise by Theon Wright $5.95
The Betrayal of Liliuokalani $7.95
The Wild Wind by Marjorie Sinclair $6.95
Hawaii: Fiftieth Star by A. Grove Day $4.95
Hawaii and Its People by A. Grove Day $4.95
True Tales of the South Seas ed. by A. Grove Day and Carl Stoven $4.95
The Trembling of a Leaf by W. Somerset Maugham $4.95
Hawaii and Points South $4.95
Horror in Paradise, ed. by A. Grove Day and Bacil F. Kirtley $6.95
Pearl $5.95
The Golden Cloak by Antoinette Withington $6.95

SOUTH SEAS LITERATURE
The Book of Puka Puka by Robert Dean Frisbie $5.95
The Lure of Tahiti ed. by A. Grove Day $5.95
The Blue of Capricorn by Eugene Burdick $5.95
Best South Sea Stories, ed. by A. Grove Day $6.95
The Forgotten One by James Norman Hall $5.95
His Majesty O'Keefe by Lawrence Klingman and Gerald Green $4.95

TRAVEL, BIOGRAPHY, ANTHROPOLOGY
Manga Reva by Robert Lee Eskridge $5.95
Home from the Sea: Robert Louis Stevenson in Samoa, by Richard Bermann $5.95
The Nordhoff-Hall Story: In Search of Paradise by Paul L. Briand $5.95
The Fatal Impact by Alan Moorehead $4.95
Claus Spreckels, The Sugar King in Hawaii $5.95
A Dream of Islands by Gavan Daws $4.95
Kalakaua: Renaissance King $6.95
Nahi'ena'ena: Sacred Daughter of Hawai'i $4.95
Around the World With a King $5.95

Orders should be sent to Mutual Publishing
1215 Center Street, Suite 210, Honolulu, HI 96816
www.mutualpublishing.com • mutual @mutualpublishing.com

For book rate (4-6 weeks; in Hawai'i, 1-2 weeks) send check or money order with an additional
$3.00 for the first book and $1.00 for each additional book. For first class (1-2 weeks) add $4.00
for the first book, $3.00 for each additional book.